AT THE MARGINS OF THE WELFARE STATE

At the Margins of the Welfare State

Social assistance and the alleviation of poverty in Germany, Sweden and the United Kingdom

CHRISTINA BEHRENDT
Researcher and Consultant for International Organizations

LONDON AND NEW YORK

First published 2002 by Ashgate Publishing

Reissued 2018 by Routledge
2 Park Square, Milton Park, Abingdon, Oxon OX14 4RN
711 Third Avenue, New York, NY 10017, USA

Routledge is an imprint of the Taylor & Francis Group, an informa business

Copyright © Christina Behrendt 2002

The author has asserted her moral right under the Copyright Designs and Patents Act, 1988, to be identified as the author of this work.

All rights reserved. No part of this book may be reprinted or reproduced or utilised in any form or by any electronic, mechanical, or other means, now known or hereafter invented, including photocopying and recording, or in any information storage or retrieval system, without permission in writing from the publishers.

Notice:
Product or corporate names may be trademarks or registered trademarks, and are used only for identification and explanation without intent to infringe.

Publisher's Note
The publisher has gone to great lengths to ensure the quality of this reprint but points out that some imperfections in the original copies may be apparent.

Disclaimer
The publisher has made every effort to trace copyright holders and welcomes correspondence from those they have been unable to contact.

A Library of Congress record exists under LC control number: 2002066594

ISBN 13: 978-1-138-73104-2 (hbk)
ISBN 13: 978-1-138-73103-5 (pbk)
ISBN 13: 978-1-315-18803-4 (ebk)

Contents

List of Figures	*viii*
List of Tables	*x*
List of Abbreviations	*xii*
Acknowledgements	*xiii*

Chapter 1
Welfare States and the Alleviation of Poverty — 1

Minimum Income Schemes and the Alleviation of Poverty	2
Combining Institutional Information and Micro-data on Poverty	5
Choice of Cases	6
Terminology	9
Structure of this Book	10

Chapter 2
Poverty and Poverty Alleviation in Industrialized Welfare States: What Do We Know? — 13

Poverty in Industrialized Welfare States	13
The Redistributional Impact of the Welfare State	17
Welfare State Efforts and the Alleviation of Poverty	25
Unsolved Puzzles and a Possible Solution	29

Chapter 3
Mapping the Reduction of Poverty through Minimum Income Schemes — 33

Evaluating the Effects of Minimum Income Schemes	33
Distribution of Means-tested Benefits within the Poor Population	37
Effectiveness of Means-tested Transfers	39
What Can Explain the Apparent Ineffectiveness of the Welfare State?	46

Chapter 4
Methodological Puzzles and Pitfalls in the Measurement of Poverty — 53

Why Do Low Income and Social Assistance Receipt Hardly Coincide?	53
Is Income an Adequate Measure of Poverty?	56
Data and Data Quality	60
Private Households: A Simple Concept with Critical Implications	69
The Concept of Income and Related Questions	76
Poverty Lines	80
A Way Out of the Methodological Problems of Poverty Research?	86

Chapter 5
Is the Entire Population Eligible for Social Assistance Benefits? — 89

The Institutional Framework: Eligibility Rules and Means-tests	89
Do Social Assistance Schemes Provide a Safety Net for All?	99

Chapter 6
Do Social Assistance Schemes Provide Adequate Benefits? — 101

The Institutional Framework: Minimum Income Standards	103
Adequacy: Evidence from the Luxembourg Income Study	127
Adequacy and the Effectiveness of Social Assistance Schemes	155

Chapter 7
Do Social Assistance Schemes Encourage Take-up? — 157

Social Assistance Schemes and the Causes of Non-take-up	158
The Administration of Social Assistance and the Question of Take-up	165
Empirical Evidence on the Take-up of Social Assistance Benefits	191
Non-take-up and the Effectiveness of Social Assistance Schemes	200

Chapter 8
Conclusion 203

Towards an Explanation of Poverty in Industrialized Welfare States 203
Mending the Holes in the Social Safety Net 206
Flawed Policies or a Flawed Measurement of Poverty? 209

Appendix 211
Bibliography *219*
Index *241*

List of Figures

Figure 2.1	Relative poverty in industrialized countries, early 1990s	15
Figure 2.2	Beckerman ratios	19
Figure 2.3	Market income poverty rates and the reduction of poverty by social transfers and taxes for the prime-age population (head younger than 55 years), early 1990s	24
Figure 2.4	Welfare state efforts and the alleviation of poverty: Social expenditure and relative poverty rates for prime-age households in OECD countries (head younger than 55 years), early 1990s	26
Figure 2.5	Welfare state efforts and the alleviation of poverty: Social expenditure and the reduction of poverty rates through transfers and taxes for prime-age households in OECD countries (head younger than 55 years)	28
Figure 3.1	Poverty lines and poverty brackets	34
Figure 3.2	Social assistance and the alleviation of poverty: a simplified model	48
Figure 3.3	Social assistance schemes and an effective alleviation of poverty: A simplified model	50
Figure 4.1	Poverty profiles in Sweden: Mapping the impact of the exclusion of students on poverty rates	72
Figure 4.2	The impact of equivalence scales on measured poverty	74
Figure 4.3	Equivalence scales in social assistance schemes and in poverty research	75
Figure 4.4	Poverty lines and poverty profiles in Britain, Germany and Sweden	81
Figure 4.5	Absolute poverty rates based on the purchasing power equivalent of the US official poverty line	82
Figure 6.1	Development of real value of social assistance benefit rates in Germany, Sweden and the United Kingdom (1985=100)	114
Figure 6.2	Development of standard benefit rates as a percentage of average production workers' take-home pay (1985 = 100)	116
Figure 6.3	Standard benefit rates for additional household members	118
Figure 6.4	Level of social assistance entitlements for different family types, after housing costs (1995)	133

Figure 6.5	Level of social assistance entitlements as a proportion of median income, Britain 1995	134
Figure 6.6	Level of social assistance entitlements in per cent of median income, Germany 1994	135
Figure 6.7	Level of social assistance entitlements as a proportion of median income, Sweden 1995	137
Figure 6.8	Poverty rates based on original and simulated social assistance benefits	145
Figure 6.9	Poverty rates for single parents based on actual and simulated social assistance benefits	149
Figure 6.10	Poverty rates for two-parent families with children based on actual and simulated social assistance benefits	150
Figure 6.11	Poverty rates for two-parent families with three or more children based on actual and simulated social assistance benefits	151
Figure 6.12	Poverty rates for the elderly based on actual and simulated social assistance benefits	153
Figure 6.13	Poverty rates for single elderly women based on actual and simulated social assistance benefits	154
Figure 7.1	Expenditure on social assistance as a percentage of total social expenditure	167
Figure 7.2	Expenditure on social assistance as a percentage of GNP	168
Figure 7.3	Recipients of social assistance as a proportion of the population in Britain and Germany (one day during a year)	170
Figure 7.4	Recipients of social assistance as a proportion of the population in Germany and Sweden (yearly sum)	172
Figure 7.5	Overlapping of non-take-up and an ineffective alleviation of poverty	192
Figure A.1	Low Income Profiles for different equivalence scales for Britain, Germany and Sweden; classical OECD equivalence scale	216
Figure A.2	Low Income Profiles for different equivalence scales (cumulated) for Britain, Germany and Sweden; square root scale	216
Figure A.3	Benefit package of social assistance recipients in Germany, Sweden and the United Kingdom (before housing costs), 1992	217
Figure A.4	Benefit package of social assistance recipients in Germany, Sweden and the United Kingdom (after housing costs), 1992	218

List of Tables

Table 2.1	The effectiveness of welfare state redistribution for prime-age households, early 1990s (household head under 55)	22
Table 3.1	Definition of poverty lines (based on disposable equivalent income; in national currency units)	35
Table 3.2	Components of cash and near-cash means-tested benefits as defined in LIS	36
Table 3.3	Distribution of means-tested benefits on households (percentage of households receiving means-tested benefits in each poverty bracket)	38
Table 3.4	Poverty rates before and after means-tested benefits and reduction through means-tested benefits	41
Table 3.5	Effects of means-tested benefits: move between poverty brackets (as a proportion of all households having received some means-tested benefits)	42
Table 3.6	Average poverty gap and average poverty gap reduction by means-tested benefits for households who were poor before having received any means-tested transfers	45
Table 4.1	Income poverty and the receipt of social assistance in Germany, Sweden and the United Kingdom: Percentage of poor households who receive social assistance benefits	54
Table 4.2	Income poverty and the receipt of social assistance in Germany, Sweden and the United Kingdom: Percentage of poor households who receive social assistance benefits (poverty status calculated on the basis of income *before* receipt of social assistance benefits/means-tested benefits)	55
Table 4.3	Undercoverage of groups of the population	62
Table 4.4	Quality of the income data in LIS (estimates based on survey data as a percentage of aggregated data in national accounts)	68
Table 4.5	Poverty rates for individuals and households	70
Table 4.6	Absolute poverty in OECD countries: results of selected studies	84

List of Tables   xi

Table 5.1	Eligibility of minors and students in the social assistance schemes of Germany, Sweden and the United Kingdom	91
Table 5.2	Employment status and eligibility in Germany, Sweden and the United Kingdom	92
Table 5.3	Eligibility of foreign nationals in the social assistance schemes of Germany, Sweden and the United Kingdom	95
Table 6.1	Provision of benefit additions (premiums) for specific groups of the population (benefit rates given as a proportion of standard benefit rates for a single adult), 1995	120
Table 6.2	Level of social assistance entitlement for different family types and poverty lines (as a percentage of median income)	139
Table 6.3	Poverty rates for an income distribution with simulated social assistance entitlements	146
Table 7.1	Possible effects of institutional structures on take-up	163
Table 7.2	Elements of the institutional framework and their effects on non-take-up	190
Table 7.3	Empirical evidence on non-take-up of supplementary benefit and income support in Britain	195
Table 7.4	Empirical evidence on non-take-up of social assistance in West Germany	197
Table 7.5	Empirical evidence on non-take-up of social assistance in Sweden	199
Table A.1	Construction of LIS datasets	211
Table A.2	Trends in effectiveness of redistribution during early 1990s: full population	212
Table A.3	Income poverty and social assistance in Germany, Sweden and the United Kingdom	213
Table A.4	Sampling methods for the LIS datasets used in this study	213
Table A.5	Definition of poverty lines for alternative equivalence scales (based on disposable income)	214
Table A.6	Distribution of means-tested benefits on households (percentage of households receiving means-tested benefits in each poverty bracket)	214
Table A.7	Distribution of means-tested benefits on households (percentage of households receiving means-tested benefits in each poverty bracket)	215

List of Abbreviations

BAföG	*Bundesausbildungsförderungsgesetz* (German Federal Education Promotion Act)
BMA	*Bundesministerium für Arbeit und Sozialordnung* (German Ministry of Social Affairs)
BMJFG	*Bundesministerium für Jugend, Familie und Gesundheit* (German Ministry for Youth Affairs, Family and Health)
CPAG	Child Poverty Action Group (United Kingdom)
DSS	Department of Social Security (United Kingdom)
E_{cl}	'classical' OECD equivalence scale
E_{mod}	'modified' OECD equivalence scale
E_{sq}	Square root equivalence scale ('LIS scale')
ECU	European Currency Unit
EU	European Union
FES	Family Expenditure Survey
GSOEP	German Socio-Economic Panel
HBL	*Hilfe in besonderen Lebenslagen* in the German social assistance scheme (aid in special circumstances)
HLU	*Hilfe zum Lebensunterhalt* in the German social assistance scheme (general social assistance)
LIS	Luxembourg Income Study
OECD	Organisation for Economic Co-operation and Development

Acknowledgements

This book is the product of many years of research, starting with a number of research papers that finally grew into a doctoral thesis and became the basis for the oral examination that took place 14 May 2001 at the University of Konstanz (Germany). The thesis was subsequently revised and shortened for this publication. Along the way, I have enjoyed many people's support and benefited from numerous discussions and critical comments.

First and foremost, this book draws heavily on the Luxembourg Income Study (LIS), the contribution of which is most gratefully acknowledged. The staff in Differdange and Syracuse – in particular Paul Alkemade, Cheri Minton, Ann Morissens, Tim Smeeding, Caroline de Tombeur and Koen Vleminckx – were most helpful in making my struggle through the LIS data an enjoyable enterprise. I should also mention that the LIS data referring to the United Kingdom is subject to Crown Copyright; it was made available by the Office for National Statistics through the ESRC Data Archive and used with their permission. Neither the Office for National Statistics nor the ESRC Data Archive bear any responsibility for the analysis nor the interpretation of the data reported here.

Some parts of the book have benefited from critical comments from participants at various conferences. Previous versions of Chapter 3, based on earlier data, were presented at the World Congress of Sociology 1998 in Montreal (Canada) and at the Common Congress of the Austrian, German and Swiss Sociological Associations 1998 in Freiburg (Germany). A revised version of this presentation was published in the Journal of European Social Policy, 10 (1), 2000. Parts of Chapter 4 were presented at the International Society for Quality of Life Studies (ISQOLS) Conference 2000 in Girona (Spain), and a summary will be published in a forthcoming special issue of Social Indicators Research, edited by Mike Hagerty and Joachim Vogel. In addition, some more recent results of this research project were presented at the ISSA Year 2000 Conference in Helsinki (Finland) and the ISA RC19 Conference in Oviedo (Spain) in 2001.

Many people were involved in this project at various stages and contributed to this study in various ways. For guidance on my way through the jungle of British and Swedish social assistance regulations, I am indebted to many people, notably Eva Bergström and Renate Minas at the Socialstyrelsen and Leif Klingensjö at the Svenska Kommunförbundet in Stockholm, as well as Sharon Jones and Cliff Newman at the Department of Social Security in London. Many people read parts of the manuscript, lent their ears for discussions, and offered valuable critical and constructive comments as well as practical help. In particular, I would like to thank Helen Bolderson, Giuliano Bonoli, Petra Buhr, Eero Carroll, Anne Erd, Martin Evans, Kristina Haaf, Björn Halleröd, Walter Korpi, Jon Kvist, Peter Krause, Frauke Kreuter, Wolfgang Lauterbach, Anders Lindbom, Kenneth Nelson, Joakim Palme, Jong-Sam Park, Saskia Richter, Matthias Sacher, Tapio Salonen, Bernd Schulte, Uwe Schwarze, Roland Sigg and Ray Thomas. My dissertation supervisor Jens Alber and second referee Ellen Immergut, together with Martin Schölkopf and Sabine Leutenecker, read and commented on the whole manuscript, and have offered their most valuable advice, guidance and encouragement. Without them, this book would never have been written. It goes without saying that remaining errors are entirely my own responsibility.

Deborah Allen, Emma Carmel, Elisabeth Coutts-Heller, Alison Herrington, Kate Taylor and Mark Webber kindly provided linguistic support for various parts of this book, but the bulk of proof-reading rested on the shoulders of Laura and Dorothy Sinfield who transformed copious germanisms into 'real English' and also helped to clarify many substantive issues. Adrian Sinfield did not only offer his generous help at these last stages of the research process, but he was, together with Richard Parry, also decisive in sowing the seed to embark on such a research enterprise many years ago during my studies in Edinburgh.

Finally, I would like to thank my parents whose support never weakened even during the most difficult times, and my husband Sven who always knows how to make me smile. To them, the book is dedicated.

Chapter 1

Welfare States and the Alleviation of Poverty

If poverty prevails, the welfare state is a failure.
(Ringen, 1987: 141)

Industrialized welfare states have established elaborate systems of income redistribution and spend a considerable proportion of their national income on social policies. In a complex wickerwork of taxes and transfers, resources are redistributed in multiple ways, between the rich and the poor, between the young and the old, between families with children and the childless, between healthy and sick people, and so forth. The redistributional impact of the welfare state is so large that some groups of the population even receive the largest part of their income from the welfare state.

Nonetheless, poverty has not been eradicated. The expansion of the welfare state during the 20th century and the economic boom after World War II led many people to believe that poverty would disappear or would at least be reduced to an insignificant minimum affecting only marginal groups of the population. Yet, a sizeable proportion of the population live in economic poverty in all industrial welfare states. According to one of the most common standards used in comparative poverty research, on average roughly one in ten households live in relative income poverty in OECD countries (cf. Atkinson et al., 1995).

Given the amount of income redistribution for social purposes, the persistence of poverty in industrial welfare states calls for an explanation. If industrial welfare states offer elaborate systems of income maintenance, why is there still a considerable amount of poverty?

The alleviation of poverty has been one of the major aims of modern welfare states, if not the most important aim. Although welfare states differ in terms of aspiration, institutional design and policies, this objective is in principle embraced by all welfare states (cf. Goodin et al., 1999: 21-36). In this vein, Stein Ringen has proposed to use the issue of poverty alleviation as a yardstick for the general effectiveness of the welfare state.

It is important to raise the issue of poverty, because of the historical significance of the problem, because its elimination has been the first priority of the welfare state, and because it offers an opportunity for discussing social policy on a basis of consensus. While there is a disagreement about the responsibility of government with regard to overall inequality, its responsibility in relation to poverty has been accepted for generations and is not seriously contested today. If poverty prevails, the welfare state is a failure. (Ringen, 1987: 141)

If modern welfare states are not effective in alleviating poverty, their very purpose is fundamentally challenged, irrespectively of whether they are effective in achieving other goals or not. Poverty is thus one important indicator for a welfare state's effectiveness and therefore deserves a more thorough analysis.

The persistence of poverty in advanced welfare states casts doubt on the fundamental operating procedures of income distribution and redistribution. What are the reasons for this apparent failure of the welfare state in alleviating poverty? Why are some countries more effective than others in this respect? What can explain these variations in effectiveness?

In spite of the strong impact of the welfare state on the income positions of individuals and private households, the mechanisms and effects of redistribution are far from clear. A number of studies have assessed the magnitude of total welfare state redistribution (cf. Beckerman, 1979; Mitchell, 1991), but could not offer a detailed explanation of the persistence of poverty in industrial welfare states.

Minimum Income Schemes and the Alleviation of Poverty

As the basic safety net of the welfare state, minimum income schemes play a critical role for the alleviation of poverty in modern welfare states. However, their role in poverty alleviation has seldom been systematically researched. This book therefore proposes to shift the analytical focus from the welfare state as a whole to minimum income schemes.[1] These schemes are explicitly designed for the purpose of alleviating poverty and are ultimately responsible for guaranteeing an adequate standard of living.[2] They step in if neither

---

[1] The Commission of the European Communities has recently re-emphasized the role of minimum income benefit schemes. One of the goals of a reform of social protection in the European Union is to 'ensure effective safety nets, consisting of minimum income benefits and accompanying provisions, with a view to efficiently combat poverty and exclusion of individuals and families' (European Commission, 1999: 14).

[2] By this token, this minimum income guarantee is closely linked to the issue of citizenship in modern welfare states. The provision of a certain minimum income for all members of a society sets out the core of social citizenship. These social rights are considered as a neces-

the primary income distribution through the market nor redistribution through social insurance and related schemes can protect people from poverty.

As the ultimate safety net of the welfare state, minimum income schemes are finally responsible for the effectiveness of the whole social security scheme. If this net does not hold, the effectiveness of the whole system is called into question. If it does, at least a minimum standard of protection is guaranteed. An effective alleviation of poverty in industrial welfare states is thus critically dependent on these minimum income schemes. A closer analysis of this basic safety net of the welfare state therefore promises valuable information on the persistence of poverty in industrial welfare states.

In spite of their importance for the alleviation of poverty, minimum income schemes have rarely been the focus of the mainstream of comparative welfare state analysis.[3] Most major studies have addressed social insurance schemes while social assistance was considered as a relic of the old poor law tradition that would subsequently be eliminated with the maturing of social insurance schemes (cf. Atkinson, 1999: 3). Nevertheless, these expectations have not been fulfilled; social assistance schemes still make up – and always have made up – a considerable portion of social expenditure in Western European welfare states. Only in recent years has rising expenditure on social assistance in a time of persistent mass unemployment in many Western European welfare states appeared to attract the interest of comparative welfare state research towards social assistance schemes and other minimum income schemes. A number of large-scale reports have sought to systematically compare the institutional design of minimum income schemes in industrialized countries.[4] Consequently, several scholars have attempted to integrate minimum income schemes into welfare state typologies or establish

---

sary extension of civil and political rights (Marshall, 1965). However, the history of minimum income schemes stands in a certain tension to this sequence of different forms of citizenship as postulated by Marshall. In many countries, provisions for the poor existed already well before the emergence of the modern welfare state, yet their focus was very different from today's minimum income schemes. Poor laws provided only very meagre benefits, often coupled with extensive policing and institutionalization of the poor in work houses (cf. Korpi, 1975; Sachße and Tennstedt, 1988, 1998). The introduction of social insurance schemes in many countries aimed to gradually replace these poor law schemes by social insurance entitlements, but means-tested benefits for the poor continued to exist in all European countries even throughout the heydays of the welfare state (cf. Eardley et al., 1996a).

[3] The two main topics of comparative welfare state research of the last years have been the historical development of social insurance schemes in Europe (e.g. Alber, 1982; Baldwin, 1990; Flora, 1986; Flora and Heidenheimer, 1981), as well as some attempts to establish a typology of 'welfare state regimes' based on their institutional design (Castles and Mitchell, 1993; Esping-Andersen, 1990; D. Sainsbury, 1999).

[4] This group of studies includes Eardley et al. (1996a; 1996b), Guibentif and Bouget (1997) and OECD (1998a; 1998b; 1999a).

new typologies of social assistance schemes (Eardley et al., 1996a; Leibfried, 1992; Lødemel and Schulte, 1992).

It is not only comparative welfare state research which has underestimated the role of minimum income schemes – poverty research has also showed little interest in these schemes.[5] Although social assistance schemes are explicitly aimed at alleviating poverty, poverty research has seldom thoroughly assessed the relationship between minimum income schemes and poverty. When assessing the causes of poverty, poverty research has largely scrutinized factors to be found in the distribution of earnings, the labour market, the social structure, and also social transfers for specific groups of the population, yet it has often neglected the basic safety net of the welfare state.

The incidence of poverty in advanced welfare states seems to have been attributed to a general mismatch of concepts of poverty and societal minimum income standards embodied in these schemes. While some observers appear to have tacitly assumed that social assistance benefits are too meagre as to provide a sufficient protection from poverty, others have sought the causes of this discrepancy rather in the measurement of poverty. The widely-used relative poverty line of 50 per cent of median equivalent disposable income in particular has been criticized as reflecting income inequality rather than a standard of subsistence, thus overstating poverty in rich countries (cf. Krämer, 1997; Blackburn, 1998).

The lack of knowledge about the relationship between minimum income schemes and poverty is only one example of a more general deficit. Whereas comparative social policy research has extensively analyzed the genesis and institutional similarities and differences of social security schemes, research into the outcome dimension is still underdeveloped. In particular, only a small number of studies have systematically evaluated the quality of social security schemes in a comparative perspective (cf. Dixon 1999).

This book makes an effort to step into this gap and to offer an evaluation of welfare state outcomes. It seeks to explain why extensive Western European welfare states are not successful in alleviating poverty. As the basic safety net of the welfare state bears the ultimate responsibility for the alleviation of poverty, this book focuses on minimum income schemes and assesses their effectiveness in protecting people from poverty. At its core is the idea that different welfare state arrangements produce different outcomes. A systematic analysis of the relationship between the basic safety net of the

---

[5] For example, this is exemplified by the fact that the recently published 'International Glossary of Poverty' devotes only the following passage to social assistance schemes: 'Social assistance consists of relief for those who are poorest, in cash or in kind [...]. Social assistance is usually subject to some kind of means-testing and may be subject to administrative or professional discretion.' (Gordon and Spicker, 1999: 121; emphasis omitted).

welfare state and the incidence of poverty thus promises to yield useful insights into the effects of the welfare state and the causes of poverty. The methodical framework of this analysis is based on a combination of qualitative information on institutional structures and quantitative micro-data on private household incomes.

Combining Institutional Information and Micro-data on Poverty

In order to gain a broad and detailed picture of the effectiveness of social assistance schemes, this book combines different types of qualitative and quantitative information. In addition to some aggregate data such as social expenditure ratios, the main focus is on micro-data from national household surveys that allow a detailed assessment of the income position of private households and the effects of redistributive policies. In order to shed some more light on this central puzzle – why is there poverty in extensive welfare states? – these data are confronted with more qualitative evidence on the institutional design of social assistance schemes. Information on the institutional frameworks stems from a broad variety of sources, including national and comparative studies on social assistance schemes and welfare states in general, national and international statistical sources, and citizen advice handbooks. For Britain and Sweden, a number of academic and administrative experts have been interviewed in order to supplement information from the literature with first-hand evidence.

This approach combines two research strategies that have been dubbed 'institution-by-institution' and 'group-by-group' approaches. The 'institution-by-institution' approach focuses on specific social security schemes – such as pension schemes or social assistance schemes – and emphasizes similarities and differences in the institutional design of these schemes. In contrast, the 'group-by-group' approach emphasizes the benefit packages available to individuals and private households (Hauser, 1997). Whereas the former approach is more focused on the organization of social policies, the second one is more concerned with the income position of individuals and households and the distributive effects of social policies.

The combination of these two approaches can help to broaden the focus of research while avoiding the blind spots inherent in each of these approaches. In addition, this allows the cross-checking of micro-data on plausibility. Survey data has often been criticized as providing a flawed basis for the assessment of poverty because of methodological problems. Confronting these data with institutional information on social security benefits and the operating procedures of these schemes can lead to a more informed interpretation of these data.

This book intentionally takes a simple stance to the analysis of the effects of welfare state institutions. It focuses only on the direct impact of social assistance schemes on poverty, and does not consider trends over time, long-term effects or side effects. A fully-fledged test of these claims would require an evaluation of the dynamic patterns of welfare receipt and poverty that would go far beyond the scope of this book.

The combination of institutional information with micro-data from the Luxembourg Income Study also governs the time frame of this analysis. As the most recent LIS data refer to 1994 (Germany) and 1995 (Sweden and the United Kingdom), this book mainly refers to the situation in the mid-1990s.

Choice of Cases

In contrast to one-country studies, comparative research allows one to depart from parochial policy analysis and to gain a new perspective on the particular characteristics of the countries under scrutiny. Therefore, three countries are analyzed in more detail – Britain, Germany and Sweden. These three countries have often been considered as paradigmatic cases for three distinct 'poverty regimes' (Leibfried, 1992) or 'social assistance regimes' (Eardley et al., 1996a; Lødemel and Schulte, 1992; Lødemel, 1992), with typical policy structures in poverty alleviation.[6]

Stephan Leibfried's proposition of 'poverty regimes' bears a strong resemblance to Esping-Andersen's (1990) welfare state regimes[7] – here dubbed as Scandinavian, Bismarck and Anglo-Saxon poverty regimes – and

---

[6] These typologies closely parallel earlier attempts to identify 'welfare state regimes'. Comparative welfare state research often uses typologies as a shortcut to describe institutional similarities and differences of modern welfare states (cf. Titmuss, 1974; Esping-Andersen, 1990, 1999).

[7] Esping-Andersen (1990; 1999) relates the institutional design of welfare states to the balance of state, market and the family. In his view, Sweden belongs to the 'social-democratic model' that is characterized by strong social rights, universalism and benefit equality. The German welfare state is depicted as a corporatist (or christian-democratic or conservative) welfare state that builds upon a fragmented system of status-based institutions and the protection of the traditional family (cf. also van Kersbergen, 1995). The British welfare state offers largely means-tested flat-rate benefits that entail a marked cleavage between state and market-based social security. Esping-Andersen's ambiguous association of the British welfare state with the 'liberal regime' together with the United States, Japan, Canada, Switzerland, Australia and New Zealand has been challenged by Francis Castles and Deborah Mitchell (1993) who argue that these countries would entail different mechanisms of income redistribution. In their view, Britain constitutes a 'radical' world together with Australia and New Zealand that are characterized by a strong degree of vertical income redistribution; a similar line of argument has been presented in a methodological critique of Esping-Andersen's typology (Obinger and Wagschal, 1997).

adds a fourth, South-European world of 'rudimentary' welfare provision (Leibfried, 1992). The critical factor in determining poverty regimes is the relationship between work and welfare as embodied in the social rights of citizens. Both the Scandinavian and the Anglo-Saxon poverty regimes put a strong emphasis on work, although in a different manner. In Scandinavia, work is considered as a social right, and strong positive work incentives are entrenched in the social assistance schemes. In the residual welfare states of the Anglo-Saxon countries, work incentives are expected to follow a different logic, as they are enforced by a very low level of benefits and negative sanctions. The 'Bismarck' poverty regime stresses the right to social security as a result of earlier contributions. Finally, the rudimentary welfare states of Southern Europe have proclaimed a right to both work and social welfare, though this right is only partly implemented.

Whereas Leibfried refers to variations in the institutionalization of social citizenship, Lødemel and Schulte address institutional arrangements of public support for the poor (Lødemel, 1992; Lødemel and Schulte, 1992). They argue that a fully-fledged analysis of welfare state regimes should consider the 'internal divisions' within welfare states, notably the relationship between social insurance schemes and means-tested social assistance. Social assistance schemes complement social insurance in the sense that they provide a minimum income with a strong emphasis on entitlement in countries with a low degree of decommodification, and are markedly separated from social insurance schemes in countries with a strong degree of decommodification (Lødemel and Schulte, 1992: 531-533; cf. Lødemel, 1989).

Countries of the 'Nordic' cluster (comprising Denmark, Finland, Norway and Sweden) are characterized by a marked division of social assistance and social insurance, as generous social insurance benefits leave a marginal or 'residual' role to social assistance schemes.[8] Unlike most social insurance benefits, social assistance is administrated at the communal level with a high level of discretion and a strong emphasis on social work treatment (cf. Ditch et al., 1997). The 'marginal' character of the Scandinavian social assistance schemes not only shows in its small significance within the welfare state, but

---

[8] A concise description of the status of social assistance in Scandinavian welfare state was given by Halvorsen and Marklund: 'Compared to other countries the target group of social assistance in the Nordic countries is more limited to the very poorest among the able-bodied. All the Nordic nations with the possible exception of Denmark are stricter in control of access but more generous in terms of the amount given to this small group. This means that social assistance has a more limited and residual ambition in the general social policy strategy, and it also means that they are less focussed on legal social rights and more concerned with assessing individual eligibility and needs for small marginal groups of the population' (Halvorsen and Marklund, 1993: 69-70). Nevertheless, there is considerable variation within the Nordic model that has led some observers to consider alternative classifications (Halvorsen, 1993: 51; Bradshaw and Terum, 1997: 245-255).

also in the stigmatizing effects of these benefits. Lødemel (1997) has denominated this aspect of the Scandinavian welfare states as a 'welfare paradox'.

Whereas these schemes funnel relatively high social assistance benefits to a small proportion of the population who slip through the mesh of the notoriously generous and universal Scandinavian welfare state, the Anglo-Saxon social assistance schemes have to accommodate a much larger group of recipients. Countries belonging to the 'British' cluster (Ireland and the United Kingdom) offer social assistance schemes that are closely integrated with non-means-tested social insurance benefits, administered at the central government level, with strong entitlements and a high degree of standardization. The continental welfare states are characterized by a medium degree of division between social insurance and social assistance. Rights positions and administrative discretion are balanced, as is the involvement of central and local units in the regulation and administration of social assistance.

In contrast to these two attempts to suggest a typology of poverty regimes that keep close to Esping-Andersen's classification, the comprehensive empirical study of Eardley et al. (1996a; 1996b; Gough et al., 1997) comes to a different conclusion.[9] On the basis of a large comparative study of social assistance schemes, they identify eight types of social assistance systems.[10] Their results suggest eight 'social assistance regimes' that partly cut across the other poverty regimes. Whereas the cluster of Scandinavian states (or the 'social democratic regime') remains unchanged, the other regimes are significantly different from earlier typologies.[11] Most surprisingly, their classification groups Germany together with 'Beveridgean' welfare states such as the United Kingdom and Ireland in the category of 'welfare states with integrated safety nets' while all other typologies mentioned place Germany in a cluster of countries clearly distinct from these Anglo-Saxon countries. In fact, the German social assistance scheme shares some of the features of this 'regime': Social assistance is largely regulated at the national level, and benefits are granted as a right, i.e. the discretion of the administering bodies is rather small. However, there are considerable differences as well. For ex-

---

[9] This study was commissioned by the Department of Social Security of the British government and the OECD.

[10] A similar but slightly modified variant of this typology has been presented by Bradshaw, joining the Japanese case with Austria and Switzerland in a cluster called 'generous but stigmatized relief' (Bradshaw, 1997: 253-255).

[11] One should take into account, however, that the small number of regimes restricts the complexity of the model. The comparison of two typologies with a considerably diverging number of regimes (three for Esping-Andersen and eight for Eardley et al.) might therefore be considered as somewhat unfair competition. However, some stark contradictions (e.g. the classification of Switzerland or the United Kingdom) cannot simply be explained by the number of regimes but must be considered as a substantial difference.

ample, unlike in the Anglo-Saxon countries, German social assistance is not only administered, but also funded by local communities.[12]

All these attempts to form distinct clusters of welfare states (with a partial exception of Eardley et al., 1996a) have in common that Britain, Germany and Sweden are part of different welfare state types, or are even considered as being some kind of archetype of this particular model. If these institutional structures have a distinctive impact on distributive outcomes, the level and profiles of poverty should also show marked variations.

Indeed, at face value, the three countries also differ in their levels and profiles of poverty. Although rankings of poverty may often lead to very divergent results dependent on the measurement methods applied (cf. Atkinson, 1998), it seems safe to conclude that Britain is among the countries with high poverty rates in Western Europe, whereas Germany displays rather low poverty rates, depending on the method of measurement. Sweden is a special case, as income data are not fully comparable to those of the other countries. Nominal poverty rates are fairly high, yet there is some strong evidence that actual poverty rates are rather low in comparison to other European countries (see Chapters 2 and 3 below).

However, I do not want to argue that belonging to a certain welfare state regime is directly related to a certain profile of poverty, although some observers have implicitly suggested a direct link between regime type and poverty (cf. Goodin et al., 1999: 90-93; Leibfried, 1992), as this relationship is blurred by a number of intervening factors. Nevertheless, there is strong evidence for a link between specific institutional characteristics of social assistance schemes and poverty, as the former are ultimately responsible for guaranteeing a societal minimum income.

Terminology

In comparative welfare state research, terminology is not always clear. Using terms common in one country to describe the welfare state in another often leads to confusion. This book is primarily concerned with one specific type of social transfer scheme: it focuses on those schemes that guarantee a minimum income not only to certain categories, but to the broad majority of the population. These benefits are not dependent on the fulfilment of any special conditions, neither in terms of previous contributions nor in terms of

---

[12] However, Eardley et al. (1996a) concede that the classification of Germany poses some problems and propose to regard Germany as a 'bridge' to the 'dual social assistance' type. Their justify this position with the existence of a separate scheme for the unemployed (*Arbeitslosenhilfe*) and wider family obligations (Eardley et al., 1996a: 169, footnote 13). Nevertheless, their more recent article does not uphold this classification (Gough et al. 1997).

personal or household characteristics, such as age, gender, nationality, disability or being a single parent. Benefits are usually means-tested, that is, are only provided upon the proof of insufficient personal resources. Therefore, eligibility depends entirely on people's need, so no other conditions are used to determine whether people should receive benefits or not. By this token, these minimum income schemes offer a universal basic 'safety net' through which nobody should fall.

These criteria are met by social transfer schemes that are often referred to as social assistance schemes; this terminology will also be followed here.[13] Examples of this type of social assistance schemes are *income support* in the United Kingdom, *Sozialhilfe* or *soziale Fürsorge* in Germany, Austria and Switzerland, and *socialhjälp, socialbistand* or *socialbidrag* in Scandinavia. In addition to social assistance schemes, many countries offer special benefits to subsidize the cost of housing for low-income groups, and some other ancillary schemes. In most countries, recipients will have the full amount of their housing costs covered (however often limited to a 'reasonable amount'), either directly from the social assistance office or by a separate housing benefit scheme (cf. Eardley et al., 1996a: 67-71). Housing benefits are therefore included in this analysis as far as these benefits add to the total minimum income package of social assistance claimants.

In many countries, there are also minimum income schemes for some categories of the population, such as the elderly, the disabled, single parents, the unemployed or the working poor. Many of these schemes provide a similar benefit level as do the general social assistance schemes or offer a even slightly higher benefit level. In addition, some countries also offer specialized schemes to foreigners with lower benefits than in the general social assistance schemes. As this book is concerned with the minimum income level in a society that applies to a broad majority of the population (cf. Veit-Wilson, 1998), the main focus is on the general social assistance schemes, but categorical schemes are also considered where relevant.

Structure of this Book

The following chapter of this book will review the existing evidence on poverty alleviation in highly-developed welfare states. Previous accounts of the poverty-alleviating power of the welfare state have largely relied on a comparison of poverty rates before and after welfare state redistribution. Whereas this approach offers a straightforward measure for the impact of the

---

[13] In the US discussion, the term 'welfare' is commonly used for this type of programme, while 'social security' is associated with social insurance schemes.

welfare state, it fails to provide an explanation for variations in an effective alleviation of poverty. In order to shed more light on the causal mechanisms of poverty alleviation, Chapter 3 then turns to those schemes that are supposed to provide the ultimate safeguard against poverty – that is means-tested benefits. Based on LIS data, it offers a first quantitative assessment of the poverty-alleviating power of the basic safety net of the welfare state and illustrates the impact of means-tested benefits on the income position of private households for three countries, Germany, Sweden and the United Kingdom. In none of these countries are means-tested benefits able to offer an effective safeguard from poverty, yet country-specific patterns of poverty alleviation can be identified. Two possible explanations may account for the apparent failure of poverty alleviation. First, an explanation may be sought in the design of means-tested benefits themselves, notably in programme structures and administrative procedures. Second, this apparent failure may also be caused by methodological problems in measuring poverty and the income position of private households. The methodological problems will be discussed in Chapter 4, focusing on the quality of available income data, the adequacy of the poverty definitions used, and the robustness of measured results.

Turning to the more substantial causes, the following three chapters will confront this quantitative data with more qualitative information on social assistance schemes and seek to establish a link between their institutional design and the profile of poverty and the structure of the poor population in Britain, Germany and Sweden. Three possible causes may explain the ineffectiveness of minimum income schemes in the alleviation of poverty: some groups of the population may not be entitled to receive benefits from these schemes; benefits may not be generous enough to push households over the poverty line; or benefits are not fully taken up by the eligible population. The following three chapters assess these questions in more detail, focusing on social assistance schemes as the very basic safety net of the welfare state. Chapter 5 compares social assistance schemes in terms of eligibility, searching for excluded groups of the population. Chapter 6 focuses on the adequacy of social assistance benefits and assesses minimum benefit levels in these schemes. At the core of this chapter, social assistance benefit levels are simulated on the basis of LIS data, thus providing an unbiased evaluation of social assistance benefit levels in relation to poverty lines for different household types. Empirical information on non-take-up in the three countries will be reviewed in Chapter 7. Finally, the concluding Chapter 8 will summarize the main results of this book and put them into a wider framework.

Chapter 2

Poverty and Poverty Alleviation in Industrialized Welfare States: What Do We Know?

Poverty still constitutes a wide-spread phenomenon in highly-developed welfare states. The following sections will present a first descriptive overview on poverty and poverty alleviation in industrial welfare states. Special emphasis is placed on the three countries that have been selected for a more detailed analysis, Germany, Sweden and the United Kingdom.

Poverty in Industrialized Welfare States

Any empirical analysis of poverty has to make choices about which concept of poverty is to be used and how poverty should be measured. Basically, poverty research has used three main concepts of poverty, focusing on low income, low expenditure or consumption, or multidimensional deprivation, each combined with absolute and relative poverty lines. Even though the variety of different concepts and methods in poverty research may suggest it, the choice is not arbitrary. Concepts and methods may be more or less appropriate for a specific purpose. I will define poverty on the basis of disposable household income for two reasons. First, this book mainly focuses on social assistance and other minimum income schemes, so income poverty naturally stands as the centre of interest. Although these schemes aim at a comprehensive improvement of a poor person's living situation, their main emphasis is on income. The second reason is a more pragmatic one. Whereas an excellent comparative database on income is available through the Luxembourg Income Study (LIS), there is no equivalent for multidimensional or consumption-oriented analyses of poverty. The following discussion of poverty will therefore predominantly focus on income poverty, yet occasionally refer to other concepts where appropriate.[14]

Most recent comparative analyses of poverty in industrial welfare states are based on the concept of relative income poverty.[15] This approach rests on the presumption that poverty is always dependent on the general welfare level in a society (cf. Townsend 1979). In most comparative studies of income poverty, this relative definition of poverty has been operationalized in a similar way, referring to a poverty line of 50 per cent of national median equivalent income.[16] However, a single poverty line provides an incomplete picture of poverty, since it does not allow for the assessment of different intensities of poverty. In addition, households may cluster just below or just above this poverty line, so the actual amount of low income may be critically under- or overstated. In order to account for varying intensities of low income, many studies also define several additional poverty lines (cf. Bishop et al., 1996). Throughout this book, households are considered as living in 'extreme poverty' if their income remains below a poverty line of 30 per cent of median equivalent income. A poverty line of 40 per cent demarcates 'severe poverty', whereas households with an income between 40 and 50 per cent of median equivalent income are considered as being in 'moderate poverty'. Households whose income exceeds the poverty line of 50 per cent, but rests below 60 per cent of median equivalent income are considered as living 'near poverty'. The intervals between the different poverty lines are referred to as 'income brackets' or 'poverty brackets'. Obviously, the bracket of 'near poverty' is not considered as poverty in a strict sense, but is included to illustrate how many households are living just above the 50 per cent poverty line.

The empirical picture of relative income poverty in industrial welfare states suggests that a sizeable proportion of the population find themselves below the poverty line, yet poverty rates and the structure of poverty vary. Figure 2.1 shows poverty profiles for a number of industrialized countries

---

[14] This chapter largely uses a methodological framework that has been established as a quasi-standard in international comparative poverty research. At this point, empirical results are presented at face value; while a more fully-fledged methodological discussion in Chapter 4 considers methodological problems, alternative measures and the robustness of results.

[15] This is at least the case for studies including more than two or three countries, e.g. Atkinson (1998); Atkinson et al. (1995); Mitchell (1991); McFate et al. (1995); Cornia (1997); Gustafsson and Lindblom (1993); Jäntti (1996); Jäntti and Danziger (2000); Oxley et al. (1999); Rainwater (1999); Smeeding et al. (1990); Smeeding and Ross (1999).

[16] A number of studies also use 50 per cent of mean household income as a poverty line, but this definition is more sensitive to extreme values at the lower and higher tails of the income distribution. For international comparisons, the median income provides more robust results. For a more detailed discussion of this poverty line, see Chapter 4.

Poverty and Poverty Alleviation   15

for the early 1990s.[17] Countries are ranked according to their poverty rate at the 50 per cent level, while the shading of the bars shows different intensities of poverty or low income.[18]

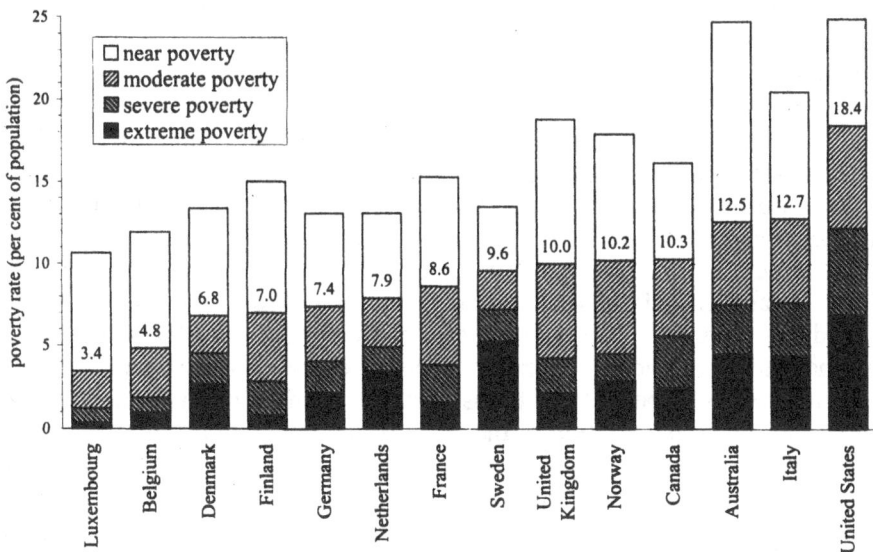

Figure 2.1 Relative poverty in industrialized countries, early 1990s

Note: Households are considered as living in extreme poverty if they dispose of a household income of less than 30 per cent of national median equivalent income, severe poverty is defined as 30-40 per cent, moderate poverty as 40-50 per cent and near poverty as 50-60 per cent of median income. Equivalence scale: modified OECD scale, attaching a weight of 1.0 to the head of household, 0.5 for further adult members of the household and 0.3 for children.

Source: LIS, own calculations.

In all industrialized welfare states, a considerable share of the population live in relative income poverty, yet with a large variation across countries.

---

[17] The choice of countries is informed by the availability of recent data in LIS (see Table A.1 in the Appendix, p. 211). In order to account for different household sizes, the poverty rates reported in Figure 2.1 are calculated on adjusted household income on the basis of the modified OECD equivalence scale. Additional household members are assumed to increase the need of the household by 0.5 for adults and 0.3 for children. Chapter 4 will discuss the use of equivalence scales in more detail.

[18] The LIS data referring to the United Kingdom is subject to Crown Copyright; has been made available by the Office for National Statistics through the ESRC Data Archive; and has been used by permission. Neither the Office for National Statistics nor the ESRC Data Archive bear any responsibility for the analysis or the interpretation of the data reported here. This disclaimer also applies to all following charts and tables based on LIS data.

16   *At the Margins of the Welfare State*

With the exception of Luxembourg and the United States, all industrialized countries in this sample display poverty rates in the range of 6 to 13 per cent of the household population if poverty is defined as 50 per cent of median equivalent household income. The lowest poverty rate of 3.4 per cent is found in Luxembourg, followed by Denmark, Finland, Germany, the Netherlands, and France. The middle ranks are taken by Sweden, the United Kingdom, Norway and Canada, where roughly one tenth of the population live in poverty. Australia and Italy have poverty rates of some 12-13 per cent, but at the very bottom of this ranking, we find the United States with a poverty rate of almost a fifth of the household population.

The profiles of poverty markedly vary across countries. Countries with similar poverty rates at the 50 per cent level do not necessarily have the same amount of extreme and severe poverty and vice versa. For example, Denmark and Canada exhibit similar levels of extreme poverty, but markedly differ in terms of overall poverty at the 50 per cent level. Likewise, Denmark and Finland have similar levels of overall poverty, but divergent poverty profiles, especially in terms of extreme and moderate poverty. Besides, there is large variation in the share of the population living near poverty just above the 50 per cent poverty line. If the poverty line was set at 60 per cent rather than 50 per cent of median income, Australia and the United States would both have poverty rates of around one quarter of the population, although poverty rates at the 50 per cent level differ by as much as 6 percentage points. These different profiles of poverty are informed by differences in the income distribution in each country, but may also be caused by differences in the underlying databases.

The three countries in the main focus of this book display particular profiles of poverty. The United Kingdom is characterized by a relatively high poverty rate at the 50 per cent level (10.0 per cent), yet with few households in extreme and severe poverty. Most poor households (5.8 per cent of the population) are living in moderate poverty. Sweden very much resembles the United Kingdom in terms of overall poverty at the 50 per cent level (9.6 per cent), but the distribution of the poor on poverty brackets shows an almost exactly reversed situation. Whereas only a small share of the poor population experience moderate poverty (2.3 per cent of the population), 5.3 per cent live in extreme poverty (2.1 per cent in the United Kingdom). This pattern can possibly be explained with the differing household definition in the Swedish data.[19] In Germany, a similar share of the population live in extreme

---

[19] It has to be kept in mind that the poverty rates reported in Figure 2.1 tend to overstate poverty in Sweden because of a differing household definition compared to other countries. Adult children are classified as separate households even if they still live with their parents and are economically dependent on them, e.g. pupils and students. For a more fully-fledged discussion of this point, see Chapter 4.

and severe poverty as in the United Kingdom, but since less households find themselves in moderate poverty (3.3 per cent), the overall poverty rate at the 50 per cent level is more than two percentage points lower. The income bracket of near poverty again is characterized by the two poles of Sweden and the United Kingdom, with Germany in the middle. Whereas relatively few households live near poverty in Sweden (3.9 per cent), more than twice as much do so in the United Kingdom (8.8 per cent). This brings Sweden close to Germany (13.5 respectively 13.1 per cent) in terms of low income rates at the 60 per cent level, whereas a much higher share of the population lives on a low income in the United Kingdom (18.8 per cent).

The general picture of the low income profiles in the three countries largely confirms earlier accounts. For example, this chart illustrates well Mitchell's (1991) earlier assessment of the British case as depicting suspiciously low poverty rates at the 40 per cent level, but much higher poverty rates at the 50 and 60 per cent level. It appears that the British welfare state is very effective in alleviating harsh poverty, yet one in ten households live in overall poverty. At face value, this finding fits very well to the common characterization of the British welfare state as belonging to the liberal welfare model where most public social transfers are confined to providing a minimum income on a rather low level. The empirical evidence for Germany and Sweden stands in a certain tension to their usual classifications. Given that the Swedish welfare state is still considered as offering a universal and generous safety net, the relatively high poverty rates call for an explanation. If the Swedish welfare states offers a more generous benefit level than the British one, why are overall poverty rates almost identical? Is there any evidence that the variations in the intensity of poverty can be directly related to characteristics of the welfare state? The German case also raises some questions. If the German welfare state emphasizes horizontal redistribution at the expense of vertical redistribution, and provides a rather mean and patchy basic safety net of minimum income schemes, what are the reasons for the relatively low poverty rates in Germany, as in most other 'conservative' or 'christian-democratic' countries? In the following sections, these questions will be dealt with in some more detail.

The Redistributional Impact of the Welfare State

The first glance at poverty rates in industrialized countries above has shown that a substantial proportion of the population live in income poverty in industrial welfare states. At face value, the persistence of poverty suggests that the welfare state thus is not effective in alleviating poverty, but this issue deserves some more attention.

International variations in poverty profiles are not only driven by variations in the effectiveness of welfare state redistribution, but also by variations in socio-demographic and socio-economic structures, as these factors put different strains on income transfer schemes. Indeed, a comparison of Scandinavia and France has demonstrated that the French poverty rate would almost be reduced to zero if social structure and labour market participation rates corresponded to the Scandinavian situation. By the same token, the Scandinavian countries would do much worse in poverty alleviation if they had the French social-economic situation (Kangas and Ritakallio, 1998b).

Rather than using aggregate social expenditure as an indicator for the impact of the welfare state, micro-data allow the effectiveness of the welfare state to be determined by comparing private household incomes before and after redistribution. This method allows us to control some external effects on poverty. By this token, a more refined analysis of the redistributional impact of the welfare state can be offered. In the following, some empirical results on the redistributional impact of the welfare state will be presented after a short methodological introduction.

Measurement of the Redistributional Impact of Taxes and Transfers

Most studies analyzing the redistributional impact of the welfare state are based on so-called Beckerman ratios. Beckerman's (1979) influential study of poverty and the impact of income maintenance programmes in Australia, Belgium, Norway and Great Britain for the first half of the 1970s has inspired a large body of research on this issue.[20] The strong impact of his work was largely due to his innovative methodological framework. His 'Beckerman ratios' developed as a widely-used measure for the effectiveness of redistribution. In principle, this method allows the comparison of the effectiveness of taxes and transfers across time, transfer schemes, and countries. The rationale of this approach is a comparison of pre- and post-redistribution poverty rates, either related to the sum of all taxes and transfers or focusing on single programmes (e.g. pensions or social assistance).[21] This broad approach side-steps a major problem in comparative research: countries have organized their social transfers differently, and therefore the same goals are approached by various means.

---

[20] However, the analysis of the redistributional impact of social transfer schemes did not start with Beckerman. Earlier studies, as for example Sawyer (1976: 34-36), attempted to evaluate the impact of transfers as well, but did not fully develop this analysis.

[21] It should be made clear, however, that only actual redistributional measures can be assessed. Further consequences of redistributional policies, such as changes in individual or collective behaviour or macro-economic performance cannot be captured by the methods employed.

Poverty and Poverty Alleviation 19

Starting from the assumption that transfers are effective if they help to prevent poverty, this approach focuses on the question of how many units (individuals or households) are catapulted out of poverty by the welfare state, or, in other words, how many units are poor before transfers and non-poor after redistribution. The effectiveness of transfers is expressed as the proportion of poverty prevented by transfers to the pre-transfer poor, as illustrated in Figure 2.2 below. The bold lines sketch the distribution of pre- and post-transfer income. Demarcated by these lines, total social security transfers are represented by areas B and C combined; the poverty line is given by the dotted line. Areas A and C together describe the extent of pre-transfer poverty: A represents post-transfer poverty, and C the amount of poverty alleviated by transfers.

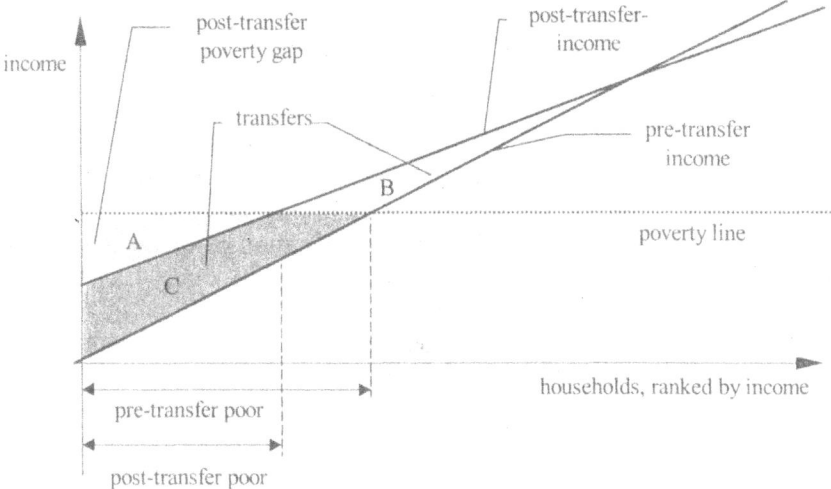

Figure 2.2 Beckerman ratios

Source: Based on the illustration in Beckerman (1979: 53).

The effectiveness of transfers can be measured as the ratio of prevented poverty and the pre-transfer poverty,[22] in short:

---

[22] In the same way, this allows to measure the efficiency of transfers, that is the transfers that actually help to lift the poor out of poverty as a proportion of the total resources spent, i.e.

$$efficiency = \frac{C}{(B+C)}$$

$$effectiveness = \frac{C}{(A+C)}$$

The effectiveness of social security transfers can be measured in two ways. The 'head count' measure provides the number of poor (households or persons) lifted out of poverty.[23] This measure captures the incidence of poverty but not its intensity. This information is provided by the 'poverty gap' which describes the amount of additional resources needed to lift the poor over a given poverty line (either on an individual or on an aggregate level). Each of these measures catches different aspects of poverty, and thus these measures should be combined to evaluate the effectiveness of social transfers.[24]

The appeal of the Beckerman ratios stems from their easy calculation and their wide range of application. In addition, these indices allow the comparison of effectiveness across countries and over time without necessarily having to account for different institutional settings. These attributes seem to have stimulated the strong influence of Beckerman's methods on later studies.[25]

Most newer studies do not confine themselves to the analysis of social security transfers, but include the tax system into their analysis. They argue that the effectiveness of the welfare state can only be judged if one allows for the fact that countries organize the redistribution of incomes in a different way. Redistribution may not only be achieved by direct transfers to clients, but also, in principle, through the tax system.[26] Focusing on either component alone (social security schemes or the tax system) would underestimate the redistributional impact of the other.[27] This argument has been brought forward most forcefully by Mitchell (1991). She criticizes the com-

---

[23] In Figure 2.2, this measure would be represented by the difference between the number of pre-transfer poor and post-transfer poor (see arrows at the bottom of the figure).

[24] For a more comprehensive account of these two measures of poverty, cf. Mitchell (1991: 43-77).

[25] In spite of its innovative methodological framework, the descriptive power of Beckerman's study was limited by serious empirical problems. The most serious of these problems concerns the data on social security benefits. The lack of available data at that time forced Beckerman to use average expenditure per recipient as a proxy for the actual social security benefits received by the households. This measure is problematic, since benefits may not be equally distributed among the recipient population. The unequal distribution tends to overestimate the poverty-alleviating effects of social security transfers especially if benefits are income related. Besides, low take-up rates might further overstate the effectiveness of benefits. Beckerman was nevertheless aware of most of these problems (Beckerman, 1979: 16-17).

[26] Obviously, some tax allowances tend to favour some groups of the population that are typically *not* the most needy, but this does not mean that the tax system as such is not qualified to achieve the same goals as direct transfers.

[27] In addition, social security transfers are taxable in some countries. Confining the analysis to transfers only would understate the impact of tax clawback of benefits.

Poverty and Poverty Alleviation   21

parative research on the redistributional impact of social transfers as too narrow in terms of a concentration on social security schemes, neglecting the redistributional impact of the tax system.[28]

Redistribution through Transfers and Taxes

When comparative micro-data on income became available in the 1980s, a number of studies scrutinized the redistributive effect of the welfare state on the basis of Beckerman ratios. While Beckerman had to rely on a suboptimal database, more recent studies could use the micro-data of the Luxembourg Income Study (LIS) for extended analyses. Mitchell's (1991) study is the most comprehensive account of the redistributive effectiveness of the welfare state based on the second wave of the Luxembourg Income Study (mid-1980s). She has identified distinct patterns of poverty reduction. Sweden, Norway, the Netherlands, France and Germany form a cluster of countries with a high effectiveness of taxes and transfers. A second, but less clear-cut cluster of low-performance countries comprises Australia, Switzerland, Canada and the US at the very bottom.[29] The United Kingdom displays a distinct pattern of effectiveness of redistribution. Applying a low poverty line of 40 per cent of the median income, effectiveness is even higher than for the high-performance countries; at the 50 per cent level, and even more for a 60 per cent poverty line, Britain is located between the two clusters, or even comes close to the low-performance cluster (Mitchell, 1991: 47, 51). A number of similar studies have largely confirmed Mitchell's results for different subgroups of the population, such as families (McFate et al., 1995; Förster, 1994), single parent families (Hauser, 1987; Hauser and Fischer, 1990), and the elderly (Shaver, 1998).

Table 2.1 shows more recent empirical results on the redistributional impact of the welfare state, based on the most recent LIS data available for selected industrial countries. Countries are ranked according to their poverty rate after taxes and transfers. As the overall redistributional impact of the welfare state is strongly dependent on the public-private mix in the pension

---

[28] In her view, the concentration on social security schemes stems from a certain eurocentrism of comparative welfare state analysis which neglects the relatively high effectiveness and efficiency of the Antipodean welfare states (see also Castles and Mitchell, 1993).

[29] The position of Australia stands in some tension to Castles' and Mitchell's (1993) redefinition of welfare state regimes that has classified Australia together with the United Kingdom as belonging to the 'radical' world of welfare. In terms of poverty reduction, Australia takes a medium position between the United Kingdom and the 'liberal' countries of Switzerland, Canada (with some characteristics of the 'radical' type) and the United States (Mitchell, 1991: 51), whereas Australia joins the United Kingdom in the reduction of inequality (Gini index) (Castles and Mitchell, 1993: 110).

22   At the Margins of the Welfare State

system, this table is confined to the prime-age population, defined as households whose head is not older than 55 years.[30]

Table 2.1 The effectiveness of welfare state redistribution for prime-age households, early 1990s (household head under 55)

Country (ranked according to poverty rate after redistribution)	Poverty Rate (rank order)		Poverty Rate Reduction (rank order)	
	before taxes and transfers	after taxes and transfers	absolute (percentage points)	relative (per cent)
Belgium 1992	13.0 (1)	2.9 (1)	-10.1 (8)	-78% (1)
Finland 1995	25.7 (10)	7.9 (2)	-17.8 (2)	-69% (2)
Germany 1994	14.7 (2)	7.9 (2)	-6.8 (11)	-46% (10)
Denmark 1992	22.6 (9)	8.1 (4)	-14.5 (4)	-64% (3)
France 1994	22.3 (8)	8.5 (5)	-13.8 (5)	-62% (5)
Netherlands 1994	19.5 (3)	9.1 (6)	-10.5 (7)	-54% (7)
Norway 1995	20.7 (5)	9.5 (7)	-11.2 (6)	-54% (7)
United Kingdom 1995	26.2 (11)	9.8 (8)	-16.4 (3)	-63% (4)
Australia 1994	20.2 (4)	10.4 (9)	-9.8 (9)	-49% (9)
Canada 1994	21.0 (6)	11.7 (10)	-9.3 (10)	-44% (11)
Sweden 1995	31.4 (12)	13.1 (11)	-18.3 (1)	-58% (6)
United States 1994	21.6 (7)	18.2 (12)	-3.4 (12)	-16% (12)

Note: Poverty rates are based on a poverty line of 50 per cent of national median income, adjusted for household size according to the modified OECD scale (weights of 1.0 for head of the household, 0.5 for each additional adult and 0.3 for each child). Italy and Luxembourg could not be considered because LIS includes only data on net incomes for these two countries. Please note that poverty rates do not correspond to poverty rates indicated in Figure 2.1 (p. 15) as Table 2.1 considers only prime-age households.

Source: LIS, own calculations.

The empirical evidence suggests that welfare state redistribution indeed has a strong impact on poverty rates among prime-age households, yet there are marked variations across countries. Some clusters of countries can be identified: A high effectiveness of the welfare state in terms of poverty reduction is found in Belgium, Finland, Denmark and the United Kingdom. Whereas

---

[30] A large part of the total reduction of poverty rates is concentrated on one specific group of the population, the elderly. Pensioners usually have very high poverty rates before taxes and transfers, because of their low market income and reliance on public pensions. Hence, the impact of welfare state redistribution is very strong for this group. An international comparison of the redistributive impact of the welfare state may be biased by variations in age cohort structure. The reduction of poverty in the welfare state is necessarily higher in countries with a higher proportion of elderly, all other things being equal.

the first three of these countries also end up with low poverty rates for disposable incomes, the United Kingdom somewhat deviates from this pattern with medium poverty rates. As in Mitchell's (1991) earlier study, the rank position of the United Kingdom is very sensitive to the poverty line chosen. An astonishing pattern of poverty reduction is also found in Sweden. Sweden achieves the highest reduction in absolute terms, but only a mediocre performance in relative terms, and ends up with fairly high poverty rates for disposable incomes. These startling results can partly be accounted for by a differing household definition.[31]

At the other end of the spectrum, a group of countries reduces poverty to a much lesser degree. The United States clearly stand out with a meagre reduction of poverty through transfers and taxes, cutting down poverty rates only by 3.4 percentage points (or 16 per cent) from 21.6 to 18.2 per cent of the population. With some distance, the Canadian, German and Australian welfare states also reduce poverty rates to a relatively small degree. Nevertheless, poverty rates after transfers and taxes are rather low in the German case, but must be attributed less to the redistributional impact of the welfare state rather than to a relatively good protection from poverty in the primary income distribution. In contrast, Canada and Australia show high poverty rates of more than one tenth of the prime-age population.[32]

The rank orders of poverty rates before and after redistribution suggest that there might be a certain trade-off between public and private sources of income. If poverty rates for market income are already relatively low, the impact of redistribution is naturally limited. Indeed, the redistributional impact of the welfare state is the stronger, the higher pre-transfer poverty rates, as Figure 2.3 shows.

The strong correlation between market income poverty rates and the redistributional impact of the welfare state points to one critical limitation of Beckerman's method. The analysis presented here has focused exclusively on the redistributional impact of actual taxes and transfers, but ignores the fact that the primary distribution of income is not independent of the welfare state.

---

[31] As indicated above, the Swedish household definition leads to an overestimation of poverty among young adults and obviously has a strong impact on poverty rates of prime-age households. A more detailed methodological discussion of this point can be found in Chapter 4.

[32] The Australian position in this rank order stands in a certain tension to Castles' and Mitchell's characterization as 'radical welfare state regime' which describes countries that spend a relatively low share of national income on social transfers and services, but nevertheless achieve a high degree of income redistribution (Mitchell, 1991; Castles and Mitchell, 1993). The results for the early 1990s put Australia closer to the bottom ranks than in Mitchell's (1991) earlier analysis, yet the distance to the United States is still apparent.

24 At the Margins of the Welfare State

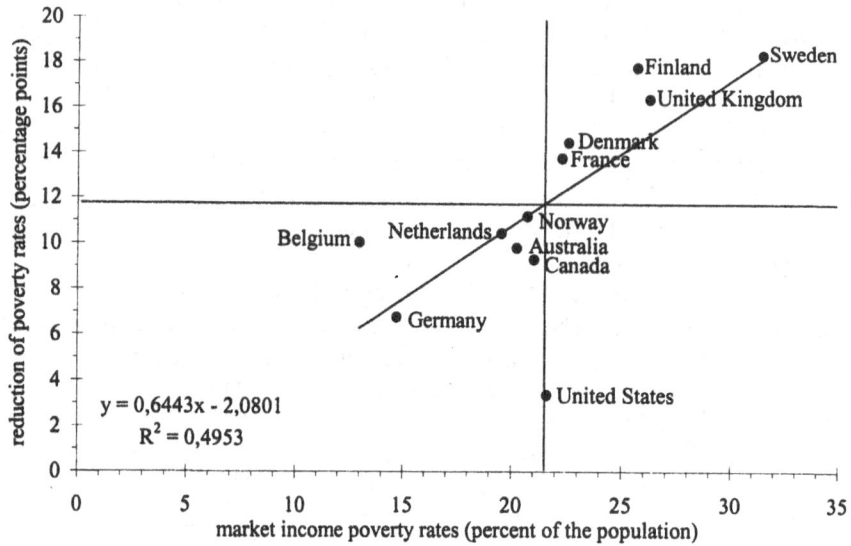

Figure 2.3 Market income poverty rates and the reduction of poverty by social transfers and taxes for the prime-age population (head younger than 55 years), early 1990s

Note: Poverty rates are calculated on the basis of 50 per cent of median household disposable income adjusted for household size according to the modified OECD equivalence scale (weight of 1.0 for head of household, 0.5 for additional adults and 0.3 for children). Data reported refer to the most recent available data for each country. Social expenditure includes public and private mandatory expenditure.

Source: LIS, OECD Social Expenditure database, own calculations.

The counterfactual of an income distribution without transfers is nothing more than a fiction that assumes that the welfare state has a merely direct effect on the distribution of income. This is, however, not necessarily the case, since individual expectations and behaviour are also reflected in the primary income distribution. Taxes and transfers may have an impact on the supply of and the demand for labour, because they provide alternative sources of income other than wages from employment. In addition, people may change their behaviour in terms of saving and consumption patterns. For example, if people expect generous pensions from a public pension scheme, they may deem it unnecessary to contribute to a private pension plan (cf. Mitchell, 1991: 43-36). Björklund (1998: 46-47) even goes one step further in claiming that a complete economic model of the redistributional impact of the welfare state should even consider changes in mating, fertility and divorce behaviour.

Nevertheless, the correlation between market poverty rates and the effects of welfare state redistribution is far from perfect. This indicates that there is indeed a certain scope for policy factors. On a given level of market poverty, some countries are more effective than others in alleviating poverty. Belgium, Denmark, Finland, France and the United Kingdom are overproportionately effective in reducing poverty in this respect, whereas the United States, but also Canada, Australia and Germany arrive at relatively low degrees of effectiveness. These results seem to partly contradict common ideas about the redistributional effectiveness of welfare states based on welfare state typologies. For example, why is the conservative Belgian welfare state so effective in reducing poverty while the German welfare state is not, although it nevertheless ends up with relatively low poverty rates?

Welfare State Efforts and the Alleviation of Poverty

What can explain different degrees of effectiveness of poverty alleviation? Are specific features of welfare states related to outcomes in terms of poverty alleviation? In particular, is there a connection between welfare state efforts and outcomes – in other words, are extensive welfare states more effective in alleviating poverty than the tighter ones?

This section will assess the relationship between welfare state efforts and poverty alleviation in two steps. The next section addresses the question of whether there is a correlation between the size of the welfare state and the incidence of poverty. Are high social expenditure rates associated with low poverty rates? We then turn to the reduction of poverty rates through taxes and transfers and its relationship to welfare effort.

Welfare State Efforts and the Incidence of Poverty

Using social expenditure as a proxy for welfare effort, the relationship between welfare state efforts and outcomes in terms of poverty has been described in a fairly succinct way: The bigger the welfare state the smaller is the poverty rate. (Gustafsson and Uusitalo, 1990: 255). This statement is based on a regression of cash social expenditure (as a percentage of GDP) and poverty rates for the time around 1980, suggesting that social expenditure accounts for two thirds of the variation of poverty rates (Gustafsson and Uusitalo, 1990: 255). Förster (1994: 20-22) has found an even stronger correlation between welfare effort and poverty rates for families with children for the mid-1980s. More recent data confirm these results in principle for the prime-age population, although the correlation is less strong than in the earlier studies (see Figure 2.4).[33] Pensions and other cash expenditure for the elderly has been excluded from the social expenditure ratios.[34]

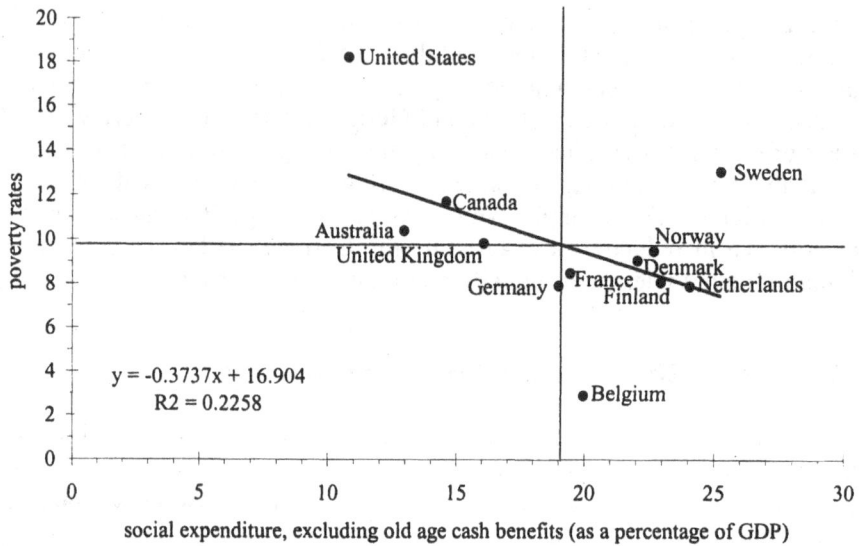

Figure 2.4 Welfare state efforts and the alleviation of poverty: Social expenditure and relative poverty rates for prime-age households in OECD countries (head younger than 55 years), early 1990s

Note: See Figure 2.3 (p. 24).
Source: LIS, OECD Social Expenditure Database, own calculations.

Figure 2.4 illustrates that there is in fact some correlation between social expenditure ratios and poverty rates. Countries with large social expenditure ratios tend to have lower poverty rates than countries with lower social expenditure ratios. Yet, social expenditure ratios only explain somewhat more than one third of the variance in poverty rates. Some countries display much higher or lower poverty rates than what would have been expected on the basis of their level of social expenditure. Notably Belgium is very effective

---

[33] In contrast to the earlier studies, Figure 2.4 includes private mandatory social expenditure, but excludes expenditure on education; the results are thus not fully comparable.
[34] It would have been more accurate to exclude *all* social expenditure on the non-prime-age household population from this analysis, since variations in socio-demographic structure obviously do not only have an effect on market income poverty rates and the redistributional impact of the welfare state, but also on the level of social expenditure. However, as aggregate data do not allow a detailed break-down, social expenditure ratios excluding old age cash benefits are taken as a proxy.

in this respect, to a lesser extent also Australia, France, Germany and the United Kingdom. In contrast, the United States and – with some methodological reservations – Sweden, as well as Norway are much less efficient.

However, this simple cross-sectional regression fails to fully elucidate the complex relationship between welfare state efforts and the alleviation of poverty. The variation of poverty levels may also be determined by the primary income distribution, reflecting variations in socio-demographic and socio-economic structures. We would therefore expect that the size of welfare effort has a stronger impact on the *reduction* of poverty through welfare state redistribution rather than on the *level* of poverty as such. The following section will address this question in more detail.

Welfare State Efforts and the Redistributional Impact of the Welfare State

As outlined above, the redistributional impact of the welfare state should also be exemplified by a clear correlation between welfare state efforts and the reduction of poverty rates. Using social expenditure as a proxy for welfare state efforts, Figure 2.5 below depicts the relationship between welfare effort and the reduction of poverty rates by welfare state redistribution for the prime-age population. Countries with high social spending tend to reduce poverty more effectively than countries with a lower social expenditure ratio. Welfare effort is more closely correlated with the reduction of poverty rates than to the level of poverty as such (Figure 2.4, p. 26). This evidence suggests that the persistence of poverty in industrialized welfare states can partly be explained by the fact that countries do not spend enough on social transfers. Consequently, a further reduction of poverty rates could be best achieved by more extensive social expenditure according to this logic.

Nevertheless, countries scatter widely and display specific patterns of poverty alleviation. Relative to their level of social expenditure, the United Kingdom, and to a lesser extent also Finland, France and Australia were overproportionally effective in alleviating poverty. In contrast, the United States, Germany, Norway and the Netherlands achieve lower levels of poverty alleviation than would have been expected on the basis of their social expenditure.

However, these simple regressions do not tell the whole story. There is large variation in the relationship between input (social expenditure) and output (reduction of poverty rates); hence, in the efficiency dimension. Countries with similar levels of social expenditure reach divergent levels of poverty reduction. For example, Germany, France and Belgium spend a comparable share of their GDP on social security for the prime-age population, yet their effectiveness in poverty reduction varies. Whereas France and Belgium are relatively successful in bringing down poverty rates, Germany is relatively inefficient in this respect and finds itself far below the regression line, both for the prime-age population only and the full population. In contrast, the United Kingdom is reaches a similar reduction of poverty rates as Finland or even Sweden, but on a markedly lower level of social expenditure.

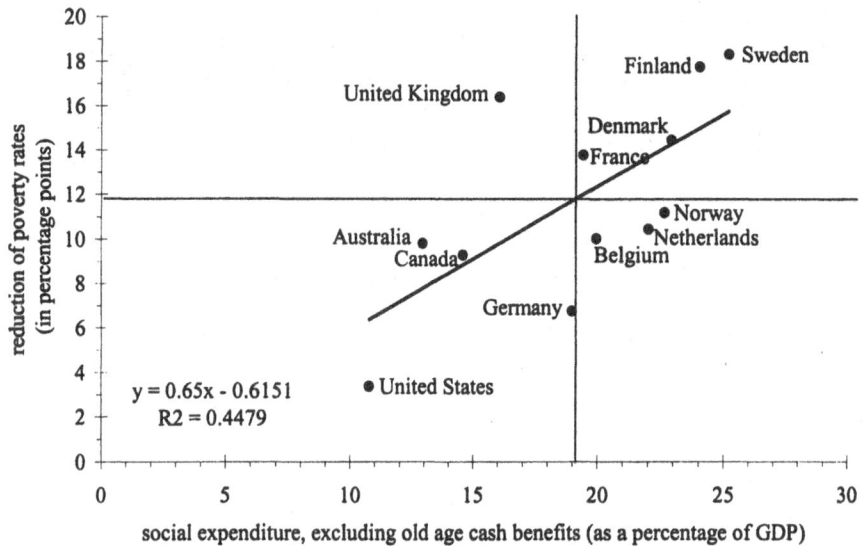

Figure 2.5 **Welfare state efforts and the alleviation of poverty: Social expenditure and the reduction of poverty rates through transfers and taxes for prime-age households in OECD countries (head younger than 55 years)**

Note: See Figure 2.3 (p. 24).

Source: LIS, OECD Social Expenditure Database, own calculations.

What can explain these large variations in efficiency? Which intervening variables can explain why some countries are more efficient than others in reducing poverty rates? Basically, these variations may be due to a number of substantial factors, including variations in policies, as well as differing socio-economic and socio-demographic contexts. The following section will elaborate further on this point.

Unsolved Puzzles and a Possible Solution

Limitations of the Existing Studies

The review of the existing evidence on the redistributional impact of the welfare state has uncovered some interesting patterns of poverty alleviation, but has sketched a pretty crude picture of poverty alleviation. In particular, this analysis suffers from three shortcomings.

First, the simple design of this type of studies embodies a very narrow view of the welfare state implying that the alleviation of income poverty is the single aim of redistribution. Yet, if one rather regards social integration as the global objective of the welfare state, there are more issues to be taken into account. The integration of the middle classes (or groups of the population with an income above the poverty line in general) may not only be considered as a waste of resources or a 'spillover' as the Beckerman model does, but also as a safeguard against a clear-cut segmentation of the society in rich and poor strata of the population, or in those who are dependent on the welfare state and those who are not.[35] A stronger emphasis on horizontal redistribution, encompassing the middle classes, may not only enhance the legitimacy of redistribution (cf. Taylor-Gooby, 1985; Roller, 1995a), but may also preclude curtailments to be concentrated disproportionately on the poor (cf. Le Grand and Winter, 1987; Pierson, 1994; Alber, 1996).

Second, as indicated above, the redistributional impact of the welfare state is dependent on socio-economic and socio-demographic conditions in each countries, so welfare states face different degrees of external pressure. Although the use of Beckerman ratios can mitigate this problem, certain flaws remain. In particular, variations in public-private mix may bias the measured effectiveness of the welfare state. Welfare states may achieve the same objectives in different ways, by regulative, distributive or redistributive policies, associated with different levels of public involvement and levels of public spending. Although outcomes of these policies do not necessarily differ, Beckerman ratios will produce different results for the poverty-alleviating effectiveness of welfare states.[36]

---

[35] Cf. e.g. Skocpol's (1991) argument in favour of universal benefits instead of rigid targeting of resources towards the poor for the case of the United States.

[36] One example for similar outcomes of different welfare state strategies can be found in pension systems. Although some countries have chosen to organize a large part of their system of old-age income security in terms of occupational pensions provided by private bodies, redistributional effects are hardly distinguishable from public pension schemes, largely because of a strict regulation and supervision of private pension schemes in some countries (cf. Behrendt, 2000c; Pedersen, 1999). It is therefore questionable whether the focus on public redistribution leads to adequate results for an evaluation of the impact of the welfare state.

Last but not least, the measured effectiveness of social transfers fails to tell anything about the causes and the conditions of an effective alleviation of poverty. Which institutional settings help to enhance or hinder redistributional effectiveness? Our knowledge on the institutional conditions of effectiveness still is astonishingly sparse. This opinion is shared by Deborah Mitchell who concludes that most of the studies analyzing outcomes of redistribution

> arrive at a set of observations which observe what has happened in each country's transfer process without making clear *how* it had happened. (Mitchell, 1991: 158, emphasis original)

Esping-Andersen takes the same line by stating that

> why welfare state structures have such different distributional consequences is left largely unexplained. (Esping-Andersen, 1990: 56)

Beckerman ratios provide a very straightforward and efficient tool for evaluating the distributive effects of public policies and allow a relatively easy comparison of redistributional effectiveness over time and across countries, but this measure does not tell anything about the mechanisms of redistribution. The evaluation of the causes of a certain outcome in terms of income distribution or poverty requires a detailed assessment of a country's institutional framework that structures redistribution, as George and Lawson have acknowledged.

> It is a sad reflection that after twenty years of unprecedented economic growth and massive government expenditure in social security, poverty is still prevalent in all EEC countries. Economic growth and increased public expenditure do not by themselves reduce inequalities and abolish poverty. Governments need to implement explicitly designed policies to achieve such ends. (George and Lawson, 1980: xi-xii)

In questioning of why welfare states fail to effectively alleviate poverty, a closer evaluation of the bottom safety net of the welfare state promises useful insights. In modern welfare states, the ultimate responsibility for the alleviation of poverty is given to social assistance schemes and other minimum income schemes. These schemes form the basic net of the welfare state and are ultimately responsible for the alleviation of poverty. If this net does not hold, the effectiveness of the welfare state as a whole is fundamentally challenged.

Focusing on the Basic Safety Net of the Welfare State

As the basic safety net of the welfare state, minimum income schemes play a decisive role for the alleviation of poverty. We would expect that minimum income benefits form an income ceiling below which no individual or household should fall. These schemes step in if the primary income distribution and social insurance schemes fail to provide a decent income level. However, the persistence of poverty in industrial welfare states suggests that this basic safety net of the welfare state fails to achieve this goal, as a sizeable proportion of the population appear to fall through this safety net and find themselves in poverty. By this token, the persistence of poverty in industrial welfare states may eventually be explained by a failure of minimum income schemes.

If minimum income schemes play a decisive role for the alleviation of poverty in industrial welfare states, our focus of analysis should shift from the welfare state as a whole to its basic safety net. A thorough analysis of these schemes can offer some more insights into the causal patterns of poverty alleviation in industrial welfare states, and can help to solve some of the puzzles that are still present in poverty research. In particular, this approach can shed some more light on the mechanisms that are responsible for the fact that a remarkable proportion of the population finds itself in income poverty. In addition, variations in effectiveness of poverty alleviation may be explained by the performance of the basic safety net of the welfare state.

This approach also allows us to complement quantitative micro-data with more qualitative institutional information on social assistance schemes in order to cross-check the quality of micro-data and to reveal causal patterns of poverty alleviation. Before embarking on a fully-fledged analysis of the interaction between social assistance schemes and poverty, the following chapter will first quantitatively explore the impact of minimum income schemes on poverty alleviation. Based on Beckerman ratios, the following chapter will give a first overview on patterns of poverty alleviation through minimum income schemes, focusing on Germany, Sweden and the United Kingdom.

Each of these three countries is characterized by a specific profile of poverty and poverty alleviation. Sweden and the United Kingdom display similar poverty rates at the 50 per cent level, yet their poverty profiles are very different. Sweden exhibits a markedly higher proportion of extreme poverty, whereas the poor in Britain are dominated by households living in moderate poverty. In addition, these similar outcomes in terms of poverty rates are produced by different types of welfare states. The two countries do not only spend a divergent share of their national income on social policies, but also differ in the general organization of social policies.[37] Whereas the British welfare state largely relies upon flat-rate benefits supplemented by private provision, the Swedish welfare state takes a more comprehensive stance with higher levels of support. It seems that different strategies of welfare state redistribution lead to similar outcomes. How can this puzzle be explained?

In terms of poverty alleviation for the prime-age population, the United Kingdom is characterized by a relatively high effectiveness in reducing poverty from relatively high market income poverty rates to rather close-to-average poverty rates after transfers and taxes. However, as the British poverty rates are very sensitive to the choice of the poverty line, measured effectiveness may not be very robust. Sweden is also characterized by a relatively high redistributional effectiveness, yet data are not fully comparable because of methodological problems and deserve a closer analysis.

The German case also calls for an explanation. Notorious for a low amount of vertical redistribution of income and lacking minimum income guarantees outside of social assistance, the German welfare state surprises with relatively low poverty rates. One possible explanation may be found in the fact that the distribution of market incomes already leaves a comparatively smaller share of the population in poverty than in Sweden and the United Kingdom. However, when the effectiveness of poverty alleviation is considered in relation to the overall effort of the German welfare state, the redistributional impact turns out to be rather limited, yet still with underproportionally low poverty rates.

The following chapter will shift the focus of analysis from the welfare state as a whole to its basic safety net in order to shed more light on these patterns of poverty alleviation and will eventually come up with a tentative explanation for these patterns.

---

[37] Compared to the United Kingdom, Sweden allocates another tenth of her GDP on social policies. In 1995, the social expenditure ratios were 22.8 and 33.4 per cent respectively (cf. OECD, 1999b).

Chapter 3

Mapping the Reduction of Poverty through Minimum Income Schemes

As the basic safety net of the welfare state, minimum income schemes play a decisive role in the alleviation of poverty. Nevertheless, these schemes have not stood in the main focus of research into the redistributional effectiveness of the welfare state so far. One could argue, however, that their effectiveness has been indirectly tested in the analyses of total redistribution presented in the previous chapter, since means-tested benefits provide for the basic layer of social security. Therefore, the existence and extent of poverty point to an ineffective alleviation of poverty through means-tested transfers. This is certainly true, but there are specific patterns of poverty alleviation through means-tested transfers that cannot be identified with the rather crude instruments used in this kind of analysis. Given that means-testing transfers are explicitly designed to alleviate poverty, a closer look at this type of benefit promises useful insights into the logic behind them.[38]

Evaluating the Effects of Minimum Income Schemes

The evaluation of the effects of minimum income schemes largely follows the methodology laid out in the previous chapter and is based on a comparison between incomes before and after transfers. Income after transfers, as used in this paper, equals the disposable income as defined by the Luxembourg Income Study, adjusted for family size.[39] The definition of the income before transfers is less obvious. Under the assumption that means-tested benefits are not taxed, the income before means-tested benefits is calculated by subtracting all means-tested benefits (cash and near cash) from the disposable income. This definition comes near to the actual calculation of

---

[38] A previous version of this chapter based on earlier data was presented in Behrendt (2000a).

[39] Households with negative and zero disposable incomes have been excluded from the study, since missing values are re-coded as zero by LIS.

means-tested benefits in most countries, considering net income after taxes in order to evaluate claimants' needs.

The income position of households is evaluated on the basis of a number of poverty lines, as used in the previous chapter. Relative income poverty is defined as income that is lower than 50 per cent of national median income adjusted for household size.[40] Furthermore, three additional poverty lines, set at 30, 40, and 60 per cent of equivalent median household income are applied for two reasons. Firstly, they allow for the assessment of different intensities of poverty, and secondly, they can be used to illustrate the degree to which the poor are pushed up the income scale by means-tested benefits. For this purpose, households are classified into 'poverty brackets' according to their incomes. The poverty brackets are defined as incomes lower than 30 per cent of the median equivalent household income ('extreme poverty'), between 30 and 40 per cent ('severe poverty'), between 40 and 50 per cent ('moderate poverty'), between 50 and 60 per cent ('near poverty') and over 60 per cent ('no poverty').

Figure 3.1 shows the lower part of an income distribution and illustrates the use of different poverty lines and poverty brackets as defined in this paper.

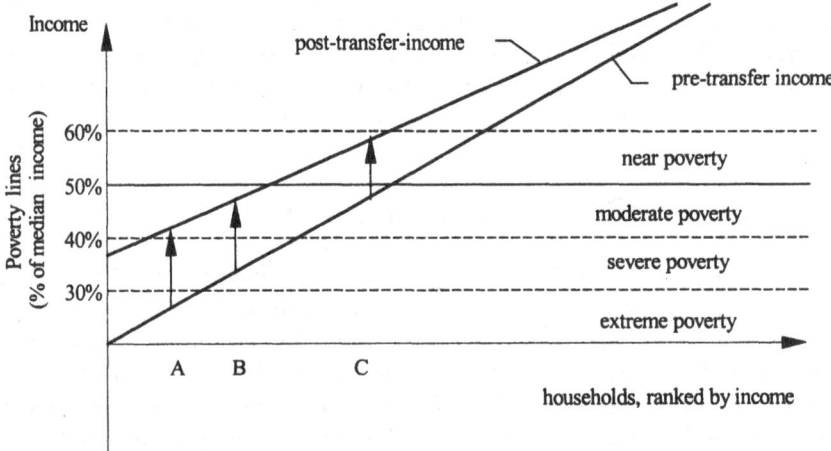

Figure 3.1 Poverty lines and poverty brackets

The effect of minimum income transfers is shown as the difference between the pre-transfer distribution of incomes (lower bold line) and the post-

---

[40] Poverty lines calculated from disposable income are applied to both income before and after means-tested transfers. Therefore, the poverty lines applied to incomes *before* means-tested transfers are not relative poverty lines in a strict sense, but are equal to the absolute value of the relative poverty lines for incomes *after* means-tested transfers.

transfer distribution of disposable incomes (upper bold line). These transfers improve the income position of households by moving them up in the income scale, as exemplified for three sample households A, B and C. Household A moves from extreme poverty into the moderate poverty bracket, thereby crossing two poverty lines (30 and 40 per cent of median equivalent income). Households B and C each move into the next-higher poverty bracket; from severe into moderate poverty for household B, and from moderate into the near poverty bracket for household C, being the only sample household to leave poverty altogether by means of minimum income schemes. In reality, the effects of minimum income schemes are less clear-cut than shown in this simplified graph, as the following analysis will demonstrate.

The comparison of disposable income with a counterfactual income before means-tested transfers provides a powerful tool to evaluate the redistributive effects of social assistance and related schemes. In contrast to the Beckerman ratios presented in the previous chapter, this measure is possibly is less sensitive to behavioural changes and different modes of provision than an analysis of welfare state redistribution as a whole. An unfettered market would not offer any private alternative to social assistance and some other means-tested benefits (as this would presumably be the case with some social insurance benefits such as pensions), though some charities may step in.

Table 3.1 Definition of poverty lines (based on disposable equivalent income; in national currency units)

Poverty lines	Germany 1994		Sweden 1995		United Kingdom 1995	
	month	year	month	year	month	year
Median	2,186.67	26,240.00	10,309.94	123,719.30	661.00	7,932.00
60%	1,312.00	15,744.00	6,185.97	74,231.58	396.60	4,759.20
50%	1,093.33	13,120.00	5,154.97	61,859.65	330.50	3,966.00
40%	874.67	10,496.00	4,123.98	49,487.72	264.40	3,172.80
30%	656.00	7,872.00	3,092.98	37,115.79	198.30	2,379.60

Note: Poverty lines are given as a percentage of median income. The values of median and the poverty lines for each country are reported in national currency units, and are based on the modified OECD equivalence scale (assumed need level of 1.0 for the head of the household, 0.5 for each additional adult, and 0.3 for children. This analysis uses household weights as provided by LIS.

Source: LIS, own calculations.

Table 3.1 displays median income and poverty lines used in this book in national currency units based on the modified OECD equivalence scale.[41] These data refer to a one-person household, the corresponding incomes of larger household would have to be augmented according to household size. The paper uses the most recent data available for each of the three countries, that is 1994 for Germany and 1995 for Sweden and the United Kingdom.

Means-tested benefits can include both cash and near-cash benefits. The means-tested benefits included in this analysis follow the definition used in the Luxembourg Income Study. For all countries examined here, general social assistance benefits and housing benefits[42] are included, as well as some categorical benefits for some countries (see Table 3.2).

Table 3.2 Components of cash and near-cash means-tested benefits as defined in LIS

	Germany 1994	Sweden 1995	United Kingdom 1995
universal social assistance schemes	– general social assistance (*Sozialhilfe: Hilfe zum Lebensunterhalt*) – social assistance in special circumstances (*Sozialhilfe: Hilfe in besonderen Lebenslagen*)	– social assistance (*socialbidrag*)	– income support
categorical schemes	– unemployment assistance (*Arbeitslosenhilfe*) – education maintenance benefits (*Ausbildungsförderung; BAföG*)	– means-tested scholarships	– family credit – school milk/welfare milk (imputed values)
housing benefits	– housing benefits (*Wohngeld*)	– general housing allowances – housing allowances for pensioners (*kommunalt bostadstillägg, KBT*) – supplementary housing benefit for pensioners (*särskilt kommunalt bostadstillägg, SKBT*)	– housing benefits – community charge benefit – rent rebate

Source: Based on LIS institutional database, variables v25 and v26.

---

[41] This equivalent scale uses a weight of 1.0 for the head of the household, 0.5 for each additional adult, and 0.3 for each child. Data for alternative equivalence scales can be found in Table A.5 in the Appendix (p. 214).
[42] Housing benefits have been included in the income measure, since they constitute an vital income supplement for many families. However, housing benefits often vary with housing costs, and we have not been able to control for different levels of housing costs due to a lack of data.

Mapping the Reduction of Poverty 37

Table 3.2 illustrates that the programmes included broadly cover the same clientele groups in all three countries.[43] The inclusion of unemployment assistance for Germany appears to be an alien element in this group at first glance, since these benefits are based on a contribution record. Its inclusion in this book may, however, be justified on two grounds: these benefits are means-tested, and they fulfil similar functions for the income maintenance of the unemployed in the same way social assistance does in the other countries.[44]

Before discussing the effects of means-tested benefits in more detail, it is necessary to investigate the role of means-tested benefits in private household budgets.

Distribution of Means-tested Benefits within the Poor Population

Means-tested benefits are not distributed evenly among the poor population, in fact, a substantial number of households do not receive any benefits in spite of low income. Table 3.3 shows the proportion of households who have received any type of means-tested transfers, according to their poverty status before the receipt of these benefits.

There is strong variation in the distribution of means-tested benefits on the poor population. The United Kingdom has very high recipient rates, especially for households living in extreme poverty, but also for the severe and moderate poverty brackets. The recipient rates tend to be significantly lower in Sweden and Germany where an astonishingly small proportion of the extremely or severely poor report to have received some sort of means-tested benefits. Sweden displays a remarkable pattern of a lower probability to receive some means-tested benefits in extreme and severe poverty, and higher rates for households in the moderate or near poverty bracket. In Ger-

---

[43] However, the Swedish means-tested scholarships somehow deviate from the other means-tested schemes because of their quasi-universal coverage. Since means-tested scholarships are means-tested based on student's income not on parents' means, most students are eligible for this program. Anyway, the LIS data do not allow to exclude this scheme from this analysis.

[44] The British unemployment benefits (now replaced by the jobseeker's allowance) do not include any second tier, claimants who have exhausted their unemployment benefits after one year have to turn to social assistance. In Sweden, there is a flat-rate unemployment assistance (kontant arbetsmarknadstöd, KAS), but this benefit expires after six months (12 or even 18 month for older workers). The German unemployment assistance is unlimited in principle, but does not fully replace social assistance, since benefits are limited to a ceiling set at certain fraction of former earnings (57 per cent of net earnings if living with children, 53 per cent if no children) (Ministerie van Sociale Zaken en Werkgelegenheit, 1995; Bundesministerium für Arbeit und Sozialordnung, 1997: 73-83).

many, two thirds of the households in the extreme poverty bracket indicated that they received some kind of means-tested benefits, but only a third in the severe poverty bracket and even less in the moderate poverty bracket. Households belonging to the near poverty or no poverty brackets were most likely to receive means-tested benefits in Sweden, and least likely in Germany.

Table 3.3 Distribution of means-tested benefits on households (percentage of households receiving means-tested benefits in each poverty bracket)

poverty bracket		Germany 1994	Sweden 1995	UK 1995
no poverty	$Y \geq 60\%$	7	24	7
near poverty	$50\% \leq Y < 60\%$	32	45	42
moderate poverty	$40\% \leq Y < 50\%$	42	47	66
severe poverty	$30\% \leq Y < 40\%$	47	52	73
extreme poverty	$Y < 30\%$	65	51	86

Note: Y = household income before means-tested transfers adjusted for household size based on the modified OECD equivalence scale. Results for alternative equivalence scales are provided in Table A.6 in the Appendix (p. 226).
Example: Among all households living in extreme poverty before means-tested transfers in Germany 1994, 65 received some kind of means-tested transfers.

Source: LIS, own calculations.

As Table 3.3 has demonstrated, means-tested benefits are not distributed equally within the poor population. Although the minimum income levels embodied in the schemes considered here may be different, means-tested benefits are designed to at least protect people from falling into the lowest poverty brackets. Three possible explanations may account for these astonishingly low recipient rates: First, some households may not have been eligible for any means-tested benefit, yet all of the countries considered provide at least some universal social assistance benefit that covers the broad majority of the population. A statutory exclusion from means-tested benefits only affects minor parts of the population in the countries considered, mainly concerning recent immigrants.[45] In addition, people working more than 16 hours per week are not entitled to receive the British income support, though they may receive family credit. Their earned income should however protect most of them from falling into the very lowest poverty brackets. Second,

---

[45] Households without permanent residence in the United Kingdom (cf. Adler, 1997) and asylum seekers in Sweden since 1988 (cf. Westerhäll, 1997; Salonen, 1993) and in Germany since 1993 (cf. Fasselt, 1997) are excluded from the general social assistance schemes, but they may receive some benefits at a lower rate. However, only a very small proportion of these people is included in the LIS database at all (cf. Atkinson et al., 1995: 124-128). See Chapter 5 for more details.

some households may not have claimed all benefits they are entitled to. Low take-up is indeed a problem that might be reflected in the low recipient rates reported here, but unfortunately, we cannot tell this because of a third problem: the under-reporting of means-tested income. Some households may not have reported all means-tested income, possibly because of the associated stigma. Therefore, we have to assume that at least some part of the non-recipients found in these data either do not claim all benefits they are entitled to, or do not report all benefits they have received.

Because the magnitude of these problems cannot be measured, non-recipient households will be neglected for the further course of this chapter. Hence, the following discussion focuses exclusively on households who have reported their receipt of any means-tested transfers. Certainly, problems of exclusion, low take up rates and under-reporting cannot be fully avoided for this group of households; however, it is assumed that salience of under-reporting is significantly smaller for households who actually have reported their receipt of some kind of means-tested benefits, rather than for households who have not reported the receipt of any means-tested benefits.[46]

Effectiveness of Means-tested Transfers

Means-tested transfers are primarily aimed at the alleviation of poverty, but their exact impact is not clear. How effectively do they reduce poverty rates? How well can they improve the economic situation of poor households? How many people are brought out of poverty by these transfers and how many remain in poverty in spite of having received them?

This section will assess the effectiveness of means-tested transfers with three complementing methods. From a broad perspective, the reduction of poverty rates (head-count measure) sheds some initial light onto the effectiveness of means-tested transfers. Second, a more detailed account follows the effects of means-tested benefits on the income position of poor households and identifies patterns of movements from one poverty bracket to another. Third, the poverty gap method focuses on the intensity of poverty and monitors how closely poor households are brought to the poverty line through means-tested transfers.

---

[46] However, we can assume that a considerable portion the problem of non-take-up and exclusion is in fact mirrored in the data used here, since households are included as soon as they reported to have received one pound, mark or krona of any means-tested benefit. Their failure to claim in another means-tested scheme for whatever reason, if so, will be reflected in the data used in the following sections.

40   At the Margins of the Welfare State

Change in Poverty Rates

A very simple measure of the impact of means-tested transfers is the reduction of poverty rates. We can compare actual poverty rates to the counterfactual of the income distribution without any means-tested transfers, and monitor their reduction, both in absolute and in relative terms. Table 3.4 shows the effects of means-tested benefits on poverty rates across various poverty brackets. Please note that all poverty rates refer to a poverty line of 50 per cent (or 30, 40, 60 per cent) of median adjusted household income *after* means-tested benefits. By this token, poverty lines are held constant even if the distribution of incomes changes. In addition, to the portion of the population in each poverty bracket, Table 3.4 also shows poverty rates for the 50 per cent poverty line, summarizing poverty rates of the lower three poverty brackets.

Under the assumption that no means-tested transfers were available in these three countries, poverty rates are expected to have been significantly higher than the actual poverty rates calculated from disposable income. Indeed, 10.5 per cent of all households in Germany had an income below the 50 per cent poverty line if no means-tested benefits were available, as opposed to 7.7 per cent when taking into account means-tested benefits. An even higher percentage, 14.0 per cent of the population would have lived in poverty in Sweden, but only 9.5 per cent did after means-tested benefits. The British poverty level of 9.5 per cent would have amounted to almost one quarter of the population if no means-tested benefits were available.

The impact of means-tested transfers can be assessed by analyzing the reduction of poverty rates by means-tested transfers. In respect to the 50 per cent poverty line, means-tested benefits have reduced poverty by 27 per cent in Germany, by 32 per cent in Sweden and by 60 per cent in the United Kingdom. A closer look reveals an outstanding reduction of the poverty rates in the United Kingdom for the two lower poverty brackets. The share of the population living in extreme poverty was reduced by 82 per cent; and by 49 per cent in the severe poverty bracket. The reduction of poverty rates is considerably less marked in Germany and Sweden. For Germany, the share of the population living in extreme poverty was reduced by half in 1994. The share of the population living in the moderate or the near poverty bracket remained almost unchanged or even increased.[47] Sweden, on the other hand, exhibited a more regular pattern: means-tested benefits reduced the percent-

---

[47] The reduction of poverty by means-tested benefits may be negative in the higher poverty brackets if the number of households entering this poverty bracket is higher than the number of households leaving.

age of the population in every income bracket; but the magnitude of the reduction varies.

Table 3.4 Poverty rates before and after means-tested benefits and reduction through means-tested benefits

Poverty Status		Germany 1994		Sweden 1995		UK 1995	
Poverty Status *before* means-tested benefits							
near poverty	50% ≤ Y < 60%	4.8		4.7		6.3	
moderate poverty	40% ≤ Y < 50%	3.2		2.9		7.9	
severe poverty	30% ≤ Y < 40%	2.2	} 10.5	2.4	} 14.0	3.9	} 23.9
extreme poverty	Y < 30%	5.0		8.7		12.1	
Poverty Status *after* means-tested benefits							
near poverty	50% ≤ Y < 60%	6.0		3.8		8.7	
moderate poverty	40% ≤ Y < 50%	3.3		2.4		5.4	
severe poverty	30% ≤ Y < 40%	2.0	} 7.7	1.9	} 9.5	2.0	} 9.5
extreme poverty	Y < 30%	2.4		5.3		2.1	
Impact of means-tested benefits in absolute terms (percentage points)							
near poverty	50% ≤ Y < 60%	+1.2		-0.9		+2.3	
moderate poverty	40% ≤ Y < 50%	+0.0		-0.5		-2.5	
severe poverty	30% ≤ Y < 40%	-0.2	} -2.8	-0.5	} -4.4	-1.9	} -14.4
extreme poverty	Y < 30%	-2.6		-3.5		-10.0	
Impact of means-tested benefits in relative terms (percent)							
near poverty	50% ≤ Y < 60%	+24%		-19%		37%	
moderate poverty	40% ≤ Y < 50%	+1%		-18%		-31%	
severe poverty	30% ≤ Y < 40%	-9%	} -27%	-19%	} -32%	-49%	} -60%
extreme poverty	Y < 30%	-53%		-40%		-82%	

Note: Y = household income before means-tested transfers adjusted for household size, based on the modified OECD equivalence scale. Results for alternative equivalence scales can be found in Table A.7 in the Appendix (p. 215).
Example: For the United Kingdom 1995, 12.1 per cent of the population were extremely poor before having received some kind of means-tested transfers and 2.1 per cent after having received some transfers. Poverty rates for this poverty bracket were thus reduced by 10 percentage points or by 82 per cent compared to the pre-transfer poverty rate. The figures right of the brackets refer to cumulated poverty at the 50 per cent level. Please note that the proportion of households in the three higher poverty brackets (severe, moderate or near poverty) can be higher after transfers if more households are moving into this bracket from lower poverty brackets than move out of this bracket into higher poverty brackets.
Source: LIS, own calculations.

Poverty alleviation appears to be achieved through differing strategies in these two countries. The German means-tested benefits appear to be more effective in reducing extreme poverty, whereas the Swedish pattern distributed benefits more uniformly across all poverty brackets. Poverty reduction at the 50 per cent level has been most effective in absolute terms in the United Kingdom, followed by Sweden, and least effective in Germany.

Measured in relative terms, means-tested benefits in Sweden appear to be almost as effective as in the United Kingdom.

Move between Poverty Brackets

The examination of poverty rates in the various poverty brackets shows the overall effect of means-tested transfers, but it fails to illustrate exactly how far households are pushed up the income scale from one particular poverty bracket to another.

Table 3.5 Effects of means-tested benefits: move between poverty brackets (as a proportion of all households having received some means-tested benefits)

poverty status after benefits ⇨ before benefits ⇩	extreme poverty	severe poverty	moderate poverty	near poverty	no poverty	total	crossing 50% line
Germany 1994						(N=473)	
- near poverty	-	-	-	64	36	100	-
- moderate poverty	-	-	28	29	43	100	72
- severe poverty	-	13	30	27	30	100	57
- extreme poverty	25	23	21	22	8	100	30
Sweden 1992						(N=2,468)	
- near poverty	-	-	-	12	88	100	
- moderate poverty	-	-	7	30	64	100	94
- severe poverty	-	18	25	19	38	100	57
- extreme poverty	17	13	14	14	42	100	56
United Kingdom 1995						(N=2,037)	
- near poverty	-	-	-	38	62	100	
- moderate poverty	-	-	23	30	47	100	77
- severe poverty	-	3	34	32	31	100	63
- extreme poverty	8	17	31	23	21	100	44

Note: Please note that households that do not receive any means-tested benefits are excluded from this subsample; the number of cases (N) refers to the number of households that have any means-tested income recorded in the given year. The 'no poverty' bracket has been omitted from the rows, since a move out of this income bracket is not possible by definition. The dotted line marks the poverty line of 50 per cent of median household income before means-tested transfers adjusted for family size. The figures do not always add up to 100 due to rounding.

Example: In Sweden 1992, of all people living in extreme poverty before means-tested transfers, 17 per cent remained in this poverty bracket in spite of having received some kind of means-tested benefits, 13 per cent moved to the severe poverty bracket, 14 per cent to the moderate poverty bracket, 14 per cent to the near poverty bracket, and 42 per cent to the no poverty bracket. Among these households, 56 per cent have crossed the 50 per cent poverty line.

Source: LIS, own calculations.

Means-tested benefits can follow different strategies. A targeting strategy would focus social transfers on the most needy in order to bring them out of poverty. A broader transfer strategy would distribute transfers more equally among the poor. This section will illustrate the impact of means-tested transfers in more detail and will demonstrate how means-tested benefits push a fraction of households from a low poverty bracket (as defined earlier) into a higher bracket. It will also demonstrate that some households do not succeed in moving to a higher poverty bracket in spite of having received means-tested transfers. The moves between income brackets are shown in Table 3.5. The table focuses on households that receive any sort of means-tested benefits; households not receiving benefits are not included. Again, poverty brackets are used to illustrate the poverty-alleviating power of means-tested benefits. The columns show the poverty status of households before means-tested transfers, and the rows the poverty status after transfers.

Table 3.5 demonstrates that the impact of means-tested benefits is not unambiguous. Only a small fraction of the poor are actually lifted over the 50 per cent poverty line, many still remain in poverty. Yet it should be noted that there is a high degree of variation across countries and over time.

In Germany, only one third of the households living in extreme poverty were lifted above the 50 per cent poverty line by means-tested transfers, while 23 per cent moved to the severe poverty bracket, 21 per cent to the low poverty bracket, and 30 per cent succeeded to leave poverty altogether. A more effective record is monitored for the severe poverty bracket, some 30 per cent of households moving to each of the three highest poverty brackets, but 13 per cent of households remained in this bracket in spite of means-tested transfers. From moderate poverty, more than 70 per cent crossed the poverty line, most of whom were pushed into the 'no poverty' bracket. One third of the households in the near poverty bracket could improve their situation and move out of poverty. In sum, Germany exhibits a pattern of poverty alleviation by means-tested transfers that is characterized by a relatively equal distribution of households onto higher poverty brackets. The Swedish and British patterns appear to be somewhat more clear-cut.

In Sweden, poor households in each poverty bracket are most likely to end up in the no poverty bracket after having received means-tested transfers. However, for a considerable proportion of households, means-tested transfers do not contribute to a discernible improvement of their economic situation. For the extreme and severe poverty brackets in particular, many households are stuck in their initial position or experience a marginal improvement of their situation without crossing the 50 per cent poverty line.[48]

---

[48] In these two poverty brackets, we would expect to find many students, due to the particular household definition in the Swedish data. If single students aged 18-21 were excluded

The most effective impact of means-tested transfers serves the moderately poor, whose chance to escape poverty may be as high as almost 94 per cent. For low-income households just above the poverty line, the effects of means-tested benefits are notable as well: almost 90 per cent left the near-poverty bracket. Overall, means-tested transfers in Sweden display an ambiguous pattern: On the one hand, they managed to catapult many previously poor households out of poverty, many of whom even crossed the 60 per cent poverty line. On the other hand, however, many households hardly improved their position at all.

The British escape rates are very high when compared to the two other countries, if movements out of the extreme and the severe poverty brackets are concerned. Almost every one of the extremely or severely poor households have been pushed into higher poverty brackets. It is noteworthy that a large fraction of this group were at least brought into the moderate poverty bracket. The United Kingdom displays the most marked relationship between the initial and the final poverty bracket of the three countries: the higher the initial poverty bracket, the higher the households are pushed up the income scale. In the moderate poverty bracket, most households are not only pushed out of poverty, but they are most likely to even cross the 60 per cent poverty line, the same applies to the near poverty bracket. Households in the lowest poverty brackets, however, only have a relatively small chance of ending up in the no poverty bracket.

The advantage of the poverty bracket method is the straightforward illustration of the effects of means-tested benefits. This approach is, however, quite sensitive to distribution effects. If households are not distributed evenly along the income scale, the use of poverty brackets may overstate or understate the effects of transfers, depending of the distance of household clusters from the – arbitrarily defined – poverty line(s). This problem could be overcome if more poverty lines were introduced in order to enhance the exactness of results. Another possibility is the application of a more precise measure: the poverty gap measure is able to reflect the intensity of poverty and can also be used to reflect the effectiveness of transfers.

Closing the Poverty Gap

The poverty gap measures the distance between a household's income and a given poverty line, in other words, it assesses the resources needed to eradi-

---

from this subsample, the movements measured would not fundamentally change, however. The percentage of households remaining in the extreme poverty bracket would be reduced from 17 to 12 per cent, and in severe poverty from 18 to 11 per cent, but the general pattern of movements into higher poverty brackets remains fairly constant.

cate poverty. This measure can be used both on an individual and an aggregate level. The effects of means-tested benefits are calculated as a reduction of the poverty gap before and after the receipt of transfers, again only for households having reported any means-tested benefits. The results are presented in Table 3.6, depicting the average resources needed to lift the poor above a poverty line of 50 per cent of median disposable household income adjusted for household size (given as a proportion of the poverty line).[49]

Table 3.6 Average poverty gap and average poverty gap reduction by means-tested benefits for households who were poor before having received any means-tested transfers

	Germany 1994	Sweden 1992	UK 1995
poverty gap before means-tested benefits	0.547	0.340	0.484
rank order (small poverty gap = 1)	(3)	(1)	(2)
poverty gap after means-tested benefits	0.009	-0.177	-0.102
rank order (small poverty gap = 1)	(3)	(1)	(2)
absolute change of poverty gap	-0.537	-0.518	-0.586
rank order (strong reduction = 1)	(2)	(3)	(1)
Relative change of poverty gap	-98%	-152%	-121%
Rank order (strong reduction = 1)	(3)	(1)	(2)
N	244	728	1,231

Note: The average poverty gap is calculated as the average resources needed to lift the poor households over the poverty line of 50 per cent of median disposable household income after means-tested transfers adjusted for family size, given as a percentage of the poverty line. Poverty gaps are negative if the average income of the (previously) poor after transfers is higher than the poverty line.

Source: LIS, own calculations.

After means-tested transfers, poverty gaps in Sweden and in the United Kingdom have become negative, thus implying that, on average, household income of the previously poor is now above the poverty line. Only in Germany is the average disposable income slightly below the poverty line. The most favourable income position was reached by previously poor households in Sweden whose average income households increased to as much as almost 18 per cent above the poverty line.

The relative reduction of poverty gaps has been greatest in Sweden, followed by the United Kingdom. Germany is clearly less efficient in relative terms. It would, however, be misleading to focus only on the reduction of the poverty gap and to ignore its absolute size. The average poverty gaps before means-tested benefits were much smaller in Sweden than in the other two

---

[49] Clearly, the poverty gap measure is not free from arbitrary decisions on the part of the researcher because this also involves the choice of a poverty line, yet this measure is less sensitive to clustering effects.

countries; in other words, means-tested benefits had a smaller gap to fill. Consequently, considering the absolute reduction of poverty gaps, Sweden displays the smallest decrease in poverty gaps, whereas the United Kingdom has most effectively managed to close its previously large poverty gap. The poverty gap before means-tested transfers was largest in Germany, but its reduction was not as effective as in the United Kingdom.

What Can Explain the Apparent Ineffectiveness of the Welfare State?

The empirical evidence presented in this chapter casts serious doubt on the poverty alleviating power of means-tested benefits. Many poor households either do not receive any means-tested benefits at all, or these benefits are not generous enough to push them over the poverty line. These results suggest that the basic safety net of the welfare state is not knit fine enough to prevent poverty, with marked differences across countries. The variation in the effectiveness of means-tested benefits across countries indicates that policy factors may have an impact on the effects of means-tested benefits, as the different patterns of poverty alleviation suggest.

The United Kingdom achieved the most marked success of means-tested benefits with an astonishingly high degree of effectiveness, especially among the lower poverty brackets. These patterns confirm earlier insights which claimed that the British welfare state was very effective in mitigating harsh poverty, but less effective in the moderate poverty sphere (Mitchell, 1991: 43-78). Obviously, means-tested benefits substantially contribute to the effectiveness of total redistribution in the United Kingdom. In fact, means-tested transfers play a much larger role in the British welfare state than they do in Germany or Sweden, yet this cannot fully explain their good performance. British poverty rates before means-tested transfers were higher than in the other two countries, but the poverty gap to be filled by means-tested transfers was even larger in Germany than in the United Kingdom.

Sweden exhibited medium poverty rates before transfers, but a considerably smaller poverty gap than in the other two countries. This indicates that social insurance benefits are relatively effective in alleviating poverty, even before means-tested benefits come into play. Means-tested transfers in Sweden are less explicitly targeted on the very poor than in the United Kingdom, but distributed fairly evenly onto the recipient population. For a relatively large fraction of previously poor households, poverty was effectively alleviated by these transfers. Others, however, could only marginally improve their income position. The Swedish data should, however, be interpreted with caution due to the differing household definition.

The record of means-tested benefits in Germany is far less impressive. The German social insurance benefits left relatively low poverty rates, but a large poverty gap to fill. The effectiveness of means-tested benefits was rather weak, especially for the poverty gap measure. The average income of formerly poor recipients of means-tested benefits still remained lower than the poverty line after transfers. However, the overall performance of the German welfare state in terms of the protection from poverty is relatively good, but this must be attributed rather to the impact of the distribution of market income and to social insurance rather than to means-tested benefits.

These divergent patterns draw attention to the impact of policy factors on the success or failure of poverty alleviation. Social assistance schemes may be designed in a way that inhibit an effective alleviation of poverty. The causes of this ineffectiveness may be found in their programme structure itself, or in an inadequate functioning of the scheme.

The outcome perspective alone is not sufficient to explain the persistence of poverty in industrialized welfare states. In order to obtain a better estimate of poverty and the effectiveness of welfare states, the following chapters will complement micro-data on poverty with other information. A more comprehensive picture on the effectiveness of social assistance schemes can be obtained by confronting the data on outcomes (poverty) with an input perspective. Information on the institutional settings that help to produce these results can shed some more light on the relationship of social assistance schemes and poverty. The reasons for the apparent ineffectiveness of social assistance schemes can thus be more thoroughly assessed and related to possible causes. In the following, the relationship between social assistance schemes and poverty will be discussed by developing a simplified model of poverty alleviation.

Industrial welfare states have established a complex system of income redistribution in order to protect people from poverty. First, social insurance schemes compensate for income losses due to invalidity, sickness, old age and unemployment. However, these social insurance schemes are not able to completely alleviate poverty. If needs cannot be met in any other way, social assistance and related schemes step in as a basic safety net. Yet, also social assistance schemes seem to fail to completely alleviate poverty. The relationship between income redistribution and poverty is depicted in a simplified model in Figure 3.2.

48   *At the Margins of the Welfare State*

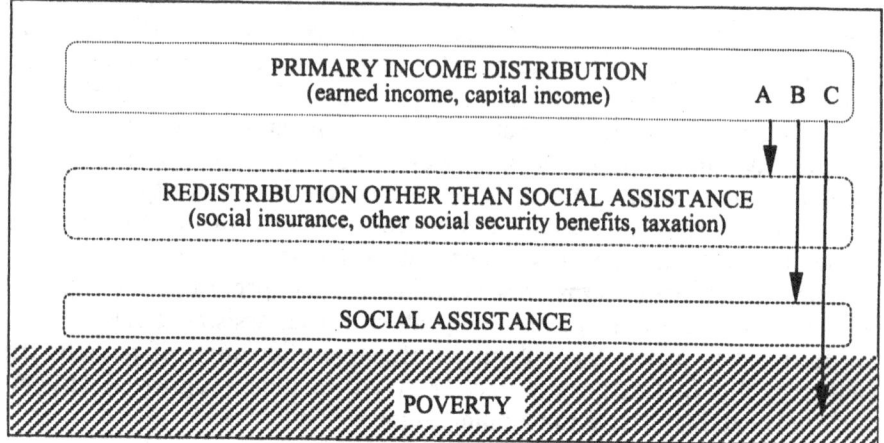

Figure 3.2 Social assistance and the alleviation of poverty: a simplified model

In this simplified model, three types of incomes may prevent people from living in poverty: first, a sufficient primary income (earned income, capital income); second, income from social transfers other than social assistance (social insurance, other social security benefits, tax benefits); and third, means-tested social assistance. These three types of incomes can be regarded as three filters in a row that hold back some units (individuals or households) and let pass others (shown here as arrows). If none of these filters can accommodate the units, they will fall into poverty. In this simplifying variant of this model, it is assumed that these filters are arranged in a strictly hierarchical order, they do not overlap with each other, nor do they overlap with poverty.

Some parts of the population are protected from poverty by their primary income, but some cannot make ends meet and fall through this filter, here exemplified as households A, B and C (see Figure 3.2). The second, more refined, filter of social transfers other than social assistance again prevents some part of the population from poverty (as household A), but still lets pass others (households B and C). The third, even more refined filter, social assistance, again holds back some households (household B), but it may be not fine enough to accommodate all, so some households pass even this last filter and eventually end up in poverty (household C).

For the alleviation of poverty, the most important filter is the last one. If this filter succeeds in comforting these units, they will not be poor; if the units pass, they will fall into poverty. As the final instance of the welfare state, this filter – social assistance – is thus ultimately responsible for the alleviation of poverty. Because of the critical significance of social assistance schemes, the following discussion will confine itself to these schemes, which represent the focal point of this book.

Although this simplified model of poverty alleviation certainly does not reflect the complexity of poverty alleviation through government redistribution, it may be helpful to illustrate the mechanisms of poverty alleviation through social assistance schemes.

Why are social assistance schemes not able to fully prevent poverty – in other words, why is this filter not fine enough to comfort all units? Basically, this shortfall occur in three dimensions: eligibility of the population, adequacy of benefits, and take-up by the eligible population. In order to be able to fully alleviate poverty, a social assistance scheme must be considered as effective in every one of these three dimensions while failure in any of these dimensions will lead to poverty. These factors appear in a certain hierarchical order. Let us assume that a household (or person) is in need because of an insufficient market income and/or insufficient social transfers. Need is defined as an inadequate level of resources that does not allow a decent standard of living. At this stage, the redistributional impact of the welfare state exclusively depends on social assistance scheme, since all other potential income sources are exhausted. The income of this household corresponds to the 'income before means-tested benefits' in the application of the Beckerman model in the previous section. If social assistance benefits were not available, the household would be poor.

Once the social assistance scheme comes into play, a three-stage process determines whether these schemes can effectively protect the household from being poor or not. First, effectiveness depends on the question whether the person or household is actually eligible for social assistance (eligibility). If this is not the case, the household will be poor, since all other income sources are exhausted in our model. If the household is entitled to receive benefits from social assistance, the second dimension of effectiveness becomes relevant: benefits must be generous enough as to cover the needs of the household (adequacy). If benefits are not adequate, poverty cannot be effectively alleviated by social assistance, the household stays poor. Finally, households can only be effectively protected from poverty if benefits are actually claimed by the household in need (take-up). If this is not the case, the household will stay poor even if the first two conditions are met. The sequence of these three conditions is illustrated in Figure 3.3 below.

The first two of these conditions are determined by the programme structure of the social assistance scheme itself. Eligibility rules and the level of benefits are determined by the responsible bodies in each country and are subject to direct political regulation. In contrast, the last dimension is not directly governed by policy factors, as take-up largely depends on perceptions and behaviour of individual claimants. However, there is firm evidence that institutional structures have an effect on take-up. Since this book is concerned with the effectiveness of social assistance schemes on poverty, it will focus on this aspect of take-up.

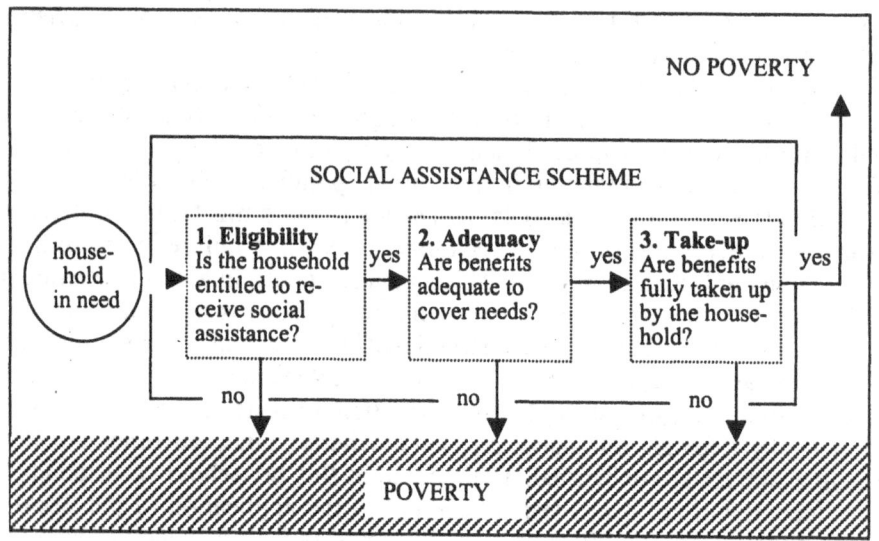

Figure 3.3 Social assistance schemes and an effective alleviation of poverty: A simplified model

Under the assumption that poverty is exclusively determined by the ineffectiveness of social assistance schemes, poverty occurs if social assistance schemes fail in any one of these three dimensions. This does not imply that social assistance schemes directly produce poverty, nor should it deny that there are other causes of poverty. Poverty may be caused by a broad variety of economic and socio-demographic causes such as low wages, unemployment, family split-up, or inadequate social insurance benefits. These causes of poverty shall not be discussed here, however. This book only focuses on the lower limits of the welfare state, that is its basic safety net. It poses the question of whether this basic safety net is able to protect people from poverty, without considering why they came to use this safety net. By this token, the economic welfare of private households is ultimately dependent on minimum income schemes, since this is the last safeguard of the welfare state. If this net does not hold, people will live in poverty. This does not mean that social assistance schemes cause poverty in a strict sense, but rather that they cannot prevent poverty.

The three dimensions of ineffectiveness outlined above match fairly well an earlier classification that discerned three types of welfare-state induced poverty: status poverty, transfer poverty, and frictional poverty (Leisering and Voges, 1993; Leisering, 1995: 84, 92). Status poverty is determined by the lack of legal entitlement for certain groups of the population and is largely consistent with the dimension of eligibility, while transfer poverty refers to insufficient transfer benefits and corresponds to the dimension of adequacy. Finally, 'frictional poverty' is caused by waiting for social security benefits caused by administrative delays and inefficiency, and is one aspect of the dimension of take-up.

Chapters 5, 6 and 7 will assess the effects of the institutional design of social assistance schemes on poverty in Britain, Germany and Sweden. They will scrutinize programme structures and administrative procedures, and confront this qualitative evidence with quantitative data on the profile of poverty in these countries.

However, variations in the effectiveness of poverty alleviation may not only be explained by differences in policy factors, but also by methodological problems in the measurement of poverty. The methodological discussion of the available micro-data for the purpose of poverty measurement has shown that the available data suffer from a number of flaws that may bias the results. These reservations raise the question of whether the measured incidence of poverty actually reflects the actual income position of private households in an adequate way. These problems can possibly lead to some inaccuracies, yet the dimensions of this bias are unknown. If the effects of these errors do not offset each other, the true extent of poverty may be critically overestimated or underestimated. Before turning to the analysis of policy factors, the following Chapter 4 will therefore discuss the methodology of comparative poverty research and review the robustness of results.

Chapter 4

Methodological Puzzles and Pitfalls in the Measurement of Poverty

In fact, however, poverty studies never risk going out of business even in rich, industrial societies, but they do face an awkward problem of definition.
(Douglas and Isherwood, 1979: 17)

The measurement of poverty is unavoidably coupled with a number of methodological choices that influence the results. Small differences in research strategies can have a large impact on measured results (cf. Atkinson et al., 1998). Therefore, this chapter follows a double objective in discussing methodological puzzles and pitfalls in poverty research. It presents a discussion of the validity of poverty research and discusses alternative methods of measurement, and, by this token, also explains the research strategy that has been chosen for the empirical analyses in this book in more detail.

Why Do Low Income and Social Assistance Receipt Hardly Coincide?

One of the major puzzles in poverty research is that income poverty and the receipt of social assistance coincide to a surprisingly small degree. This gap has often been interpreted as an indicator for the flaws of income as a measure of economic well-being. Only a small part of the poor claim social assistance, and only a small group of claimants are poor. Critics of the income poverty concept have repeatedly pointed to this fact to demonstrate the flaws of income as an indicator for poverty. Halleröd (1991) has shown for a Swedish sample that only one in sixteen respondents living in income poverty received social assistance, while only a sixth of recipients were considered as poor.[50] Similar results were found by Kangas and Ritakallio (1998a) for Finland, indicating that only 18 per cent of respondents who were poor

---

[50] Cf. Halleröd (1991: 111, 220-221), own calculations. Income poverty was defined by a political standard, referring to the national social assistance recommendations.

54   At the Margins of the Welfare State

by relative income measures have also received social assistance, and only 17 per cent of recipients of social assistance lived in income poverty (Kangas and Ritakallio, 1998a: 187). A similar pattern is found for the three countries in this book, as Table 4.1 shows.[51]

Table 4.1 Income poverty and the receipt of social assistance in Germany, Sweden and the United Kingdom: Percentage of poor households who receive social assistance benefits

	Germany 1994	Sweden 1995	UK 1995
Social assistance			
-- percentage of poor households in receipt of social assistance	18.5	14.9	38.3
-- percentage of recipient households living in poverty	40.1	20.2	22.0
Any means-tested benefit			
-- percentage of poor households in receipt of means-tested benefits	38.0	28.9	46.1
-- percentage of recipient households living in poverty	22.0	9.4	17.7

Note: Based on a poverty line of 50 per cent of national medial equivalent disposable income and the modified OECD equivalence scale. Social assistance includes cash social assistance payments (LIS variable V25S1); any means-tested benefits encompasses cash and near cash benefits (LIS variables V25 and V26).

Source: LIS, own calculations.

The weak correlation of social assistance receipt and income poverty calls for an explanation. Both indicators focus on income as an indicator of poverty, either directly in the case of income poverty, or indirectly in the case of social assistance receipt. In the latter case, social assistance offices act as an intermediate instance who decide whether a person or a household is living in (politically defined) poverty or not. Although this procedure is certainly not free from flawed judgements, measured poverty should largely overlap. Remaining divergences are supposed to largely stem from the fact that these poverty lines are positioned at different levels. For example, if the relative poverty line is lower than the level of social assistance benefits, only a small share of poor will receive social assistance, but, in turn, the proportion of the poor among recipients should be close to 100 per cent.

There are, however, two important reservations. First, a small degree of overlapping may be considered not as an indicator for the failure of measures of poverty, but rather as a proof of the effectiveness of the basic safety

---

[51] Table A.3 in the Appendix (p. 213) shows the overlapping of poverty and social assistance receipt as a proportion of the population.

net of the welfare state. If social assistance schemes succeed in bringing previously poor households over the poverty line, recipients will not be classified as poor, and social assistance receipt and poverty therefore do not coincide. If this kind of analysis is used to demonstrate deficiencies in the measurement of poverty, it would therefore be wiser to use household income before social assistance (or means-tested benefits) rather than disposable income after receipt of these benefits (see Table 4.2).

Table 4.2 Income poverty and the receipt of social assistance in Germany, Sweden and the United Kingdom: Percentage of poor households who receive social assistance benefits (poverty status calculated on the basis of income *before* receipt of social assistance benefits/means-tested benefits)

	Germany 1994	Sweden 1995	UK 1995
Social assistance			
-- percentage of poor households in receipt of social assistance	25.1	27.1	60.2
-- percentage of recipient households living in poverty	74.5	51.2	78.9
Any means-tested benefit			
-- percentage of poor households in receipt of means-tested benefits	55.5	50.7	78.6
-- percentage of recipient households living in poverty	44.0	22.8	69.0

Note: Based on a poverty line of 50 per cent of national medial equivalent disposable income and the modified OECD equivalence scale. Whereas the poverty line has been calculated on the basis of disposable income, the poverty status has been evaluated on the basis of equivalent household income before receipt of these benefits (disposable income minus social assistance benefits or means-tested benefits). Social assistance includes cash social assistance payments (LIS variable v25s1); any means-tested benefits encompasses cash and near cash benefits (LIS variables v25 and v26).

Source: LIS, own calculations.

A more subtle problem concerns the fact that both income and social assistance receipt can vary over time. Recent evidence from dynamic poverty research shows that there is indeed a considerable variation for most countries (e.g. G. J. Duncan et al., 1995; Leisering and Walker, 1998). The measurement of relative poverty usually refers to yearly income. Since households are considered as poor if their yearly income falls below a certain level, they may well experience short poverty spells without being considered as poor in a yearly account of poverty, provided that their income in the remainder of the year is high enough to compensate for periods of low income. Social assistance receipt usually is evaluated in a different way in these samples. People are classified as recipients if they have received social

56   At the Margins of the Welfare State

assistance at least once during the year, irrespective of their income status during the rest of the year. These different ways of measurement lead to a systematic bias, as the following example will show. A household has an income below the relative poverty line during one month of the year and receives social assistance during this month (assuming that the relative poverty line and the level of social assistance coincide), but has a higher income in the remaining eleven months that pushes its yearly income over the relative poverty line, and is thus not eligible for social assistance for this period. In this case, this household would be classified as non-poor, yet receiving social assistance. If the circumstances of the household had been stable throughout the year, both measures would have pointed in the same direction.

Nevertheless, it is questionable whether these methodological reservations can alone explain the large divergences found in the data. This issue calls for a further analysis. The following sections will discuss methodological problems in poverty research in more detail.

Is Income an Adequate Measure of Poverty?

The measurement of poverty is fundamentally dependent of the choice of the basic indicator of the standard of living of an individual or household. Different approaches often produce divergent empirical results, and even more, the degree of overlapping of poverty measured by several indicators is suspiciously small.[52] Each of these different approaches to measure poverty highlights another aspect of poverty while neglecting others.

As do most other studies in comparative poverty research, this book uses income as the basic indicator of poverty, yet some observers have fiercely disputed the validity of this measure for a number of reasons. The following paragraphs will review these arguments and discuss alternative measures.

Is Expenditure a Better Indicator of Poverty?

Rather than measuring poverty on the basis of low income, one could argue that the level of consumption offers a more direct way to measure standards of living. Indeed, several studies have relied on consumption for poverty studies, among them studies of poverty in the European Union (Haagenaars et al., 1994, 1998). Compared to the low income approach, this measure is less sensitive to short-term fluctuations and problems of measurement. Yet,

---

[52] For empirical analyses of the overlapping between different measures of poverty and deprivation, cf. Halleröd (1991), Kangas and Ritakallio (1998a), Andreß (1999), and Burchardt (1999).

many studies do not observe consumption as such, but rather household expenditure, and this measure often is no less sensitive to methodological choices than income. In addition, consumption may be easier to observe than income in some contexts, for example in societies where many people grow their own crops or in countries with a large black economy (cf. Room, 1990: 41). Like income, consumption reflects a flow of resources, but does not provide a sufficient picture of the actual welfare at any point in time. This point is relevant if one compares different age cohorts. Older age cohorts may have had the chance to accumulate material assets over the years, even on a relatively low income, and may thus live more comfortably on the same level of consumption than younger age cohorts. Besides, this approach produces an inadequate picture of welfare levels of private households if savings are accumulated or liquidated.

Are Multidimensional Deprivation Measures Better Indicators for Poverty?

Many scholars prefer to measure poverty more directly by evaluating the living conditions of the population (e.g. Townsend, 1979; Muffels et al., 1992).[53] This type of studies is based on the assumption that poverty is closely associated to deprivation in several dimensions of life, including food, housing, and so forth. The pioneering study of Peter Townsend has established a comprehensive poverty index of 60 items ranging from household amenities to children's birthday parties (Townsend, 1979: 248-262). Responding to the argument that the lack of certain items does not necessarily reflect deprivation, but is also governed by individual preferences, later studies reformulated their survey questions in order to isolate items that people could not afford (Mack and Lansley, 1985; Gordon and Pantazis, 1997).

Multidimensional analyses may sketch a more exact picture of the overall living situation of poor people, yet this approach also has some specific weaknesses. First, multidimensional analyses of deprivation do not agree on the question of which the relevant dimensions of deprivation actually are, and how they relate to poverty. For example, some studies include a social dimension of deprivation, referring to the individual health status, leisure, integration in the labour market etc. Deprivation in one or more dimensions can be closely linked to poverty, but deprivation has to be clearly distinguished from poverty (Townsend, 1987: 140). A bad health condition can be associated with poverty (and we know that there actually is a certain correlation), but many people are sick without being poor and vice versa (cf.

---

[53] More recent studies include Halleröd (1991; 1995a; 1995b), Deleeck et al. (1992), Callan et al. (1993), Muffels et al. (1992), Mayer (1995), Nolan and Whelan (1996a; 1996b), Whelan (1993).

Ringen, 1987: 144-145). However, proponents of the multidimensional poverty approach argue that material poverty is closely associated to cumulated deprivation in several dimensions (Townsend, 1987).[54]

Second, as in other approaches, multi-dimensional analyses of poverty are not free of some arbitrariness by the part of the researcher. Which aspects of living conditions are chosen, which items are selected for the measurement of deprivation, and what weight do they have in a comprehensive measure of deprivation? For comparative analyses, the operationalization of a multi-dimensional poverty approach is even more critical. Not only variations in climate and regional settlement patterns have to be considered, but also cultural traditions and societal perceptions of what constitutes a decent living standard.[55]

Third, the lack of comparable data hampers cross-country studies for methodological reasons. Although a growing body of empirical studies on living standards and multidimensional deprivation has been accumulated over the last years for many countries,[56] comparative research is still rare. Other than for income poverty, multidimensional analyses of poverty still cannot rely on a large body of comparable data, although some efforts have been made to fill this gap (cf. Halleröd, 1996a, 1998; Mayer, 1995; Muffels, 1993).

Finally, multidimensional analyses of deprivation are sensitive towards life-course effects, yet the consequences of this bias are not clear. Multidimensional analysis tend to produce markedly higher poverty rates for young

---

[54] Peter Townsend has put this issue as follows: 'People can experience one or more forms of deprivation without necessarily being in poverty. People with the same resources may display a different relationship to forms of deprivation. And people with fewer resources than others may be more likely to experience forms of deprivation even when their resources remain considerably above the 'poverty line'. However, it is assumed in this conceptualization that at a certain point in descending the scale of income or resources, deprivation is likely to grow disproportionate to further loss of resources and that this 'threshold' properly marks the beginning of a state of objective poverty. Thus, while people experiencing some forms of deprivation may not all have low income, people experiencing multiple or single very severe forms of deprivation are in almost every instance likely to have very little income and little or no other resources.' (Townsend, 1987: 130-131).

[55] Halleröd (1996a, 1998) could demonstrate that perceptions on a decent standard of living vary even among countries with a similar socio-economic context, such as Britain and Sweden. Whereas Swedes considered commodities as e.g. a car or a television set as absolutely necessary, Britons ranked social activities such as regularly meeting friends in a pub or celebrations on special occasions higher. Andreß and Lipsmeier (1995) found a similar effect for East and West Germany, as did more recently Böhnke and Delhey (1999) for the two parts of Germany and the United Kingdom.

[56] To give some examples, cf. for Britain Townsend (1979) and Mack and Lansley (1985); for Germany Glatzer and Hübinger (1990), Andreß and Lipsmeier (1995), and Andreß (1999); for Sweden Halleröd (1991).

people than income-based measures, and lower poverty rates for the elderly (cf. Andreß and Lipsmeier, 1995). This effect is due to the fact that people can accumulate some goods (e.g. household amenities) over the years. However, the lack of disposable income can not necessarily be compensated for by the possession of these amenities, since goods cannot always be liquidated in order to buy food or to cover other current needs. Therefore, some people may be considered as non-poor on the basis of their general living standard although they cannot make ends meet from their current income. In addition, the perceived adequacy of a certain standard of living may change over the life course. For example, young students may consider it fairly normal to live in a single room and not having a car, whereas this way of life would be considered as inadequate by older cohorts.

Justifying Income as an Indicator of Poverty

Comparative poverty research largely uses low income as the main concept of poverty, since it is relatively easy to measure and to compare across countries (there are some pitfalls, however, that will be discussed below).[57] This approach constitutes an indirect indicator of poverty, since financial resources do not determine deprivation as such, but the command over resources allows the acquisition of goods that enhance the standard of living. In contrast to approaches that directly measure deprivation, the use of income is based on the concept of equality of opportunity rather than equality of result (Ringen, 1988: 355). People are considered as having the same welfare position if they have command over the same amount of financial resources, irrespective of their ability to reach the same standard of living. If people choose to save parts of their income rather than spending them on food or housing, or if they do not use their income in an economic way, the loss in observable standard of living is not considered as deprivation but as a product of their own choice. In this sense, the indirect measurement of poverty is more open to different ways of life than direct concepts.

In addition, as this book is concerned with the effectiveness of the basic safety net of the welfare state that aims at guaranteeing a minimum income, it is obvious that income is a 'natural choice' for evaluating the performance of these schemes.

An income-based indicator of poverty is not without flaws, however. This approach has often been criticized as providing an inadequate measure of poverty, since money as such cannot satisfy the most elementary needs people have. First, households with equal income may have different standards

---

[57] In some studies, income poverty is also referred to as 'economic poverty' or 'financial poverty'.

of living because of inequalities in financial and material assets, as well as access to other resources (social services, help of relatives or friends). In addition, non-cash resources usually are inadequately taken into account in most studies, with some exceptions (cf. Smeeding et al., 1993). Second, households have different levels of expenditure that are not fully reflected in analyses of income poverty (e.g. expenditures for housing, health or childcare). Third, short-term fluctuations in income may be buffered by other resources (e.g. financial assets, family support) and therefore do not necessarily have an immediate effect on living conditions. Fluctuations of income may bias the measured income, so the actual welfare level of households with a strongly fluctuating income (e.g. some self-employed) may deviate strongly from the measured income status. Finally, poverty lines used in analyses of financial poverty hardly account for regional variations in income and expenditure levels.

Data and Data Quality

The Luxembourg Income Study provides a very useful basis for the comparative analyses.[58] The LIS project has assembled a large number of national micro-data that contain detailed information on socio-demographic characteristics and incomes of private households. Where possible, the variables in the LIS database have been standardized in order to allow cross-national comparisons. However, the LIS data operate with some definitions that impose certain restrictions on the subsequent interpretation of the data. This section presents the methodology used in this paper and discusses some methodological problems.

Sources and Construction of Database

Although LIS has gone a long way to make the national datasets comparable to each other, the data unavoidably retain some characteristics of their national 'parent study'. These national studies are the Family Expenditure Survey (FES) for Britain, the Socio-Economic Panel (GSOEP) for Germany, and the Household Survey (Inkomstfördelningsundersokningen, HINK) for Sweden. The Family Expenditure Survey was established by the British government in 1953-54 and includes a broad variety of income as well as expenditure variables. It has been principally intended for the computation of

---

[58] For a detailed description of the database, cf. Smeeding and Schmaus (1990); Atkinson et al. (1995). Some basic information on the LIS datasets used in this paper is provided in Table A.1 in the Appendix (p. 211). A more detailed description of this database can be found at http://www.lis.ceps.lu.

the Retail Price Index (Office for National Statistics, 1998a), but has been used for a broad range of applications. Other than the British data, the German data stem from a large panel survey that was launched in 1984. The GSOEP covers a large spectrum of the living conditions of private households, including household composition and change, income, health and attitudes.[59] The Swedish data originate from a sample of tax records, with specific implications for the quality of the data (see below). The income data from the tax files is supplemented by additional information drawn from a telephone survey (cf. Jansson, 1994, 1998).

Every large dataset embodies some specific methodological problems that impose certain restrictions on the subsequent interpretation of the data, and LIS is no exception to this rule. The methodological flaws of each of the national datasets unavoidably spill over to the LIS datasets, yet in different ways and to a different degree. The following paragraphs will discuss the main methodological problems and lay out the methodological strategies chosen to deal with this problems in this book.

Income surveys are not an ideal source for the assessment of poverty for three reasons. First, low-income strata of the poor population tend to be poorly represented in surveys, and second, they often have lower response rates than the middle classes. In addition, some types of income – some of which are in particular relevant for this book – tend to be under-reported in some surveys.

The following sections will provide a discussion of methodological problems of poverty research based on datasets to be used in this book (cf. Smeeding and Schmaus, 1990; Atkinson et al., 1995). These problems are supposed to be partly counterbalanced by the use of sample weights and other data editing procedures, yet some of these problems unavoidably will go uncorrected. Nevertheless, in spite of all flaws, there are hardly any alternatives to the use of these data for a quantitative analysis of income poverty. The LIS data still provide the best available evidence for comparative studies. However, as with any data, we must be aware of the limitations of the data in order to be able to execute a thorough analysis of the data and interpret the results carefully. For this purpose, the following sections will summarize the available evidence on methodological limitations of the data used in this book.

---

[59] This survey has been initiated by a group of researchers at the University of Frankfurt/Main and is administered by the German Institute for Economic Research (Deutsches Institut für Wirtschaftsforschung, DIW). For a more detailed description of the German Socio-Economic Panel, cf. Hanefeld (1987); Wagner (1991); Wagner et al. (1994); Rendtel (1995); GSOEP (1996); Pannenberg and Rendtel (1996).

Undercoverage

For quantitative poverty research, it is critical that low-income groups are adequately represented in the sample. Yet, this is not always the case, as these groups often are not covered to a sufficient degree. This problem largely is determined by the sample design of the survey.[60]

Table 4.3 Undercoverage of groups of the population

	Germany 1994	Sweden 1995	UK 1995
Persons living in institutions			
– People living in residences for students, apprentices, etc.	Included	excluded	excluded
– Soldiers	excluded if not living in private households[b]	excluded	excluded
– People in care or nursing homes	partly included[b]	largely included if under age 74	excluded
– Hospitals	Excluded[b]	excluded	excluded
– Prisoners	Excluded[b]	mostly included	excluded
– Private households within institutions (e.g. caretaker)	Included	excluded?	excluded?
Foreigners and ethnic minorities			
– Permanently resident foreigners	included	included[a]	included
– Refugees and asylum seekers	included?	included[a]	included
– Members of the diplomatic service	included?	some excluded	excluded
– Foreign soldiers	included?	some excluded	excluded
Other groups			
– Homeless	largely excluded	largely excluded	largely excluded
– Domestic servants	included	included?	included
– Roman catholic priests	included	included?	excluded
– People over the age of 74	included	excluded	included
– People living in remote geographic areas	included?	included	Scilly and Scottish offshore islands excluded

[a] People who have not been resident in Sweden for an entire calendar year will not have any annual income recorded (missing) (Jansson, 1998).
[b] For the SOEP: sample members remain in the sample if they move into an institution during the course of the panel survey.

Source: Based on LIS country-specific documentation of datasets; Office for National Statistics (1998a); Harris (1998); Hanefeld (1987: 162-201); Wagner (1994: 75-78); Jansson (1994; 1998).

---

[60] For a discussion of sampling effects in poverty research, cf. Howes and Lanjouw (1998); for a general discussion of survey errors, cf. Groves (1989). Sampling methods used for the surveys in this study are summarized in Table A.4 in the Appendix (p. 213).

Many surveys exclude some relevant groups of the population from the sampling frame altogether. These sampling errors may occur at different stages of the sampling process. First, some groups of the population may be *a priori* formally excluded from the sampling frame, as e.g. persons living in institutions, the – homeless or some categories of foreigners.[61]

As Table 4.3 illustrates, none of the three datasets perfectly covers the resident population, but every one entails some degree of undercoverage. Many groups with high poverty risks are indeed *a priori* excluded from the sample, such as the homeless or persons living in institutions. Sampling errors for poverty-prone groups of the population may lead to underestimating poverty, yet this bias may at least be partly compensated by sampling errors for the better-off. For the three countries covered in this book, sampling errors do not perfectly coincide, so the comparability of the data is limited. Possibly, the magnitude of sampling effects is broadly similar, but there are important differences for some groups of the population. The exclusion of very old people from the Swedish sample in particular is important in this respect.

Second, the procedure of selecting potential respondents from the sampling frame may also contribute to the undercoverage of some parts of the population. For example, the selection of respondents from telephone registers will systematically exclude people who do not possess a phone; similar selection effects apply for electoral registers or administrative registration records. In addition to these sampling errors, a number of non-sampling errors further reduce the quality of survey data for poverty research.

Non-response

The poor representation of some low-income groups in surveys is reinforced by a certain non-response bias. Non-response may occur either as a failure to be included in the survey at all (unit non-response) or may be confined to certain survey questions (item non-response).

Although being included in the sampling frame, low-income households may not be included in the sample for a number of reasons. Some groups tend to be disregarded because their life circumstances make it unlikely to be included in the sample.[62] This applies in particular to homeless and very mobile people (e.g. construction workers, travellers), but also to the self-employed (Foster, 1996). Although most surveys operate with strict rules for

---

[61] For a very careful and comprehensive analysis of undercoverage effects cf. Schnell (1991); also Hanefeld (1987: 162-168) for a description of these effects in the German Socio-Economic Panel.

[62] The underrepresentation of married prime-age men in many surveys can possibly also be explained by this effect (Schnell, 1997: 200-201).

the selection of sample households, compliance on the part of the interviewers is hard to control (cf. Schnell, 1991, 1997). In addition, some parts of the sampled population are not able to take part in an interview, such as people with a serious illness or handicaps. Although these non-response effects do not exclusively affect people at the lower end of the income scale, some groups of the population with high poverty risks tend to be poorly represented in these surveys.

Some observers believe that surveys are an unsuitable instrument for assessing the life situation of these groups: complex questionnaires would exceed their intellectual or communicative skills, and fear of stigmatization or administrative sanctions prevents people to uncover their precarious life situation to interviewers (cf. Goyder, 1985, 1987; Schnell, 1997: 204-205; Andreß, 1999: 29). For the British FES, the demands upon respondents are particularly high, since respondents are required to keep a two-week diary in order to record their incomes and expenditures (Foster, 1996: 9).[63] Although non-response rates cannot be associated with a general 'middle class bias' (cf. Goyder, 1985: 80-88; Schnell, 1997: 198-209), there is some evidence for a correlation with the level of education and unemployment.[64]

People with very low and very high incomes are also more likely to drop out of a panel study (panel attrition). For the German GSOEP, this was the case for the transition from the first to the second wave of the panel (1984 to 1985), but panel attrition for the poor has been similar to the average panel attrition in subsequent waves (Habich et al., 1991: 493; cf. Rendtel, 1990). However, Riphahn (1998) could show for the years 1984-1996 that panel attrition is associated with a low level of education, unemployment and female headship of the household. For foreign nationals, the risk of moving abroad is one additional factor that may lead to dropping out of the panel. In addition, the probability of non-response tends to be higher for immigrant or ethnic minority households and households with more than two adults, at least in the British context.[65] Although there is hardly any evidence that low income as such prevents people from taking part in these surveys, the factors that have been found to foster problems of non-response are strongly correlated to low income and poverty. Therefore, even if a general middle class

---

[63] In the 1994/1995 FES, non-response amounted to some 30% of the sampled population (Central Statistical Office, 1999).

[64] Cf. Foster (1996) for the British 1991 FES, and Rendtel (1995) and Berntsen (1992: 104-107) for the German SOEP. For the latter, Rendtel et al. (1995) could show in response to Lipsmeier (1993) that persons in households receiving social assistance indeed were more likely to leave the panel survey (panel attrition) than the average over all households, whereas the effect of unemployment was ambiguous.

[65] Cf. Foster (1996); Hansbro and Foster (1997), quoted in Office for National Statistics (1998b: Section 1 part 4).

bias is not supported in the data, problems of non-response for low-income groups tend to limit the quality of survey data for poverty research. However, systematic evidence on the effects of this non-response bias on the quality of the measurement of poverty is very sparse (Andreß, 1999: 30).

Other than the British and German surveys, the Swedish data are partly based on tax files and are supposed to be less sensitive to biased non-response. Although the latter uses telephone surveys to supplement the income data from the tax files by additional socio-demographic information, non-response in these interviews does not lead to the exclusion of the household from the sample, since some information on household composition, housing and employment can also be derived from the tax files.[66] The Swedish data are therefore supposed to be more reliable in this respect.

Generally, these errors can be partly accounted for by the use of sample weights.[67] These weights are supposed to balance the under- or over-representation of certain socio-demographic groups, yet the effect of this procedure is fairly limited, since these weights can only achieve a partial correction of errors on certain variables (e.g. family type), but cannot reflect the full complexity of sampling and non-sampling errors. In this book, sample weights provided by LIS will be used in order to mitigate possible errors.

Quality of the Income Data

Income data on the basis of surveys also suffer from the problem that not all income is reported properly, especially for the lower and higher ends of the income strata, as the evidence compiled by Atkinson, Rainwater and Smeeding shows (1995: 142-154). The under- or overreporting of certain types of income is partly a function of specific patterns of general non-response (unit non-response), as discussed above. In addition, people may refuse to indicate their income (item non-response), since income is considered as a very sensitive issue in surveys. Respondents may either not know the exact amount of their household income, or hesitate to disclose it to the interviewer (cf. Ross and Reynolds, 1996). In addition, the answers given by respondents may be incorrect for any reason.[68] Respondents may 'forget'

---

[66] Kjell Jansson, Statistiska Centralbyrån, personal communication, 11 March 1999.

[67] These sample weights are supposed to account for different probabilities of selection (cf. Atkinson et al., 1995: 21; Krause, 1997b: 54); for a critical discussion of survey weights cf. Schnell (1993).

[68] An earlier analysis of this issue reported for the German *Einkommens- und Verbrauchsstichprobe (EVS)* that only one third of all households had classified themselves in the same income category when the reported amounts given in an unspecified income question and the results of the much more specific income questions of the income and expenditure diary were compared. A full 58 per cent of respondents underestimated, but only 8 per cent of house-

66   At the Margins of the Welfare State

some types of income because they do not consider it as income, as for example some types of social transfers (Habich et al., 1991: 494). Moreover, if several social security benefits are paid out together, respondents may not be able to distinguish them in the survey (Fry and Stark, 1993: 11-13).[69] People give flawed answers if they either do not know the exact value of a certain income component, or if they want to conceal certain types of incomes.[70] The latter is most probable to affect incomes from illegal activities and some transfer incomes that may be regarded as stigmatizing, such as some means-tested benefits. Missing data due to item non-response is not distributed equally in the population, but tends to be most marked for very low and very high incomes (Atkinson et al., 1995). There is also some variation with household types and age (cf. Johnson and McCrae, 1998; Rendtel et al., 1995).

The extent of this bias appears to vary across countries, however. For the German data, there were concerns that means-tested benefits were subject to under-reporting. There is some evidence that low-income households are slightly underrepresented in the GSOEP (cf. Berntsen, 1989: 21; Lipsmeier, 1993). It is not clear, however, which portion of the under-reported income must be accounted to sampling errors, and which portion is due to 'real' under-reporting (item non-response and incorrect data). Eventually, concerns on under-reporting led to the decision to use a synthetic estimate of the

---

holds overestimated their income (Euler, 1983). A similar bias was found not only for the EVS, but also for the GSOEP and the *Mikrozensus* in a more recent study (Bedau and Krause, 1998).

[69] Fry and Stark report that there has been a large problem of under-reporting of income support for pensioners in Britain, since state pensions and income support are paid out in the same order book. For 1989, the data of the FES reflected less than half of the number of income support recipients among pensioners. For other groups of the population, such as the sick, the unemployed and single parents, this problem is less virulent and there has also been a overestimation of income support in some years (Fry and Stark, 1993: 11-13).

[70] The effects of incomplete or flawed reported income may be reduced by using certain interview strategies. First, questions on income should be ascertained as 'close to the source' as possible, which means that income components that accrue at the household level (e.g. housing benefits) should be included in the household questionnaire and be reported by the household head, whereas income components with a more individual character (e.g. earnings) should be reported by the respective household member (cf. Habich et al., 1991: 494). Second, respondents should be informed during the interview that their responses are treated confidentially and anonymously, and that their answers will not provoke any negative consequences whatsoever. By this token, it should be made clear that respondents do not have to fear stigmatization or criminal prosecution when reporting any 'sensitive' income. Third, interviewers can permit or urge respondents to look up income components in their documents in order to enhance the quality of the data. This does however take additional time that the interviewer may not be willing to allow. Tight restrictions in money or time for the interviewers and a lack of control by the research institute may result in 'quick and dirty' interviews with poor results.

amount of social assistance for the 1994 wave.[71] In the United Kingdom, the under-reporting of transfers seems to be less problematic (Atkinson and Micklewright, 1983: 43-48), although still existent. There is some evidence that income from employment (especially part-time employment), self-employment, investment and occupational pensions is under-reported. Generally, the data provided by the FES do not markedly deviate from other national statistics (Office for National Statistics, 1998a: Section 1 part 5). For the Swedish data, we would expect a markedly smaller bias, as the data are based on tax files rather than on survey data. Tax files are generally assumed to provide more reliable data than surveys, since reporting errors may be minimized. However, there are some typical potential errors associated with administrative data, such as tax evasion in the case of tax records (Atkinson et al., 1995: 25-30). In addition, coverage of income components is dependent on the national tax rules. For example, realized capital gains from capital are only included in if this type of income has to be included in income tax assessments, and if it actually is declared (cf. Björklund, 1998: 45).

The quality of reported income data is usually evaluated by comparing the reported amounts of income to aggregate data from national accounts or expenditure on social transfers. The use of this method is not unproblematic, since it is based on a number of assumptions that tend to limit the quality of the comparison. Moreover, the quality of external data is not necessarily superior to survey data (Atkinson et al., 1995: 34-37). Table 4.4 below summarizes the available evidence on the quality of income data in Britain, Germany, and Sweden for the mid-1990s. Where available, older results are also reported if they provide a more detailed account of the quality of the income data. The external validation of survey data is based the national accounts, the 'Blue Book' and administrative statistics in the British case, the '*Volkswirtschaftliche Gesamtrechnung*' (VGR) in the German case, and the Nationalräkenskaper series for Sweden.

The data assembled in Table 4.4 below show a divergent pattern of data quality in Britain, Germany and Sweden, especially for government transfers. Whereas the British FES and the Swedish tax files come close to the national account data, the GSOEP produces a flawed estimate of social transfers, notably for unemployment benefits and social assistance (Berntsen, 1989; Kassella and Hochmuth, 1989).[72]

---

[71] Means-tested benefits were estimated on the basis of the legal entitlements, but only for households who have reported the receipt of social assistance payments (Krause, 1997a; Krause et al., 1996). Some earlier studies on the basis of the GSOEP have also used simulated amounts of social assistance (Berntsen, 1992).

[72] For the British data for 1977, data were adjusted for differing age distributions in the FES sample and the total population (Atkinson and Micklewright, 1983).

68   At the Margins of the Welfare State

Table 4.4 Quality of the income data in LIS (estimates based on survey data as a percentage of aggregated data in national accounts)

	Germany		Sweden		United Kingdom	
	1983	1993	1995	1977	1992	1995/96
Wages and salaries	108.8	92.4	98	93.7	96.2	94
Self-employment income	}36.3	}52.4	40	75.7	74.1	67
Property/investment inc.			96	50.6	60.3	52
Occupational pension inc.	..	..	110	74.5	98.7	49
Government transfers	50.6	62.1	101	88.6 (90.9)	96.4	82
-- public pensions	56.6	..	..	95.8 (108.4)	..	..
-- unemployment benefits	37.4	..	..	103.1 (101.4)	..	..
-- social assistance	38.4	..	..	92.9 (95.0)	72.0/93.3*	
-- housing benefits	84.8	..	..	..	..	..
Total	76.9	89.5	..	89.0	92.9	..

Note: The data for Sweden do not include property income from capital gains, and transfer incomes from private pension schemes and student loans, since these types of income are not available in the national accounts. Values in parentheses age-weighted (Atkinson and Micklewright, 1983).
* For Britain 1992, social assistance benefits have been validated on the basis of administrative data for the 1991/92 fiscal year, for all other types of income the national accounts. The second figure relates to administrative statistics for the household population only.

Source: Atkinson et al. (1995: 34); Atkinson and Micklewright (1983: 43-48); Stuttard (1996); Johnson and McCrae (1998); G. Harris (1998); Berntsen (1989: 21); Kassella and Hochmuth (1989); Bedau and Krause (1998: 232); Jansson (1998).

Notably social assistance benefits tend to be underestimated in survey data, along with property income and income from self-employment. One source of error for this type of transfer income is the fact that a relatively large share of social assistance benefits are claimed by persons living in institutions, and this group of the population is not or only poorly represented in the surveys considered here (Johnson and McCrae, 1998: 26-27). Johnson and McCrae could show for the 1992 data on Britain that once the institutionalized population is excluded from the aggregate expenditure figures, the FES produces a much better result (Johnson and McCrae, 1998: 29-31).[73] Moreover, they could also demonstrate that under-reporting of social assistance benefits does not occur at random: social assistance expenditure on pensioners was much less probable to be reflected in the FES survey than expenditure on non-pensioners (63.8 versus 98.3 per cent for 1991/92). Many pensioners seem to have indicated their income from income support with their retirement pension (cf. Fry and Stark, 1993: 11-13). Their total income would thus

---

[73] Their estimate however suffers from the fact that Johnson and McCrae (1998) had to use administrative data reflecting 'one day in May', while the FES data relate to a whole year. This may lead to errors due to seasonal effects.

not be underestimated, but their income from social assistance actually is (Johnson and McCrae, 1998: 29-35).

It has to be noted, however, that some of the external comparisons for the government transfers that could be presented here are fairly outdated, so more recent data may possibly have reduced the problem of under-reporting, since new standards of national accounts allow a better estimate (van der Laan, 1998). It appears that the quality of the income data in the GSOEP has indeed improved as the less detailed data for Germany 1993 would suggest (Bedau and Krause, 1998). However, as a more recent break-down by income component is not available to my knowledge, readers should be aware of this problem for the interpretation of empirical results.

These large divergences between the British and the German surveys could be found in different interview strategies that may influence the exactness of results, or in the methodology of the external comparison itself. Within the scope of this book, however, it is not possible to clarify this issue. Therefore, the results of this study should be interpreted with due respect to the limits of the survey data.

Private Households: A Simple Concept with Critical Implications

Unit of Analysis: Individuals or Households?

Studies of income distribution and poverty have to define a basic unit of analysis of economic welfare, such as families, households or individuals. Some types of incomes usually are collected by individuals (e.g. wages or pensions), but other types accrue at the family or household level (e.g. housing benefit). By the same token, many types of household expenditure can be related to the income-sharing unit (e.g. rent), other types of expenditures are more strongly associated with individual members of the household or family (e.g. clothing). Generally, it is assumed that income is pooled on the household or family level and shared equally within the household. Under this premise, all members of the household enjoy the same level of economic well-being, intra-household inequality is not taken into account.[74]

Poverty can be measured either on a household/family basis or on an individual basis. In the latter case, the equivalent income of the household is assigned to each household member as their individual welfare level. Some observers hold that this approach would be superior to the household ap-

---

[74] For a discussion of intra-household transfers and the effects of this assumption on the measurement of individual welfare, cf. Pahl (1989), Thomas (1990), Findlay and Wright (1996).

proach, since it is less sensitive to social structure effects for international comparisons (cf. Task Force on Statistics on Social Exclusion and Poverty, 1998). Nevertheless, a large part of poverty research refers to the household level. Since this book is concerned with the effects of social assistance on poverty, and social assistance payments are usually granted to the household as a whole and not to individual members of the household, the household will also be used as the primary unit of analysis throughout this book. Nevertheless, it is interesting to see how robust poverty measures are. In fact, poverty rates markedly differ depending on whether households or individuals are chosen as unit of analysis (see Table 4.5).

Table 4.5 Poverty rates for individuals and households

	Germany 1994		Sweden 1995		UK 1995	
	households	individuals	households	individuals	households	individuals
near poverty	5.7	5.3	3.9	3.0	8.8	8.8
moderate poverty	3.3	3.0	2.3	1.6	5.8	5.6
severe poverty	1.9	1.4	1.9	1.3	2.1	2.1
extreme poverty	2.2	1.9	5.3	3.1	2.1	2.6
poverty (50% level)	7.4	6.3	9.6	6.1	10.0	10.3

Note: Poverty rates are computed on the basis of the modified OECD equivalence scale.

Source: LIS, own calculations.

Whereas British poverty rates for individuals hardly deviate from poverty rates on a household basis, the choice of the unit of analysis actually makes a remarkable difference for Germany and Sweden, but less so for Britain. In the former countries, poverty rates are lower if measured on an individual basis, most markedly in Sweden. Sweden even changes its rank position. Whereas Swedish poverty rates come second to the British one if poverty is measured on a household basis, individual poverty rates are lowest in Sweden. The large divergence between both poverty measures can possibly be explained by the specific household definition for Sweden (see below). If small households dominate among the poor population, household poverty rates will be higher than individual poverty rates. In contrast, the relationship between individual and household poverty rates in Britain suggests that larger households make up a higher share of the poor population.

A more subtle methodological pitfall is the question which type of the income-sharing unit – households or families – can be used. Some datasets allow to identify both families (usually defined as persons related by blood, marriage or adoption who are living together) and households (usually defined as people who share a dwelling and food, but are not necessarily re-

Household Definitions and their Impact on Measured Poverty

Although the Luxembourg Income Study is deeply committed to ensuring cross-national comparability, some problems still remain, since the construction of national surveys does not allow a perfect streamlining ('lissification') of the data. Differing household definitions are one of the most crucial problems that limit comparability across countries. Since income is usually collected and shared within private households, discrepant household definitions can make a significant difference for the measurement of income levels and poverty. For our purpose, it is most important to acknowledge that the Swedish household definition deviates from the household definition used in Britain and Germany. The Swedish survey considers all young adults from the age of 18 still living with their parents as independent households, although they might still live with their parents and be economically dependent on them. Consequently, the poverty rates tend to be higher than if a household definition more similar to that of other countries had been applied.[75]

The following exercise will help to clarify the consequences of the differing household definition. Figure 4.1 shows two alternative poverty profiles for Sweden. The bold line displays the poverty profile for the full household sample, whereas the dotted line shows a poverty profile for a sample without single students aged 25 or younger.[76]

Figure 4.1 illustrates that the inclusion or exclusion of students has a strong effect on measured poverty. Poverty rates are markedly lower if students are excluded from the sample. For a poverty line of 50 per cent of median equivalent income, the exclusion of students reduces poverty rates from 9.8 to 5.6 per cent of the population. At the 40 per cent level, poverty rates would decrease from 7.4 to 3.4 per cent, and from 13.4 to 9.9 per cent at the 60 per cent level.

---

[75] Earlier estimations have indicated that in 1979, one sixth of the poor in Sweden were students aged 18-24, and they accounted for 0.8 percentage points of the poverty rate (5.0 per cent instead of 4.2 per cent) (Smeeding and Schmaus, 1990: 6-7).

[76] This definition excludes almost 74 per cent of student households from the sample. The remaining student households include other adults or children are living in the same household, and older students.

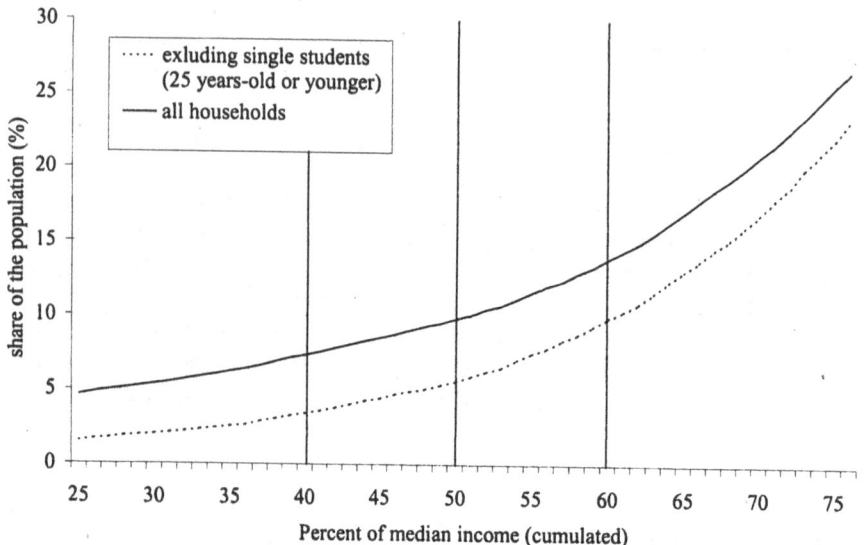

Figure 4.1 Poverty profiles in Sweden: Mapping the impact of the exclusion of students on poverty rates

Source: LIS, own calculations.

Nevertheless, this problem cannot simply be solved by excluding students from the sample. Whereas poverty tends to be overstated if students are included in the sample, the exclusion of students from the sample would understate poverty for two reasons: first, poverty rates of these young people themselves would certainly be understated, since we do not know how many students are not supported by their parents and are actually living in poverty. Second, the income of their parent households would be overestimated, since these students would have to be added to their parents' household and increase the number of persons in the household. Thus, equivalent household income would decrease. Hence, a truly comparable measure of poverty would lie somewhere between these two profiles, but its exact level is not clear. Any interpretation of the results of this book should therefore take into account that the comparability of the Swedish data is limited due to differing household definitions.[77] Keeping these methodological problems in mind, the

---

[77] In order to interpret the Swedish data, one should also take into account the institutional rules of entitlement in Sweden. In some counties, young adults are entitled to social assistance (socialbidrag) independently of their parents' income even if they are living with them, yet benefits tend to be lower to account for lower rents and other household-related costs. Students are generally not entitled to social assistance (with some exceptions during the term holidays), since they are eligible for means-tested scholarship grants and additional

following accounts of poverty in Sweden draws on the full sample of Swedish households, including students.

Adjustment for Household Size

When analyzing private household income, researchers have to make decisions about the adjustment of data for different household sizes and variations in need. A given disposable income does not necessarily lead to equal levels of welfare for households with different needs.[78] Studies of income inequality and poverty therefore use equivalence scales in order to adjust household income according to the size and composition of the household. Most equivalence scales discriminate between adults and children, some also according to the age of household members.[79] The elasticity of equivalence scales ranges between 0 (additional household members do not increase the need of the household) and 1 (per capita income calculated as household income divided by the number of its members).

The choice of equivalence scales has a considerable impact on the measured poverty, since the level of median income is sensitive to the choice of equivalence scale. Poverty rates vary with equivalence scales, but the direction of the bias is indeterminate, depending on the distribution of poverty risks among the population.

Figure 4.2 presents poverty rates for three widely-used equivalence scales. The 'modified OECD equivalence scale' attaches a weight of 1.0 for the head of the household, 0.5 for additional adults, and 0.3 for children under 18 years. Compared to other equivalence scales, this scale embodies a medium elasticity of need (cf. Atkinson et al., 1995). This equivalence scale has been recommended by the EU Task Force on Social Exclusion and Poverty (1998) and will also be used throughout this book. In addition, most empirical results will also be presented for two alternative equivalence scales, in order to account for the sensibility of results for the choice of the equivalence scale. These scales are the older OECD equivalence scale and the square root scale. The older OECD scale ('classical OECD scale') attaches a weight of 1.0 for first and 0.7 for further adults in the household,

---

scholarship loans. However, students may receive social assistance under certain circumstances.
[78] Subjective poverty research has shown that marginal need of additional household members varies with the income level of the household. Since poorer households allocate a larger share of their household income on food and clothing, additional household members increase the household need level more markedly than for richer households (cf. Van Praag and Van der Saar 1988; Aaberge and Melby, 1998).
[79] For an overview on widely-used equivalence scales, cf. Buhmann et al. (1988: 120) and Atkinson et al. (1995: 18-21).

and 0.5 for children.[80] The square root scale (also dubbed 'LIS scale') calculates equivalent incomes on the basis of the square root of the number of persons in the household, without differentiating between children and adults.[81] These three equivalence scales are the most widely-used equivalence scales in comparative poverty research.

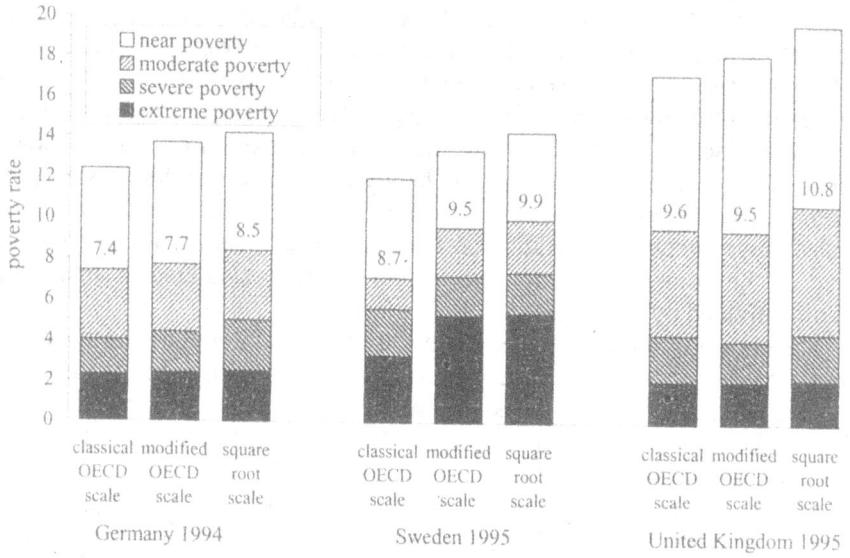

Figure 4.2 The impact of equivalence scales on measured poverty

Source: LIS, own calculations.

Figure 4.2 illustrates that poverty rates are sensitive to the choice of the equivalence scale. Overall poverty rates vary by more than one percentage point. For example, whereas the modified OECD equivalence scale produces higher poverty rates than the classical OECD equivalence scale in Germany and Sweden, the latter are higher in the United Kingdom. The distribution of the poor onto poverty brackets is relatively stable, except in the case of extreme poverty in Sweden. In all countries considered here, however, poverty rates are highest if the square root scale is used.

Whereas the overall level of poverty often is only marginally affected by the choice of equivalence scales, poverty rates for specific groups of the population may change dramatically (cf. Buhmann et al., 1988; Burkhauser

---

[80] The classical OECD scale has been used in a number of influential studies, such as e.g. Mitchell (1991).

[81] This scale has been applied in many recent studies, e.g. Atkinson et al. (1995); Burniaux et al. (1998).

et al., 1996; Burniaux et al., 1998: Annex 2). Basically, equivalence scales that attach a large weight to additional household members produce higher poverty rates for large households, whereas equivalence scales with a low elasticity result in high poverty rates for single person households. These effects do not only apply for income-based poverty analyses, but also for expenditure-based studies (de Vos and Zaidi, 1997).

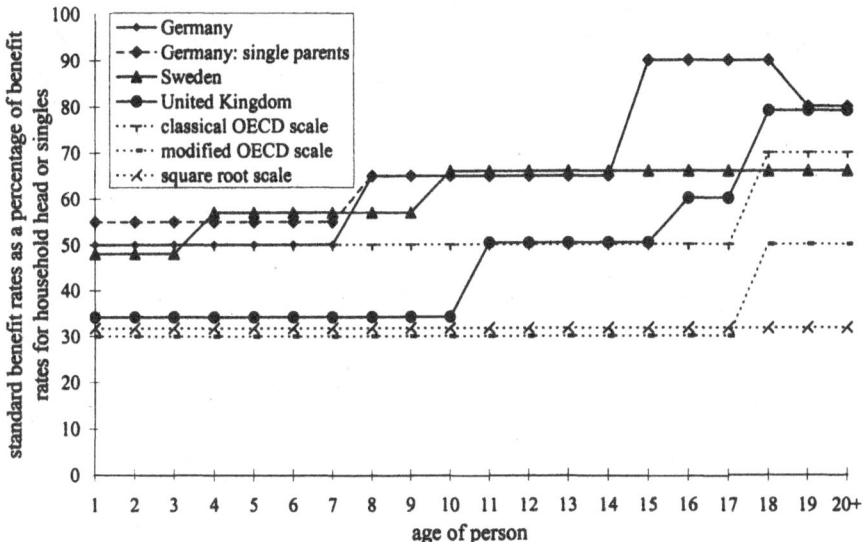

Figure 4.3 Equivalence scales in social assistance schemes and in poverty research

Note: For Sweden: Standard benefit rates as recommended by the National Board of Health and Welfare. Germany: children of single parents receive 55 per cent of the adult rate up to the age of 7. The weight assigned to additional household members assigned by the square root scale is dependent on the total number of persons in the household. The value presented here refers to the third person in a household, the additional weight of the second household member would be higher (0.41), for further household members slightly lower.

Source: Own calculations based on national statistics and social assistance regulations.

For the assessment of the effects of means-tested benefits, an additional issue has to be taken into account. Means-tested benefit schemes usually also embody equivalence scales. In fact, some national poverty studies use equivalence scales based on institutional equivalence scales of the respective social assistance scheme.[82] If equivalence scales used do not perfectly match

---

[82] Cf. e.g. Hanesch et al. (1994: 128-145), Hauser and Wagner (1996) for Germany, or Björklund (1998) for Sweden.

76 At the Margins of the Welfare State

the equivalence scales institutionalized in the benefit schemes, measured poverty is very sensitive to the choice of the equivalence scale and the poverty line applied. To illustrate this point, Figure 4.3 displays the equivalence scales institutionalized in the social assistance schemes of Germany, Sweden and the United Kingdom in 1995. Benefit rates for additional household members are given as a percentage of the single person's rate. To allow a direct comparison, the equivalence scales described above are depicted as well.

Figure 4.3 shows that institutional equivalence scales vary markedly across countries, depending on the age of the additional household members. Nevertheless, institutional equivalence scales attach a higher weight to household members than both the modified OECD scale and the square root scale. Only the classical OECD scale matches the institutional equivalence scales more closely.

In order to avoid the bias caused by different equivalence scales, would national institutional equivalence scales produce more robust results than the general equivalence scales? Do the latter underestimate household needs, given that social assistance scales are often based on a more thorough evaluation of household consumption patterns than general equivalence scales? This is not necessarily the case. The institutional equivalence scales presented here only reflect some part of the total benefit package of recipient households, but the complete picture is more complicated. Most recipient households also receive some part of their benefit on a household basis, such as allowances for housing costs or for irregularly occurring needs. If these allowances were to be included in the calculation of institutional equivalence scales, their elasticity of need would probably shrink, in other words, they would move closer to the equivalence scales used in poverty research. The reason is that the value of these allowances tends to be higher for small households because of economies of scale. In addition, the benefit package may be made up by benefits from other transfer schemes which possibly incorporate different equivalence scales. Therefore, the full picture is more complex than the simple comparison of institutional equivalence scales embodied in standard benefit rates and other equivalence scales would suggest.

The Concept of Income and Related Questions

The definition of income is of crucial importance to the measurement of income poverty. As an indicator of economic well-being, this book focuses on disposable income of private households, as defined by LIS.

Disposable Income and its Components

Disposable income is defined as market income plus public and private transfers, net of taxation. Market income includes income from employment, self-employment, and from capital or other property. Public and private transfers include benefits from social insurance and other public transfers (cash and near-cash), as well as private transfers such as alimony. Taxes and social security contributions are then deducted from gross income (cf. Atkinson et al., 1995: 13-15).

Households with negative or zero disposable income have been excluded from the analysis, since missing values have been recoded as zero by LIS. No other adjustment for extremely low or extremely high incomes has been made.

Non-cash Income

The measurement of non-pecuniary income components poses a difficult problem for the measurement of income, especially for cross-country comparisons. The inclusion of non-cash benefits may have a strong impact on measured poverty for some countries. Smeeding et al. (1993) have incorporated some non-cash benefits (mostly health and education) into the assessment of poverty and have found that these benefits considerably reduce poverty rates in some countries, especially for single parents and the elderly. This effect was particularly marked in the United Kingdom.

The integration of non-cash benefits into the assessment of poverty has to operate with a number of assumptions that invariably limit the interpretative power of these data. Estimating non-cash income is a very difficult task, since micro-data generally are not good enough to reflect the access to these benefits and the use of these goods and services for every household in the sample. First, it is not clear whether the value of non-cash benefits can be equalled to the possession of money income at all, because non-cash benefits cannot be traded against other goods. People may prefer to spend money on other goods or services if they could have disposed of the money equivalent of non-cash benefits (Smeeding et al., 1993: 237). Besides, some types of non-cash incomes are associated with needs that are not fully reflected in common poverty measures and equivalence scales (cf. Radner, 1997). For example, if people are ill and therefore in need of health care, this need is normally not reflected in these measures. As far as non-cash benefits are used to cover unmeasured need, the omission of non-cash income is not problematic as such. For international comparisons, however, there is indeed a problem of comparability if the mix of public and private provision varies across countries.

Second, any estimation of the value of non-cash benefits has to distinguish between actual cost of the actual use and the value of potential access of these benefits. For example, how can the cash value of free or subsidized health services be measured? Under the assumption that people without access to these non-cash benefits would have to pay for these services, we would try to estimate the value of the services used. But would it not be more realistic to assume that people would buy a health insurance if health services were not free at the point of use, rather than directly paying for these services? In this case, we would try to estimate the cost of a health insurance rather than the value of the actual use of these services. Given that the use of health services varies markedly by age and gender, these methods will produce very divergent results for the measurement of poverty, especially when evaluating poverty for subgroups of the population or comparing countries with a different socio-demographic structure of the low-income population. Similarly, there are good reasons to argue that the free access to education as such enhances the welfare of all households, rather than only for current users, but we know that the use of education is unequally distributed in the population and therefore may bias measured poverty.

Time Frame

The Luxembourg Income Study provides income data on a yearly basis. Income dynamics within shorter periods of time are thus not fully reflected. The use of yearly data rather than monthly or weekly data evens out short-term fluctuations in income. Generally speaking, the longer the period of observation, the smaller the measured income inequality and the more stable appears the distribution of incomes.[83] Households may balance short-term fluctuations of income by adjusting their consumption behaviour or by accumulating or liquidating capital, without necessarily changing their general welfare position. In addition, households may deliberately shift their income between different periods.[84] Indeed, income inequality tends to be lower if measured over a longer period or even over lifetime, and the same is true for poverty rates (cf. Björklund, 1998; Burkhauser et al., 1997).

Some observers have claimed that even the period of one year is too short for an adequate analysis of the well-being of households and individuals (Alessie et al., 1997; Salas and Rabadan, 1998; J. Falkingham and Hills, 1995). For the analysis of poverty, this argument is problematic, since choosing a very long period of observation can lead to a stark underestima-

---

[83] Cf. e.g. Burkhauser et al. (1997) for a comparison of Germany and the United States.

[84] Björklund (1998: 43) has given the example of a person who accumulates income during some years in order to embark on a long journey around the world.

tion of poverty. The ability to re-distribute incomes over longer periods of time is limited, and is not equally distributed among the population. Generally, we can assume that households in a comfortable welfare position in terms of current income, financial assets, consumption goods and human capital will find it easier to balance their income over a longer period of time. Households that do not dispose of these attributes – and many poor households will belong to this category – tend to be less easily capable of compensating for temporal income losses by surpluses of a previous or latter period, because they lack of these very compensation mechanisms. Moreover, the equalization of income over a longer period of time requires some information (or at least expectations) about future developments. Again, we can assume that these are distributed in an unequal way: People in stable jobs of the primary labour market may find it easier to plan for the future than people in precarious employment or unemployment who generally also run a higher risk of being poor.

Poverty is a condition of deprivation at a certain point in time that cannot infinitely stretched into the future. To put it bluntly, a hungry person will not be prevented from starving by the knowledge of having plenty of bread in five years' time. This extreme example illustrates that, at least for analyses of poverty, extending the period of observation does not necessarily produce better results. Although the income position of a household may appear relatively good from an ex-post perspective averaging income over several years, households may have experienced periods of extreme deprivation.

For analyses of poverty, a period of one year may thus be a reasonable approximation of household budgeting and planning periods. It constitutes an acceptable compromise between equalizing short-term income fluctuations and the accounting for the immediate effects of low income on groups of the population.

In cross-national research, the time horizon of the surveys should ideally coincide. However, this is not fully the case for this study. Whereas the German and the Swedish income data report yearly income, the British Family Expenditure Survey refers to a period of two weeks.[85] The yearly income measure provided in the LIS data is based on the information on weekly income that has been re-calculated for the period of one year. The discrepancy between weekly and yearly income may occur as a merely technical problem, yet it may make a difference for the quality of the income data. The shorter the period of observation, the more sensitive the income data are towards short-term variations. Thus, incomes measured over a shorter period of time tend to be more dispersed than yearly data (cf.

---

[85] Seasonal variations are accounted for by spreading out the interview periods over the year (Office for National Statistics, 1998a).

80 At the Margins of the Welfare State

Atkinson et al., 1995: 16). It is not clear whether the use of weekly income in the British data has any effect on poverty rates, but a comparison of poverty rates for monthly and yearly income based on the German GSOEP has revealed that poverty rates tend to be higher for monthly data (Habich et al., 1991: 495). This effect may also be found in the British data, but there is no systematic evidence on this issue.

Poverty Lines

Where to Draw the Line? Poverty Profiles in a Comparative Perspective

Measures of relative income poverty have often been criticized of sketching a flawed picture of poverty, since relative poverty lines involve arbitrary decisions on the part of the researcher. Moat frequently, a household is considered as poor if it commands over less than 50 per cent of national median income adjusted for household size. Why should one choose 50 per cent of median income rather than 49 or 51 per cent? Apart from the argument of having at least one quasi-standard yardstick for international comparisons, there is no empirically or theoretically founded argument for or against choosing any of these alternatives. In addition, these poverty lines are also sensitive to clustering effects, so a small shift of the poverty line may cause a large variation in measured poverty. To account for these effects, some researchers also report poverty rates at alternative levels that are slightly higher or lower than the 50 per cent poverty line, often at 40 and 60 per cent of median income. This improves the quality of measured results, but it is still far from perfect. Confined to a small number of poverty lines, these approaches only sketch an incomplete picture of the profile of poverty. Figure 4.4 depicts the distribution of income among the low income strata for Britain, Germany and Sweden and shows the profile of poverty for each possible poverty line between 25 per cent of median income and 75 per cent of median income adjusted for household size.[86] Three poverty lines are shown as vertical lines in the chart, 40, 50, and 60 per cent of median equivalent income. The lowest part of the income distribution has been cut off in order to allow a closer focus on the most interesting part of the income distribution, between 25 and 75 per cent of median equivalent income.

---

[86] Figure 4.4 is based on the modified OECD equivalence scale. Again, these low income profiles may also be biased by the choice of the equivalence scale. in the Appendix present the same results with alternative equivalence scales.

Methodological Puzzles and Pitfalls 81

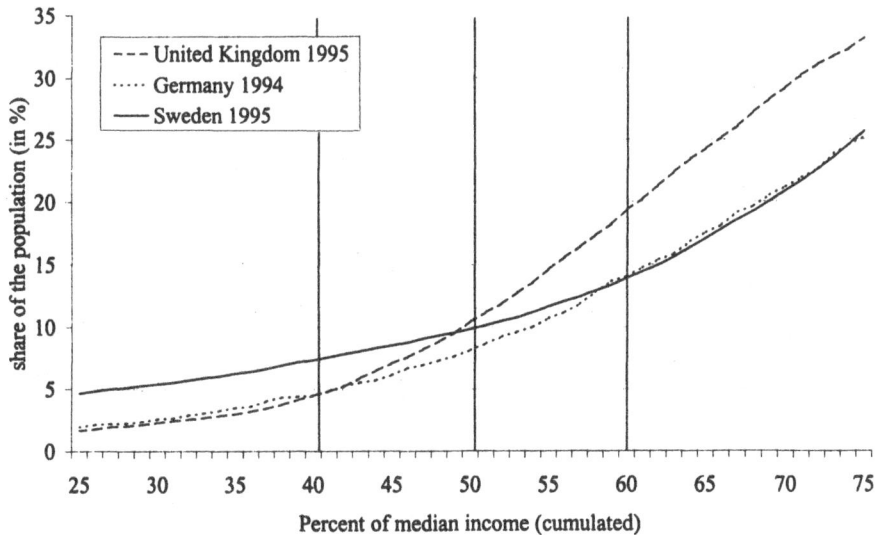

Figure 4.4 Poverty lines and poverty profiles in Britain, Germany and Sweden

Source: LIS, own calculations.

Figure 4.4 illustrates that the distribution of income in the lower strata of the population is far from forming an unambiguous picture. Rather, there is a marked variation that makes the choice of a poverty line a hazardous enterprise. Poverty rates are extremely sensitive to their position in the distribution of income. If one was to shift the poverty line slightly to the left or to the right, not only poverty rates itself may markedly change, but also the rank order of the three countries. For example, if the poverty line was moved from 50 to 48 per cent of median equivalent income, Sweden and the United Kingdom would swap places. Likewise, the graphs for Germany and the United Kingdom intersect at around 41 per cent of median income. Below this point, these two countries display a very similar profile of poverty. Poverty profiles for Germany and Sweden intersect at 58 per cent of median income, and almost perfectly parallel each other from this income level.

A Superior Measure of Poverty? Absolute Poverty Lines

Proponents of the absolute poverty approach argue that absolute measures provide a better measure of poverty, since they are able to map variations in overall societal welfare, rather than reflecting structures of inequality within a specific society.

82 At the Margins of the Welfare State

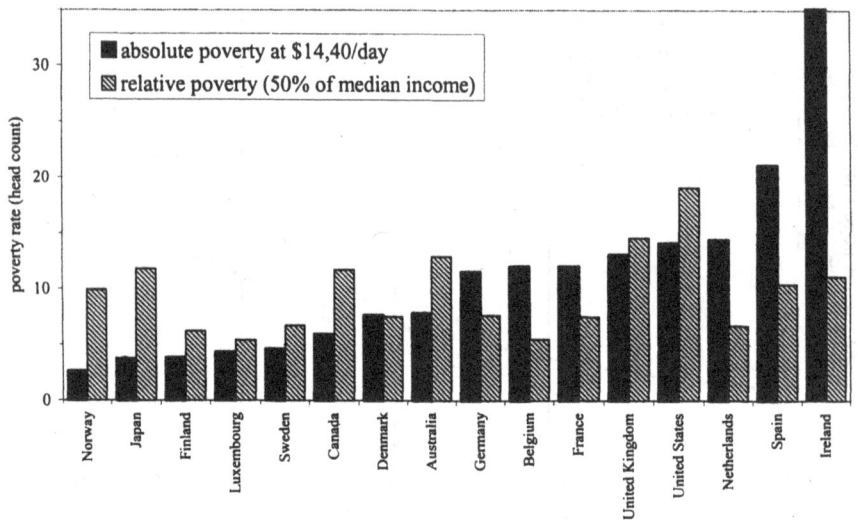

Figure 4.5 Absolute poverty rates based on the purchasing power equivalent of the US official poverty line

Note: The absolute poverty line is the purchasing power equivalent of the US official poverty line for a single person ($14.40), based on purchasing power parities of the Penn World Tables. Equivalence scale: e = 0.5.

Source: Smeeding (1997: 22); relative poverty rates computed on LIS datasets by Koen Vleminckx, 1998.

Studies of absolute poverty apply the same poverty line – net of variations in purchasing power – in absolute terms to all countries in the sample. Most studies on absolute income poverty have based their assessment on the purchasing power equivalent of the US poverty line. In a tentative analysis, Smeeding (1997) attempted to directly compare income poverty in industrialized and developing countries. Applying the purchasing power equivalent of the US poverty line, Smeeding found much higher poverty rates for many European countries, whereas the US poverty rate almost halved compared to a relative poverty line of 50 per cent of median income. Figure 4.5 shows his results and compares them to relative poverty rates.

The comparison of absolute and relative poverty rates does not produce a consistent picture of income poverty in advanced welfare states.[87] Countries

---

[87] Relative poverty rates presented in Figure 4.5 can slightly deviate from poverty rates in Figure 2.1, since different equivalence scales are used in order to make these data comparable to Smeeding's results.

with similar relative poverty rates have divergent absolute poverty rates and vice versa. Among the countries with the lowest absolute poverty rates – the Scandinavian countries, Luxembourg, Japan, Canada and Australia – are both high and low performers in the relative poverty dimension. Together with Austria, the United Kingdom and the United States (and with the exception of Denmark), all these countries have lower absolute than relative poverty rates. At the other extreme of the spectrum, we find Ireland and Spain with much higher absolute than relative poverty rates, a fact that may be due to the somewhat lower standard of economic development in these countries. Higher absolute than relative poverty rates are also found in Germany, Belgium, France and the Netherlands which are positioned in the middle ranks in terms of absolute poverty. As Smeeding (1997) rightly acknowledges, international comparisons of absolute poverty are critically dependent on the quality of the purchasing power parities used (cf. Brungger, 1996). This point is illustrated by a comparison of absolute poverty rates as computed in a number of studies that all u the same set of LIS data (yet partly referring to different years). Table 4.6 illustrates that their results markedly differ from each other, although at least some of these studies have used similar methods to measure poverty.

The poverty rates assembled in Table 4.6 suggest that absolute poverty lines are no less sensitive to methodological choices than relative poverty lines. Two types of absolute poverty lines have been applied, either based on the US official poverty line (Blackburn, 1998; Smeeding, 1997), or based on a certain percentage of median income in the US (Blackburn, 1994; Kenworthy, 1998, 1999). This allows a relatively easy comparison of these studies, since the US official poverty lines is generally held to correspond closely to 40 per cent of median income (Smeeding, 1997: 8). The absolute value of these poverty lines is then 'exported' to the other countries by use of purchasing power parities.

Blackburn's (1998) and Smeeding's (1997) data should match each other fairly well, since they are both based on the US official poverty line for a single person. Blackburn (1998) found that most industrialized countries even exceeded the US poverty rate of 20.8 per cent, especially the United Kingdom with more than 40 per cent, and the Netherlands with even 50 per cent of the population.[88] Among the countries assembled in Table 4.6, only Canada had lower poverty rates than the United States.

---

[88] Curiously, Blackburn's more recent results (1998) produced higher poverty rates than the earlier ones (1994), although being based on a supposedly lower poverty line.

84 At the Margins of the Welfare State

Table 4.6 Absolute poverty in OECD countries: results of selected studies

Poverty line	Blackburn (1998) US off. pov. line for single person			Smeeding (1997a)			Kenworthy (1998, 1999) 40% of ...			Blackburn (1994) 50% of US median income		
	Y	P	R	Y	P	R	Y	P	R	Y	P	R
Australia	1985	38.4	(6)	1989	7.8	(3)	1989	11.9	(7)	1985	29.9	(4)
Canada	1987	13.6	(1)	1991	5.9	(2)	1991	6.5	(3)	1987	11.3	(1)
France	1984	37.1	(5)	1984	12.0	(5)	1989	9.8	(5)	1984	29.8	(3)
Germany	1984	34.4	(4)	1989	11.5	(4)	1989	4.3	(1)	1984	30.6	(5)
Netherlands	1987	50.0	(8)	1991	14.4	(8)	1991	7.3	(4)	1987	42.4	(8)
Sweden	1987	34.0	(3)	1992	4.6	(1)	1992	5.8	(2)	1987	34.9	(6)
United Kingdom	1986	41.1	(7)	1991	13.1	(6)	1991	16.8	(8)	1986	35.9	(7)
United States	1986	20.8	(2)	1994	14.1	(7)	1991	11.7	(6)	1986	17.7	(2)
Mean		33.7			10.4			9.3			29.1	

Note: Y = year; P = poverty rate (head count); R = rank order (1 = country with lowest poverty rate). The table excludes countries that have not been covered by all cited studies. All studies are based on LIS data, but partly refer to different years and are partly based on different methods: The results published in Blackburn (1998) are based on the official US poverty line (as used by the Census Bureau) for a single person household for 1985, adjusted with purchasing power parities from the OECD National Accounts; equivalence scale e=0.75. Smeeding (1997) used the purchasing power equivalent of the official US poverty line ($14.4 per day), the purchasing power parities provided by the Penn World Tables and an equivalence scale of e=0.5. Kenworthy (1998) has used a poverty line set at 40 or 50 per cent of the US median adjusted with purchasing power parities from the OECD National Accounts, and an equivalence scale of e=0.5. Blackburn (1994) applied 50 per cent of US median income in 1985 as an absolute poverty line, adjusted for purchasing power with OECD purchasing power parities; equivalence scale not stated. For Australia, the correct year must be 1985, not 1987 as stated by Blackburn, since LIS does not provide data for 1987.
Source: Blackburn (1994, 1998); Kenworthy (1998, 1999); Smeeding (1997: 22); own calculations.

The magnitude of Smeeding's (1997) poverty rates correspond more closely to common measures of relative poverty for most of these countries, yet the rank order of countries markedly deviates from these measures, as Figure 4.5 above has illustrated. Even though Blackburn and Smeeding have based their analyses on the same reference poverty line, their results show large divergences that cannot fully be explained by the fact that their analyses partly refer to different years and use different equivalence scales. Poverty rates differ by as much as 30 percentage points, especially in the cases of Australia, France, Germany, the Netherlands, Sweden and the United Kingdom. Possibly, a large part of this divergence can be accounted for by different purchasing power parities.

Kenworthy (1998; 1999) has applied the purchasing power equivalent of 40 per cent of median equivalent income in the United States as an absolute poverty line, which roughly corresponds to the US official poverty line. His results generally come close to Smeeding's, but are slightly lower on average, and display large divergences for some countries, especially for Australia, Germany and the Netherlands.[89] In addition, he employed a poverty line of 50 per cent of US median equivalent income, as did Blackburn (1994). Again, Blackburn's results produced markedly higher poverty rates than the other study.

The large variance of poverty rates based on broadly similar absolute poverty lines has illustrated that the measurement of absolute poverty are also critically dependent upon methodological choices, notably purchasing power parities. Purchasing power parities are established for different purposes and are not necessarily suitable for the assessment of the income position of the poorest strata of the population for different reasons. Some purchasing power parities are based on a basket of goods, but this approach often inadequately reflects the consumption patterns of low-income households. In addition, the exchange rates chosen to price the basket of goods possibly may paint a flawed picture of the purchasing power in the respective countries during a certain period of observation. Kangas (2000: 11) claimed that purchasing power parities tend to overestimate the cost of living in countries with a high level of public services. Because of these methodological problems associated with purchasing power parities, absolute poverty lines are not necessarily more reliable than relative poverty lines. To my knowledge, there has not been any systematic research into conditions under

---

[89] Own calculations. Their analysis overlaps to a large degree in terms of covered countries and years. However, Smeeding's analysis refers to the year 1984 for France and 1994 for the US while Kenworthy's refers to 1989 for France and 1994 for the US. Countries that do not appear in both studies (Italy, Switzerland, Luxembourg, Japan, Spain) have been excluded from the calculation of average poverty rates.

which purchasing power parities are suitable for poverty research. Thus, the following discussion will confine itself to relative income poverty.

A Way Out of the Methodological Problems of Poverty Research?

The discussion of methodological problems in poverty research has illustrated that the measurement of poverty is highly sensitive to methodological choices. Different methods produce different empirical results, and even more, that the degree of overlapping of poverty measured by several indicators is suspiciously small.[90] Each of these different approaches to measure poverty highlights another aspect of poverty while neglecting others. Kangas and Ritakallio (1998a) have put this point as follows:

> [D]ifferent methods produce different pictures of poverty. Despite differences in results, each of these pictures may be equally correct and realistic. They only map a different slice of reality. Therefore, a simultaneous use of various measures may be advisable. One measure gives one result, another reveals something else. By concentrating on one single 'correct' measure, a great deal of valuable information may be lost. A full analysis requires a multidimensional method of measurement. In that way, we can reveal that many faces of poverty and social exclusion that, in turn, can be combatted by different remedies. (Kangas and Ritakallio, 1998b: 199)

A simultaneous use of several poverty measures, as proposed by Kangas and Ritakallio, may certainly shed some light on the advantages and deficiencies of different methods to measure poverty and illustrate different types of poverty, yet this approach does not help to explain the causes of these discrepancies.

An alternative approach may elucidate at least one small facet of the puzzle of poverty in industrialized welfare states. Turning back to the original question of the effectiveness of the welfare state in alleviating poverty, quantitative data on private household incomes and the incidence of poverty can be combined with more qualitative evidence on institutional arrangements. Confronting data on poverty with information on social assistance schemes can shed more light on the mechanisms that account for the persistence of poverty in advanced welfare states and help to provide a better estimate of the quality of the available income data.

---

[90] For empirical analyses of the overlapping between different measures of poverty and deprivation, cf. Halleröd (1991), Kangas and Ritakallio (1998a), Andreß (1999), and Burchardt et al. (1999).

The following three chapters will assess the three dimensions of ineffectiveness of social assistance schemes, that is eligibility, adequacy and take-up, as outlined in the last section of Chapter 3.

Chapter 5

Is the Entire Population Eligible for Social Assistance Benefits?

On the basis of the three dimensions of effectiveness outlined at the end of Chapter 3, this and the following chapters will evaluate social assistance schemes in Germany, Sweden and the United Kingdom. An informed description of the institutional framework identifies causal links between institutional structures and outcomes in terms of poverty alleviation.

The first of the three dimensions, the dimension of eligibility, possibly is the most straightforward parameter to measure the effectiveness of social assistance schemes in terms of poverty alleviation. If the institutional framework excludes some groups from social assistance, and they therefore will not receive any social assistance benefits, they are not sufficiently protected from poverty. This does not mean that people who are not entitled to social assistance benefits necessarily are poor, but they run a higher risk because they lack the basic safety net of social assistance.

The Institutional Framework: Eligibility Rules and Means-tests

The institutional framework of social assistance schemes provides for certain rules that regulate access to social assistance schemes. Basically, two mechanisms determine entitlement to social assistance: First, social assistance schemes stipulate rules of entitlement that grant eligibility to some categories of the population while denying it to others. For example, in some countries, certain groups of foreign nationals may not be fully eligible for social assistance. Some groups of the population may thus be *a priori* excluded from the general social assistance scheme. In a second step, means-tests guarantee that social assistance is only paid to the most needy groups of the population. Since institutional arrangements regulating access to social benefits vary considerably across countries, we expect that this first dimension has a substantial impact on the effectiveness of social assistance schemes and that the different institutional frameworks explain why minimum income schemes are more effective in some countries than in others.

The following sections will systematically compare the institutional regulations regarding eligibility and means-tests in Britain, Germany and Sweden.

General Eligibility Rules

An effective alleviation of poverty through social assistance schemes depends on the scope of this program in terms of coverage of the population. If large parts of the population are excluded from social assistance and equivalent schemes, poverty may not be effectively alleviated.

This proposition has been at least implicitly accepted by many industrial countries. Social assistance schemes are indeed virtually universal in most countries, among them our three relevant cases, Germany, Sweden and the United Kingdom (cf. Eardley et al., 1996a). As a rule, social assistance benefits in these three countries cover all residents whose income does not meet certain minimum standards. There are some important exceptions, however, focusing on three categories of the population that are partly excluded from entitlement: foreign nationals, young people and students, and some groups of the population with a specific work status. For some of these groups, there is a special minimum income scheme with lower benefit rates. Whether poverty of individuals within these groups can effectively be alleviated then depends on the adequacy of received benefits.

Young People and Students Turning to another distinct group, which is not per se eligible for social security, most countries have stipulated a minimum age for claimants of social assistance benefits. Frequently, minors are allowed to claim social assistance independently of their parents only under certain conditions. In the United Kingdom, young people aged 16 and 17 are in principle eligible for income support at a reduced rate. However, this is hardly relevant in practice, since unemployed young people are eligible for a Youth Training Scheme and a 'bridging allowance' when waiting to enter this scheme.[91] In Sweden, young people are in principle entitled to social assistance from the age of 18 as soon as they finished their secondary education without having their parents' income taken into account.[92] The German

---

[91] The provision of these Youth Training Schemes appears to embody some problems, since placements are not always available or suitable. Some observers claim that these schemes even have contributed to a increase in youth homelessness (cf. Eardley et al., 1996b: 392).

[92] With growing costs of social assistance, municipalities have become more reluctant to granting social assistance to young people living with their parents. Generally, they are entitled to the standard benefit rate, but will not get any allowance for housing costs unless their parents are on social assistance as well. Most social assistance offices will not support a young claimant wanting to move out of the parental household without good reasons (Socialstyrelsen, personal communication, 20 August 1998).

social assistance scheme has no lower age limits, but minors are normally only eligible if their parents cannot provide for them.[93]

Table 5.1 Eligibility of minors and students in the social assistance schemes of Germany, Sweden and the United Kingdom

	Germany	Sweden	United Kingdom
Minimum age	no formal minimum age, but strong parental responsibility	18, in exceptional cases 15	16 (but special rates for people aged 16-17)
Students	no (with some exceptions)	under some circumstances	only if part-time student and available for work

Source: Own compilation based on Eardley et al. (1996b).

Students in the three countries are another group of the population that underlie specific restrictions when claiming social assistance. The exclusion of students from social assistance schemes is often justified by the availability of student grants and loans, or the parental obligation to pay for their children's education. Students in Germany usually are not eligible for social assistance, since they may receive benefits under the Federal Education Promotion Act (*Bundesausbildungsförderungsgesetz, BAföG*). This allowance is means-tested not only for the students' but also for their parents' income, although the parental means-test can be suspended under certain circumstances. It is granted as an interest-free loan that must be repaid after subsequently taking up employment. In some cases, the total sum to be repaid can be reduced (e.g. if students have finished their studies very quickly or very successfully) or postponed (if the earned income, adjusted for family size, is below a certain level). However, under certain circumstances, students may claim social assistance for their children or if they have special needs. In the United Kingdom, part-time students may claim income support if they are available for work, but full-time students cannot (CPAG, 1998: 19-22). Students in Sweden do not have to rely on their parents' income but have an independent right to social security benefits including social assistance after their 18th birthday. However, since most students in Sweden are entitled to student grants during term time, they usually are not entitled to benefits during this period. During vacation, students are expected to work to make their living, but they may claim social assistance during this period

---

[93] Yet, if they can prove a complete break-down of the relation to their parents, they enjoy a separate entitlement (Eardley et al., 1996b: 162-163). Pregnant teenagers and teenage mothers of young children are allowed to claim social assistance independently from their parents' income since August 1996, even if they continue to live with their parents (Bundesministerium für Gesundheit, 1996).

under some circumstances.[94] However, municipalities have been more and more restrictive in this point in recent years.

As most students whose income is below a certain minimum standard are covered by specialized student grant or loan schemes in every one of the three countries, we can assume that there is no serious problem of exclusion for students.

Employment status In all three countries considered, eligibility is, in principle, not dependent on the employment status of claimants, yet there is a work hours limit in the United Kingdom. Claimants working more than 16 hours a week are not eligible for income support, but they may receive family credit or disability working allowance.[95] In Germany and Sweden, there are no restrictions on work hours; even claimants in full-time employment may top up their earned income by social assistance if their income is below the stipulated amount. There are, however, variations in the degree earned income is disregarded in the calculation of social assistance (see below). However, able claimants refusing to work are subject to certain sanctions. Social assistance payments may be notably reduced but are normally not withdrawn altogether.

Table 5.2 **Employment status and eligibility in Germany, Sweden and the United Kingdom**

	Germany	Sweden	United Kingdom
Work hours	no restriction	no restriction	not more than 16h/week
Self-employed	no restriction	normally not eligible	no restriction

Source: Own compilation based on Eardley et al. (1996b).

Another restriction applies to the self-employed in Sweden. Self-employed claimants usually are expected to give up their business and look for a regular job if they need to claim social assistance (Halvorsen and Marklund, 1993). In Britain and Germany, no formal restrictions apply for this group.

However, employment status is an attribute that is, to a certain degree, subject to individual deliberation. We can assume that British full-time employees or Swedish self-employed would adjust their work status to eligibility regulations if they are in serious financial troubles and if there are no other social security benefits available to them. Therefore, we can assume

---

[94] Students are only entitled to social assistance if they cannot make their living by any other means (see footnote 92 (p. 90); Socialstyrelsen, personal communication, 20 August 1998).

[95] However, the partners of claimants are allowed to work up to 24 hours per week (CPAG, 1997b: 13). The working hours limit used to be 24 hours for claimants before 1992.

that there is no serious problem of exclusion for these employment categories.

Migrants Although social assistance payments are not strictly limited to nationals in any of the three countries, certain restrictions apply to some categories of migrants such as refugees or asylum seekers. This policy exemplifies well that social assistance is considered as a public grant that is not easily bestowed to strangers or follows harsher criteria for non-members of society. There is a certain logic in this, well explained by Freeman (1986). He argues that there is a fundamental conflict between the construction of European welfare states and the free movement of labour, each with a different 'logic of distribution'. The main driving forces of these two spheres are equal chances and individual performance in the market, and bonds of mutual aid and the principle of need in the welfare state. Whereas the first allows or even requires the openness of a society, the latter runs the risk of being stretched too far if extended beyond a closed community (Freeman, 1986: 52). Yet, this dichotomy does not catch one important division within welfare states. In most industrial welfare states, two different forms of mutual aid co-exist that are exposed to migration in a different way. Where the principle of mutual aid is institutionalized in social insurance schemes with a strong link between individual contributions and benefits, migration generally does not overburden the system as benefits depend on a previous contribution record. Much more exposed are those parts of welfare states in which the principle of mutual aid is not mediated by contributions, but where a community is directly confronted with the needs of new members. Social assistance schemes are examples of this type of welfare state programmes. These schemes will quickly come to their limits when rising needs are putting ever higher demands on the members of the community. This might be one possible interpretation of the tendency to confine eligibility for social assistance to the permanently resident population that can be found in many countries in recent years, as in the three countries considered here.

In Sweden, asylum seekers are not eligible for the general social assistance scheme, but are covered by a separate scheme with lower benefits established in 1988 (*ekonomiskt bistånd till asylsökande*).[96] Benefits are lower than in the general scheme, 75 per cent of the basic amount (*basbelopp*) for single people, that is about two thirds of the normal recommended rate for

---

[96] Before the introduction of the Assistance for Asylum Applicants Act (*lagen om bistånd för asylsökande*) in May 1988, applicants for political asylum were entitled to the regular social assistance benefits (cf. Gustafsson, 1986b). Benefits were paid by the municipalities who could recover them from the government for the first 3-4 years of residence. For a general overview on recent Swedish immigration policies, cf. Hammar (1999).

non-refugees.[97] If people are living in institutions and are not cooking for themselves, they receive only 25 per cent of the basic amount. This scheme is organized similarly to the general social assistance scheme, but the costs largely accrue at the central government level (Gustafsson, 1993: 264).[98] Since 1991, municipalities receive a yearly block grant from the government for each asylum applicant during his or her first three years in Sweden (SEK 135,500 per adult and SEK 83,100 per child) in order to provide an incentive for quick integration into the labour market (Salonen, 1993: 119).[99] Refugees are not included in the social assistance statistics any longer (Halvorsen and Marklund, 1993: 86).

The German government followed a similar strategy and gradually restricted social assistance for asylum seekers and some other categories of foreigners. Spurred by the rising number of asylum seekers during the late 1980s and early 1990s, a specific social assistance scheme for asylum seekers has been introduced in 1993.[100] Since then, social assistance for this group is governed by the Assistance for Asylum Seekers Act (*Asylbewerberleistungsgesetz*). The reduced rates of benefits stipulated by this law applied to asylum seekers during the first year of their stay in Germany and to foreigners without valid residency permit. In 1997, the scope of this scheme has been extended towards asylum seekers during their first three years of residence in Germany as well as to the group of civil war refugees and some foreigners with the lowest residency status (*geduldete Ausländer*). Social assistance for asylum seekers and these other groups is usually paid in kind, together with a personal allowance of 40 DM (€20.12) per month for children and 80 DM (€40.23) for adults (Schoch, 1995: 51). If asylum seekers are not living in an institution, the head of the household receives 360 DM (€184.07) per month, 220 DM (€112.48) for young children under the age of 7, and 310 DM (€158.50) for every other additional household member, in addition to the personal allowance (Bundesministerium für Gesundheit,

---

[97] Cf. Salonen (1993: 117-118); own calculations. The benefit levels for refugees have been curtailed as part of the Swedish government's 1992 crisis package. Before December 1992, benefit rates used to be 85.7 per cent of the basic amount (*basbelopp*) for self-catering singles and 33.1 per cent for non-self-catering singles (Salonen, 1993: 117-118).

[98] Before May 1988, when Sweden introduced a special social assistance scheme for refugees and asylum seekers, applicants for political asylum were entitled to the regular social assistance benefits (cf. Gustafsson, 1986b). Benefits were paid by the municipalities who could recover them from the government for the first 3-4 years of residence.

[99] For eligibility rules for EU-nationals in Sweden, cf. Westerhäll (1997).

[100] Until 1993, social assistance used to be granted to all foreigners living in Germany, yet subject to some restrictions which have been subsequently tightened (cf. Fasselt, 1997; Minderhoud, 1999; Voges and Weber, 1996).

1997).[101] Additional benefits are limited to emergency help, e.g. recipients are entitled to medical treatment only in case of acute illness, but not for prophylactic medication.

Table 5.3 Eligibility of foreign nationals in the social assistance schemes of Germany, Sweden and the United Kingdom

	Germany	Sweden	United Kingdom
Asylum seekers	Special scheme since 1993, with lower benefits	Special scheme since 1988; with lower benefits	Not eligible, but urgent cases payment during the processing of their application
Refugees	Special scheme only after 1997; with lower benefits	Special scheme since 1988; with lower benefits	Eligible if recognized under the UN convention. Possibly urgent payments
Other foreigners	No restriction but special scheme for *geduldete Ausländer* (after 1997)	No restriction	Eligible only if 'right to abode' or if legally resident in the UK with indefinite leave to remain

Source: Own compilation based on Eardley et al. (1996b).

In the United Kingdom, refugees are generally eligible for income support if recognized under the UN convention, but asylum seekers are not. Yet, they may receive 'urgent cases payment' during the processing of their application under some circumstances (Eardley et al., 1996b: 393). A special feature of the British system is further that only actual – but not legal – residence in the United Kingdom is required in order to receive income support, unlike in Germany and Sweden (Guibentif and Bouget, 1997: 11). From August 1994, claimants are subject to a 'habitual residence test' assessing whether the claimants' 'centre of interests' actually lies in the United Kingdom on the basis of past behaviour and future intentions (cf. CPAG, 1998: 66-87). This procedure has been heavily criticized because of the discretionary nature of the test and its administrative costs (cf. Adler, 1997; Bolderson and Roberts, 1995).[102] Claimants having failed the habitual residence tests may be eligible for emergency payments from the social fund. In February 1996, a further restriction was posed upon asylum seekers. New asylum seekers are eligible

---

[101] These benefit rates amount to 81-96 per cent of the average standard benefit rates in the regular social assistance scheme, depending on the individual's age (own calculations based on Bundesministerium für Arbeit und Sozialordnung, 1997: 674 and Bundesministerium für Gesundheit, 1997).

[102] Indeed, the majority of legal appeals against benefit refusals on the basis of this habitual residence tests has been successful, so most claimants had to be granted income support (cf. Adler, 1997: 56-60).

for urgent payments only if they have applied for asylum immediately at the port of entry. In addition, if asylum seekers appeal against the refusal of their application, they may not receive any social security benefits during the appeal process (CPAG, 1998: 80-85). After a vigorous public discussion of this issue, the High Court ruled in October 1996 that local authorities are responsible for providing the very basic necessities of life to these excluded groups under the 1948 National Assistance Act that has been confirmed by the Court of Appeal in February 1997 (Minderhoud, 1999: 136-140). Table 5.3 summarizes the main regulations for foreign nationals in the three countries.

Responding to increasing fiscal pressures during the last years, each of the countries considered here has restricted eligibility for certain categories of foreign residents.[103] Under certain circumstances, these groups are *a priori* excluded from the general social assistance scheme, yet they may be eligible for specific social assistance benefits at a lower level. Although these special benefits constitute an effective bottom floor against extreme forms of deprivation, these benefits do not match the general minimum income level institutionalized in social assistance schemes for the permanently resident population (cf. Veit-Wilson, 1998). If one assumes that the general minimum income level provides for a standard of living that can be considered as some kind of poverty line accepted in society, these special benefits for asylum seekers and related groups necessarily will not provide for an equally acceptable standard of living. In relation to this standard, lower benefits for migrants will therefore lead to poverty.

Eligibility and effectiveness As this section has shown, social assistance schemes cover the vast majority of the population, yet are not fully universal in any of the three countries considered. Parts of the population are excluded from eligibility because of their age, residence status or employment status. However, some groups might be entitled to some other benefits, such as in-work benefits (e.g. family credit in the United Kingdom), or for student loans or grants. It is not always clear, however, whether these alternative schemes can protect claimants from poverty. Yet we can assume that those schemes augment their own resources to a sufficient degree and will not leave these groups in poverty. There is however one major exception. Special social assistance benefit schemes for foreign nationals usually offer

---

[103] It seems that not only increasing expenditure on social security benefits for asylum seekers has provided the motivation for these policies, but these decisions can also be seen – at least in the United Kingdom and Germany – as a reaction against the growing number of legal appeals against negative decisions on asylum applications. Without formally restricting rights of appeal, people may find it much harder to appeal against these decisions if they do not have access to larger sums of cash money because benefits are provided in kind (Germany) or withheld altogether (United Kingdom).

markedly lower benefits than the general social assistance level. Usually, claimants will not be eligible for other schemes either. In this case, their income level is likely to remain below the poverty line.

Yet, the discussion of these regulations has uncovered relatively small differences between the countries considered. We can therefore assume that exclusion from social assistance does not greatly vary across countries, yet there are differences for some specific groups.

Means-tests and Income Disregards

After general eligibility for social assistance is determined, means-tests seek to ensure that benefits are targeted on the very needy. In this sense, means-tests provide some kind of fine-tuning of eligibility. Basically, social assistance benefits are granted if household income falls below a certain minimum income standard (see Chapter 6 below). For the assessment of claimants' income, certain types of income are disregarded in some countries, such as financial assets, other social security benefits or earned income. These income disregards are relevant for the effectiveness of social assistance schemes, as some claimants may be excluded from entitlement to social assistance because of the level of their own resources.

Disregards for assets allow claimants to receive social assistance while keeping a certain amount of property in cash or kind. Although they primarily aim at improving the efficiency of social assistance schemes – assuring that resources are directed towards the most needy parts of the population – these provisions are also relevant for the eligibility dimension of effectiveness. The lack of disregards for assets may constitute an effective barrier to protect all prospective claimants from poverty. This may be the case if people are unable to liquidate their assets quickly enough to balance shortfalls in their current income. If claimants are excluded from eligibility on these grounds, the effective alleviation of poverty may be at stake. Certain disregards for assets may thus improve the effectiveness of social assistance schemes in the eligibility dimension.

Whereas the British and the German social assistance schemes consider income or assets only if exceeding a certain amount, means-tests are strictest in Sweden. Principally, all income and financial assets are taken into account. Some municipalities may, however, allow claimants to keep their car or owner-occupied housing under some circumstances (for example, if they absolutely need the car to get to work or if they cannot find another flat). These strict means-tests ensure that people with low income first turn to alternative sources of income before they apply for social assistance in order not to be forced to liquidate all assets (OECD, 1998a). By this token, relatively generous social assistance benefits may be granted without necessarily facing serious poverty trap problems.

The British income support scheme offers the most generous disregard for financial assets which are fully disregarded up to the amount of £3,000.[104] Between £3,000 and £8,000, benefit entitlements are reduced by £1 for every £250 or part thereof. Households with assets above the limit of £8,000 will not receive any income support benefits before they have liquidated their belongings (OECD, 1996: 395-396). However, only one in twenty non-elderly claimants were reported to have some savings in 1994 (OECD, 1998a: 32). Disregards in the German social assistance are much smaller. Generally, financial assets have to be taken into account when calculating benefit rates, but there are some exemptions specified in national regulations. Small amounts of capital and 'reasonable' owned housing are disregarded for most claimants; but there are more generous regulations for some categories of claimants (the handicapped, blind, persons in long-term care) (Bundesministerium für Arbeit und Sozialordnung, 1997: 674-675).[105] In Sweden, financial assets are fully taken into account, as a rule.

Income from other social security schemes is generally not disregarded in social assistance in the three countries considered, but the German *Sozialhilfe* provides certain exemptions, most importantly parents' benefits (*Erziehungsgeld*) (Bundesministerium für Arbeit und Sozialordnung, 1997: 683).[106] The British income support also provides for a disregard for contributions to private pension schemes, yet contributions are only disregarded at a rate of 50 per cent.

Disregards for earned income may also enhance the effectiveness of social assistance schemes. Many observers argue that disregards for earned income, may contribute to a high effectiveness of social assistance schemes (cf. e.g. Blundell, 2000; Boss, 1999). This is not necessarily the case for a static assessment, as wage earners usually can supplement their earned in-

---

[104] Assets taken into account are all financial assets and the market income of land or property, except owner-occupied housing (OECD, 1996: 395-396).

[105] Generally, capital assets are disregarded up to an amount of DM 2,500 for younger and able-bodied claimants, and up to DM 4,500 for the elderly and the disabled, cf. Deutscher Verein für öffentliche und private Fürsorge, 1992; Breuer and Engels, 1998).

[106] This scheme has been introduced in 1986 and provides a flat-rate benefit of DM 600 for mothers or fathers who stay at home or only work part-time during the first two years after the birth of their child (it is also available for adopted children). The parents' benefit is not means-tested for the first six months and is then reduced or even withdrawn depending on the parents' income (tapered reduction at a rate of 40 per cent for income exceeding DM 29,400 for couples and DM 23,700 for single parents). The parents' benefit is linked to a parents' leave for up to three years with a job guarantee (Bundesministerium für Arbeit und Sozialordnung, 1997: 610-616). Some federal states have set up their own schemes supplementing the national scheme and may extend the period parents' benefit is paid to up to three years.

come with social assistance benefits in all three countries, but there may be beneficial long-term effects. If claimants can keep at least part of their income in addition to social assistance benefits, they will be more prone to take up work or to stay in low-paid employment. By this token, working claimants can retain a link to the labour market and conserve or even enhance their occupational qualifications.

In Germany, earned income has been disregarded up to roughly DM 270 per month (€138), the equivalent of half the standard benefit rate since 1993 (Bundesministerium für Arbeit und Sozialordnung, 1997: 683; Sell, 1998; Bäcker and Hanesch, 1998).[107] The British income support scheme allows claimants to retain a weekly income of £5 (€35 per month) per individual or £15 for lone parents (€106 per month), non-elderly long-term recipients (more than two years), recipients of disability or higher pensioner premium and some reserve or emergency workers (Eardley et al., 1996b: 396). In addition, a bonus system introduced in 1996 allows claimants to accumulate earnings up to a limit of £1,000 (€1,630) to a 'back to work bonus' that will be paid when the client definitely leaves the income support scheme for employment (OECD, 1998a: 191). In Sweden, however, earnings are normally taxed away at a rate of 100 per cent, thus offering no financial incentive for taking up employment.

As far as disregards for earned income and assets play a role in the effectiveness of social assistance schemes, the Swedish strategy of very strict means-tests is assumed to have a more negative impact on the alleviation of poverty than in Britain and Germany. If claimants with a low current income are excluded from eligibility because of their assets, poverty might occur. However, it is questionable whether a sizeable proportion of the population is affected by these problems, so the effects of this provision may be rather limited.

Do Social Assistance Schemes Provide a Safety Net for All?

The analysis of eligibility regulations has started from the assumption that the full coverage of the population by social assistance schemes and related schemes is essential to effectively fight poverty. If some parts of the population are excluded from this basic net of social protection, however, they run a higher risk to be poor than those parts of the population covered by social assistance. This does not mean that people necessarily are poor, but rather

---

[107] Previously, the disregard for earned income was calculated as an addition to the standard benefit rate (*Mehrbedarfszuschlag*), i.e. employed persons used to receive an addition of 20 per cent of the standard benefit rate.

that they are exposed to market forces without the protection of strong social rights. If these groups are also confronted with other unfavourable conditions such as restricted access to the labour market or specific needs, their lack of any social safety net increases their poverty risk.

The institutional assessment of social assistance schemes above has shown that the broad majority of the population is in fact covered by social assistance in each of the countries considered. Restricted eligibility could only be testified for some categories of foreign nationals, minors living alone, students, the full-time workers in Britain, and the self-employed in Sweden. However, serious deficits in the dimension of eligibility exist only for some categories of foreigners, as they usually do not have any opportunities to take advantage of any other social security schemes, or to adapt individual attributes to comply with eligibility conditions. The effects of means-tests outlined above has demonstrated that the lack of disregards for earned income and assets in Sweden can also have some negative effects in the dimension of eligibility, yet its quantitative impact tends to be rather limited.

Because of the complexity of eligibility regulations and the lack of suitable statistical material, however, it is impossible to quantify exactly the population that is excluded from entitlement to social assistance benefits in either country. It would have been interesting to estimate the effects of the eligibility regulations on poverty rates based on household micro-data, but the available data in the Luxembourg Income Study do so for two reasons. On the one hand, sample sizes are too small as to engage in such an undertaking. In addition, some of these groups are not only excluded from the mainstream minimum income schemes, but – formally or *de facto* – excluded from surveys that could tell us anything about their income situation. For the LIS datasets, some categories of foreigners are in fact formally excluded, and others may have a smaller probability of being included in the survey than the mainstream population (see Chapter 4). Causes for a *de facto* exclusion can be found in their housing conditions, with a higher probability of living in institutions, in multi-family households, and in poor urban areas, all of these factors increasing the potential of being poorly represented in surveys. Besides, non-response rates tend to be higher for ethnic minorities because of language problems and cultural differences.

Although a more detailed account is precluded by imperfect data, we can conclude that the eligibility dimension cannot contribute much to the explanation of the incidence of poverty in the three countries considered. The only sizeable effect could have been expected from the group of non-nationals with restricted entitlement rights, but their partial exclusion cannot account for the apparent ineffectiveness of social assistance schemes because of data problems.

Chapter 6

Do Social Assistance Schemes Provide Adequate Benefits?

If the eligibility dimension, as described in the previous chapter, is the first fundamental dimension of effectiveness of social assistance schemes, the second dimension is the question of whether these benefits are adequate to protect people from poverty. As outlined in Chapter 3, social assistance benefits are considered as adequate if they guarantee a standard of living equal or higher than the poverty line. Should the level of social assistance be lower than this standard, social assistance must be considered as ineffective for the alleviation of poverty. Thus, the effectiveness of social assistance schemes essentially depends on the level of benefits. How much money is actually paid to claimants? Is this benefit level generous enough as to guarantee a decent standard of living? Can social assistance benefits bring claimants out of poverty?

The persistence of poverty in extensive welfare states has often spurred concerns about whether minimum income schemes are able to provide for a decent standard of living. At face value, the mere existence of poverty would suggest that social assistance benefit levels are indeed too low as to provide for an adequate protection from poverty (leaving aside for the moment the dimensions of eligibility and take-up). Indeed, several lines of argumentation support this claim. Various political economy approaches agree that low social assistance benefits are crucial for the functioning of modern societies, yet their reasoning is very different. Neo-marxists would argue that social assistance benefits are low in order to ensure a large 'reserve army of labour' necessary for the functioning of capitalist systems, but benefits must be still high enough to ensure the re-production of labour (cf. Block, 1987, Piven and Cloward, 1971). From a neo-liberal perspective, too generous social assistance benefits undermine work incentives for individuals and increase labour costs for employers eventually weakening international competitiveness of the national economy (cf. Atkinson and Mogensen, 1993; Havemann, 1996; Moffitt, 1992). Because they set an effective minimum wage, social assistance benefits should be low in order not to distort the functioning of the economy.

Although neither line of argument explicitly argues that social assistance benefit levels should be below a – however defined – poverty line, it is plausible to assume that a benefit level below the poverty line would even enhance economic efficacy, provided that the physical reproduction of labour is not endangered. Assuming that most poverty lines used in comparative research for industrialized countries are intended to match a basic threshold for a decent standard of living that also considers cultural and social needs, a social assistance benefit level that would comply with both lines of argumentation would not guarantee this, although the mere physical subsistence should be ensured. Thus, the benefit level that is suggested by these approaches would not be considered as adequate by our standards.

Another line of argument focuses on the long-term development of social assistance benefit levels, suggesting a systematic downward trend in the context of welfare state curtailments. Social assistance schemes are believed to be more prone to retrenchment than other programmes for several reasons. Firstly, recipients of social assistance usually are a small minority of the population without sufficient economic and political power. Thus, they cannot easily defend their interests and mobilize support against curtailments (cf. Piven and Cloward, 1971). Secondly, social assistance is a social transfer programme where beneficiaries and financiers of the scheme hardly overlap, which makes a broad public support of the programme even less probable. In addition, there are hardly any provider interests associated with the scheme that could mobilize middle class support (Le Grand and Winter, 1987; Alber, 1996). Thirdly, since social assistance schemes set an effective minimum wage, employers are strongly interested in low benefits, especially in the context of a more and more internationalized economy, paralleling the political economy arguments presented above. These three factors suggest that there is an inherent dynamic towards low social assistance benefits.

However, Pierson (1994) has argued that social assistance schemes tend to be spared from curtailments because of two reasons. On the one hand, these schemes provide a very limited potential for curtailments because of their relatively small expenditure volume. On the other hand, cuts in social assistance programmes may be perceived as 'unfair' within the population because of the already low income status of claimants, and may mobilize support from advocating groups. Yet, Pierson's objections do not fully invalidate the proposed trend towards ever less adequate social assistance benefits. His two safeguards against curtailments are the more powerful, the lower the benefit level already is. In countries with a relatively generous benefit level, these mechanisms may not take effect. In this sense, his argument can be interpreted as postulating some kind of lower threshold for cur-

Adequacy 103

tailments rather than an overall impediment against curtailments in these schemes.
Both broad lines of arguments – political economy approaches and retrenchment approaches – would suggest that social assistance schemes tend to provide a benefit level that is not high enough to bring people out of poverty (if poverty is defined as taking into account needs other than mere physical subsistence). Empirical tests of this assumption are sparse, however. When discussing poverty in industrialized welfare states, many observers appear to tacitly assume that social assistance benefit levels are too low as to effectively alleviate poverty, yet this issue has hardly been assessed in more detail. The following sections will step into this gap and test the presumption of an inadequate social assistance benefit level on the basis of an informed description of the institutional framework. After assessing the composition of the social assistance income package, the equivalence scales embodied in the institutional regulations, and indexation mechanisms, the adequacy of social assistance benefits are analyzed in two steps. First, following Eardley et al. (1996a), social assistance benefit levels are analyzed on the basis of a number of model families. In a second step, this approach will be complemented by a more comprehensive simulation of benefit levels on the basis of the data of the Luxembourg Income Study. Rather than confining itself to a number of pre-defined household types, this approach allows the assessment of income packages of all households in the sample.

The Institutional Framework: Minimum Income Standards

An international comparison of minimum income standards is a very complex task. Benefits usually are based on a combination of a standard benefit rate for each member of the household, an allowance for housing costs, possibly a supplement (premium) to account for special needs such as disability or old age, and some one-off benefits for irregularly occurring needs. The exact level of benefits depends on the specific needs of the household in question and can thus hardly be standardized. In addition, the benefit package often is not only made up by social assistance benefits only, but also draws on other schemes, such as housing allowances. Rather than comparing standard benefit rates as such, the evaluation of social assistance benefit levels should scrutinize income packages available for the poor population. The following sections thus assess the definition and the composition of minimum income packages in Britain, Germany and Sweden, encompassing not only social assistance benefits in a narrow sense, but the full benefit package recipients of social assistance are entitled to. In other words, it assesses minimum income standards, i.e. the level of benefits a person without any income can expect to receive.

Defining the Level of Social Assistance Benefits

Social assistance benefits are informed by societal notions of adequacy, and are, in turn, also an expression of this concept. They define a socially accepted minimum income standard below which no member of the community should fall. Theses benefits are often also used as a reference point in other benefits schemes.[108] The level of these benefit rates has to meet two basic goals. On the one hand, minimum income standards should guarantee a decent standard of living for the low-income population, but, on the other hand, benefits should not undermine work incentives. In a way, these two goals set a lower and an upper limit for social assistance benefits, which are, however, not easy to integrate.

How are minimum income standards defined in each country? There is a large range of possible instruments and procedures used to define these standards. Governments may rely on dietary requirements or baskets of goods, on empirical data on income or consumption of the low-income strata, or on mere political deliberation. Social assistance benefit rates may provide for a uniform minimum income standard or may allow for a certain degree of variation of benefit rates across the country. Accordingly, benefit rates may be fixed at the national, regional or municipal level. In a comparative perspective, we find a strong variation in the procedures used for the definition of standard benefit rates. They differ in terms of the mode of calculation, the agencies responsible and the variation of benefit rates within a country (Veit-Wilson, 1998; Eardley et al., 1996a).

In regard to the alleviation of poverty, neither of these different procedures can be regarded as being *a priori* more effective than another. The adequacy of benefit rates is dependent on the level of benefits, rather than on the procedure of defining benefit levels as such. Some general principles can be laid out, however. A basket of goods approach defines a minimum subsistence standard for the population that should at least guarantee the physical subsistence of recipients, provided that the basket of goods is satisfactorily selected, priced and up-rated. If empirical income or consumption data of specific groups of the population are taken as a reference value for social assistance, or if social assistance rates are defined by mere political

---

[108] For example, the German Constitutional Court has held in 1991 that a certain minimum income of families should be exempted from taxation, and referred to the social assistance benefit rates as a yardstick. Since the child benefit and the tax allowances for families did not meet this requirement at that time, the government was obliged to undertake a major reform of these benefits in 1995.

deliberation, this bottom safeguard of physical subsistence is lacking, so external mechanisms have to be found to secure an adequate minimum income standard. For these reasons, a basket of goods approach can be considered as being superior to other approaches in principle, but the actual effectiveness of these procedures essentially depends on the exact design of these mechanisms, so no *a priori* qualification of these methods can be made. What is the nominal basis for social assistance benefit rates in Britain, Germany and Sweden?

In Britain, benefit levels are centrally set by the national government and are uniform for the whole country. The level of income support is based on 'normal living expenses' (Guibentif and Bouget, 1997: 145), and is intended to cover most expenses.[109] When initially setting up national assistance rates, the Beveridge Committee had referred to Rowntree's seminal work on subsistence minima, but had to reduce the originally envisaged income standards because of budgetary restrictions. Since then, the definition of social assistance benefit rates has been predominantly informed by political deliberation; yet has been regularly indexed to inflation (cf. Atkinson, 1990; Veit-Wilson, 1992, 1998: 27). Responding to concerns that social assistance rates did not secure a decent standard of living, the predecessor of income support, supplementary benefit, was complemented by an additional long-term benefit rate in 1966 (Veit-Wilson, 1998: 90). Today's income support scheme, however, does not incorporate any special rates for long-term claimants.

The German social assistance has also seen a recent change in the definition of benefit rates. Until 1990, standard benefit rates were based on a basket of goods as established by the German Association for Public and Private Welfare (*Deutscher Verein für öffentliche und private Fürsorge*).[110] In order to cover the 'socio-cultural minimum', this basket comprised food, electricity, smaller household goods and goods for 'personal needs' including personal hygiene, transport, books, papers, and leisure (Brühl, 1992: 15-24; cf. Bundesminister für Jugend, Familie und Gesundheit 1985). The basket was first established in 1955, and subsequently thoroughly revised in 1962, 1970

---

[109] There seems to be no formal basket of goods that is supposed to be covered by the income support scheme, as the government was determined to simplify the very complex benefit structure of the income support's predecessor, supplementary benefit (cf. N. Harris, 2000b: 125-129; Rahilly, 2000).

[110] This association was founded in 1880, driven by the aspiration to co-ordinate the welfare activities of the municipalities in the absence of national legislation and to avoid welfare-induced migration (cf. Orthbandt, 1980). It assembles virtually all public and private institutions concerned with social assistance in Germany, including representatives of federal and state ministries, municipalities and charities (*Wohlfahrtsverbände*).

and 1985.[111] In the meantime, the basket of goods was regularly adapted to the development of prices. After a long debate about the revision of the basket of goods during the 1980s, the *Länder* decided to fundamentally reform the calculation of standard benefit rates (cf. Tschoepe, 1987).[112]

Since 1990, benefits are supposed to be determined according to the so-called 'statistics model' (*Statistikmodell*) which is based on the average expenditures of a strata of low-income groups whose income position is clearly above the social assistance level,[113] rather than on a basket of goods (cf. Brühl, 1998: 28-36).[114] The expenditure data are taken from a large survey of incomes and expenditure of private households that is usually conducted every five years (*Einkommens- und Verbrauchsstichprobe, EVS*). By referring to the expenditure of a reference group of households, standard benefit rates now institutionalize the principle of 'less eligibility' without any reference to the notion of need that had been inherent in the basket of goods model. Although the 'statistics model' has not yet been fully implemented, benefit rates have seen a slight decrease since then (see Figure 6.1 below). Both under the previous and the new system, these standard benefit rates do not have the character of fixed legal entitlements, but can be modified according to the individual needs of the claimant (cf. Brühl, 1998: 56-61), provided that individual circumstances of claimants are evaluated in a correct and fair way.

---

[111] For a historical overview of the early and the more recent debates on social assistance benefit rates in Germany, cf. Heising (1995 [1990]) and Orthbandt (1986).

[112] To make a long story short: The revised basket of goods proposed by the *Deutscher Verein für öffentliche und private Fürsorge* in 1981 was heavily criticised, both for being too generous and being too stingy. The municipalities, fearing increasing financial strains, advocated a reduction of benefits, whereas the charities, claimants' organizations and some academic experts favoured higher benefit levels. Since the protagonists could not agree on a basket of goods, the federal government set the standard benefit rates by law until the federal states eventually issued a new 'alternative' basket of goods in 1985. This basket of goods reworked the outdated composition of the basket but sought to underestimate the value of goods in order to prevent a sudden rise in expenditure. By 1990, the long-discussed proposition of a 'statistic model' was realized in a three-stage process (cf. Oberbracht, 1993: 32-38; Orthbandt, 1980, 1986).

[113] In order to avoid circularity in the adaptation of social assistance benefits, the reference group is supposed to have an income clearly above the social assistance level (10-15 per cent higher than social assistance).

[114] However, the reform of the base has not been fully implemented. The envisaged implementation of the third stage of the reform planned for 1993 has been suspended, and benefit rates have since been adjusted on the basis of political decisions (cf. Schellhorn, 1989; Wienand, 1997a). The liberal-conservative government had envisaged that the calculation of standard benefit rates would eventually be based on the 'statistical model' from 1999, but the incoming government has decided to suspend this procedure for another two years. In the meantime, the database for the calculation of standard benefit rates will be thoroughly assessed before a new mode of calculation is installed.

In Sweden, social assistance benefit rates build upon the basic amount within the social security system (*basbelopp*). Basically, the level of benefits is based on recommendations from the National Board for Health and Social Services (*socialstyrelsen*)[115] which in turn are based on advice from the Tax Board and the Consumers Board (Halvorsen, 1993: 40; Veit-Wilson, 1998: 57-58).[116] According to these standards, benefits are supposed to cover expenses for food, clothing, health and personal hygiene, medical and dental expenses, leisure activities, furniture, electricity, accident and home insurance, newspapers, TV, telephone, and public transport (Halvorsen, 1993: 42-43). The standard benefit rate thus also includes some items, as e.g. furniture, that are supposed to be covered by one-off benefits in Germany and Britain (cf. Buhr, 1999: 226). However, municipalities are free to remove some of these items from this list and grant them separately, so the benefit rates actually paid by the municipalities may markedly deviate from these recommendations. One in three municipalities grants a lower rate of benefit to short-term recipients (*korttidsnorm*), but this practice has often been subject to legal appeals (OECD, 1998a: 27, 175-177). Claimants with severe difficulties in using the money responsibly because of drug addiction or other problems may receive a reduced norm (*reducerad bruttonorm*) while regular bills are paid directly by the social assistance administration (Schwarze, 1994: 50-55).

In January 1998, a new social assistance scheme (now named *försörjningsstöd*) was implemented after a long discussion. This reformed scheme introduced a more uniform social assistance standard (Socialstyrelsen, 1997a). There are personal allowances for each person in the household, depending on their age, as well as an allowance for the household as a whole, according to its size. Benefit rates for young children depend on whether they receive lunch in a child-care facility or not. The personal allowances cover expenditures for food, clothing and shoes, personal hygiene and leisure activities; the household allowances offsets costs for household consumer goods, daily newspaper, telephone and a TV licence (cf. Socialstyrel-

---

[115] The origins of the National Board of Health and Welfare lie in an early regulation of medical services (Socialstyrelsen, 1998). Today, it is responsible for steering a broad variety of medical and social services.

[116] The recommended standard rates have been set according to a basket of goods on the basis of a major study of consumer prices undertaken in the first half of the 1980s. Since the establishment of this practice in 1985, the underlying basket of goods has not been reassessed, but the standard benefit rates have been adapted to the development of prices. In 1995, however, the rise in prices was only considered at a rate of 60 per cent when adjusting benefit rates (OECD, 1998a: 27).

sen, 1997a; Ditch et al., 1997: 50-53). In addition, municipalities may grant additional benefits on a discretionary basis.[117]

In every one of the three countries, institutional safeguards seek to ensure that social assistance benefits remain well below earnings from paid work ('principle of less eligibility').[118] While in all three countries benefit rates are supposed to meet this condition, benefit rates for larger households in Germany shall be effectively capped if their benefit entitlement exceeds the incomes of working families of a similar size since 1996. In Sweden, a government recommendation lays out that benefit levels shall remain below earnings from full-time work (cf. Schwarze, 1994: 50; Ditch et al., 1997: 52-53).

Responsibilities for Regulation and Funding of Social Assistance

In the procedure of setting standard benefit rates, institutional arrangements may have a decisive impact on the effectiveness of social assistance – notably the allocation of decision-making powers and funding responsibilities at the central versus the local level is deemed to influence the long-term adequacy of benefit rates (cf. Alber, 1996, 1997). Decentralized schemes may tend to lower benefit levels for the following reasons. If federal states or municipalities are free to set their own benefit rates, and if they are also responsible for funding social assistance benefits, they have a double incentive to grant low benefit rates. They can avoid benefit-induced migration of the poor to their territory ('welfare tourism'), and they hope to attract enterprises because of their ability to offer low tax and wage levels. Therefore, the definition of social assistance rates at the local level may have a built-in dynamic towards a very low level of benefits, an effect that has been dubbed 'race to the bottom'. It would be misleading to suggest a simple causal relationship between the degree of centralization of a social assistance scheme and the probability of benefit curtailments or a low level of benefits. In centralized schemes, the government may as well tend to cut benefit levels, provided

---

[117] Additional benefits are divided into two categories. The costs of housing, electricity, household insurance, medical treatment, acute dental treatment, glasses, contributions towards unions and unemployment insurance are supposed to be covered by the municipalities as they occur, and can be challenged before administrative courts (*förvaltningsbesvär*). The same applies to the costs for transport, home helps and other services for the elderly or handicapped. Municipalities enjoy a larger scope of discretion for the following items: the costs of moving, new furniture and household appliances, TV set, psychotherapy, non-acute dental care, recreation, vacancies and debt payment. In these cases, decisions may not be challenged before the courts, but clients may claim a re-consideration of the decision taken (*kommunalbesvär*) (Kommunförbundet, personal communication, 18 August 1998).

[118] This principle is known as 'Lohnabstandsgebot' in Germany and 'respektavstand' in Sweden.

Adequacy 109

that its financial interests are at stake. But if regulatory and financial powers are dispersed on different levels of government, benefits are less prone to curtailments, since the regulator has no immediate financial gain from retrenchment (cf. Alber, 1996, 1997). Variations in the adequacy of social assistance benefits may thus be explained by differences in the institutional design.

Based on the distribution of regulatory and funding responsibilities, one could expect that benefit levels are lower in countries where these responsibilities are united at either the national level or at the local level, but there might be an even stronger long-term trend towards low benefit levels if municipalities are relatively autonomous in setting benefit levels. In contrast, a system in which funding and regulatory responsibilities are dispersed on different levels of government might provide more generous benefits in the long run.

Indeed, one of the most marked differences between the social assistance schemes of Germany, Sweden and the United Kingdom can be found in the institutional distribution of regulatory and funding responsibilities. In the United Kingdom, both regulatory and financial responsibilities for social assistance are unified at the national level. Unlike most other social assistance schemes in Western Europe, the British income support is entirely financed out of national general taxation. The ancillary scheme for the provision of one-off benefits, the social fund, is also funded out of the central budget, but is administratively strictly separated from the income support budget. Only housing benefit and council tax benefit is borne, to a small extent, out of local authorities' funds.[119]

In marked contrast to the United Kingdom, we find Sweden with a strong variation of standard benefit rates. Municipalities enjoy a relatively large degree of discretion which allowed them, until the 1998 reform, to set their own social assistance benefit rates.[120] Neither the amount recommended by the National Board nor the list of items that are supposed to be covered by social assistance are binding for the municipalities. Inconsistencies occur in particular when some municipalities have excluded costs that do not occur on a day-to-day basis from the standard benefit rates but rather grant them

---

[119] The local authorities receive a block grant from the government, largely based on the number of claimants (Department of Social Security, personal communication, 22 October 1998).

[120] The 1998 reform has eventually restricted the degree of discretion of municipalities and introduced a national minimum standard of social assistance. The minimum benefit rates are now fixed on the national level, but the municipalities continue to finance and to administer the scheme. With the partial nationalization of benefit rates, responsibilities are divided more strongly between the central and local level while the funding of social assistance is still in the hands of the municipalities.

separately when applicable (Byberg, 1998: 83-84).[121] Yet, their autonomy is limited by the jurisdiction of the Supreme Administrative Court which held in several decisions that social assistance benefits should at least match the subsistence standards set by the Federal Taxation Authorities in order to guarantee a decent standard of living (*skälig levnadsnivå*) (Halvorsen, 1993: 36; Byberg, 1998: 83).[122]

The benefit rates actually paid by the municipalities may deviate considerably from the national recommendations and show a large degree of variation. In 1992, the recommendations of the National Board of Health and welfare proposed benefit rates at the level of 116 per cent of the basic amount for singles and 192 per cent for couples (Eardley et al., 1996b: 358; own calculations). According to a report of the Swedish Association of Municipalities (*Svenska Kommunförbundet*) assessing benefit rates in 25 municipalities, the average rates actually paid by the municipalities were slightly lower, 113 per cent for singles (median: 115 per cent) and 187 per cent for couples (median: 190 per cent). The lowest benefit rates were paid in Södertälje (97 per cent for singles and 160 per cent for couples) whereas the highest rates were provided in Umeå (125 per cent for singles) and Uppsala (207 per cent for couples) (Svensson, 1993: 44-45; own calculations). Some 40 per cent of municipalities paid less than stipulated by the National Board of Health and Welfare (OECD, 1998a: 175).[123] The determinants of the variation of benefit levels across municipalities are not completely clear. The political decisions on benefit levels seem to be governed by the composition of the municipal assembly and the general financial situation of the municipality, but the direct costs of social assistance have no discernible effect on standard benefit rates (Aguilar and Gustafsson, 1989).

---

[121] These items include for example the costs of medical and dental care, household equipment and furniture. In a court ruling of 1994, this practice was confirmed to be legitimate. The National Board of Health and Welfare subsequently revised its policy and removed these items from the standard benefit rate from 1996 (Socialstyrelsen, personal communication, 20 August 1998). Apparently, this procedure has resulted in a reduction of total expenditure (OECD, 1998a: 27-28, 33).

[122] This standard was set in two rulings by the Supreme Administrative Court in 1984 (Halvorsen, 1993). The relatively high discretion of the Swedish municipalities in fixing the amount of social assistance benefits is not necessarily a common feature of the Scandinavian welfare states. In Denmark and Finland, the level of benefits is set centrally by law respectively Cabinet directives (introduced 1987 respectively 1983). In Norway, municipalities enjoy a greater degree of discretion that had been narrowed during the 1980s with a closer coupling of social assistance to the minimum old age pension, but this trend has been reversed since 1989 (cf. Halvorsen, 1993: 36-37, 41).

[123] However, these different standard benefit rates could not explain differences in total cost of social assistance across municipalities (Bergmark and Sandgren, 1998).

Adequacy 111

The development of benefit rates over time does not display a general trend towards higher or lower benefits, at least for the first half of the 1980s.[124] Expenditure on social assistance is funded by local taxes and block grants from the government (Halvorsen, 1993: 38).[125] These block grants are intended to cover all kind of municipal activities and are not dependent on the number of social assistance recipients (OECD, 1998a: 169). In addition, the municipalities receive block grants for the support of refugees.[126]

In Germany, standard benefit rates (*Regelsätze*) are set by the federal states (*Länder*), while the equivalence scales embodied in the social assistance rates are regulated in the federal law. However, in spite of the lack of central regulation, standard rates hardly vary across states.[127] The small variation of benefit rates across states can be attributed to the characteristics of the decision-making process. The decision about the standard benefit rates is taken by the state ministers of social security[128] on the basis of recommendations by an independent association, the German Association of Public and Private Welfare. Thus, the existence of this co-ordination procedure – which is not formally institutionalized in the Federal Social Assistance Law – may explain why the federal states do not fully use their formal autonomy to underbid the benefit rates of other states in the context of strained public budgets. In addition, the courts also oversee the adequacy of social assistance benefit rates based on the principle of human dignity stipulated in the Basic Law (*Grundgesetz*). There is no variation of social assistance rates within federal states, with the exception of Bavaria and Saxony.[129] Variations in the

---

[124] Cf. Gustafsson (1986a); Schwarz (1986); both quoted in Gustafsson (1993: 254).

[125] The financial autonomy of the municipalities has been tightened during recent years. Not only the country's economic problems limited the financial intake of local communities, but also a decision of the national government that prevented the municipalities from increasing local taxes from 1990 to 1994 (cf. Jahn, 1997: 118-119).

[126] Payments are made for the refugees' first 3.5 years of residence in Sweden, but on a diminishing scale in order to provide incentives for a quick integration (Ditch et al., 1997: 49).

[127] Yet, the level of benefits used to be considerably lower in the five 'new Länder' and East Berlin (former GDR), but this gap is closing as the general standard of living rises. The small variation across states is an important difference from other federally organized social assistance schemes, such as AFDC/TANF in the United States or the Swiss social assistance (cf. Eardley et al., 1996a, 1996b).

[128] In some states, other ministries have to be consulted prior to the decision about standard benefit rates: the Minister of Interior in Bavaria, and both the Minister of Interior and Finance in the Saarland and Schleswig-Holstein. In addition, a hearing of social assistance experts is required in Hesse, Rhineland-Palatinate, Brandenburg, Saarland and Bavaria (Oberbracht, 1993: 23).

[129] In these two federal states, the state government sets the minimum level of standard rates while the municipalities are free to decide to top up these rates. This scope of discretion has actually been used by a number of municipalities. In Bavaria, most large cities and many

price levels between urban and rural regions are thus hardly taken into account (Oberbracht, 1993: 23-24).

The German social assistance scheme is financed jointly by the municipalities, the federal states, and to a very small degree also by the central government. The source of funding depends on the type of assistance and the agency responsible for the administration of this benefit. Three different modes of financing contribute to the total expenditure on social assistance. General social assistance is mainly administered and financed through the municipalities. Their funds originate from local taxes and funds distributed among the municipalities through a complex financial redistribution mechanism (*kommunaler Finanzausgleich*). The regional social assistance agencies (*überörtliche Träger*) cover the majority of costs for social assistance in special circumstances (*Hilfe in besonderen Lebenslagen*). Their costs are born partly by the municipalities and partly by the federal states.[130] The third type of funding includes federal contribution for social assistance paid to Germans staying abroad (Bundesministerium für Arbeit und Sozialordnung, 1997: 677-687).

In conclusion, the institutional arrangements of setting benefit rates may favour or hinder the effectiveness of social assistance schemes in the long run. Whereas the British system of central funding and regulation is assumed to be relatively immune against structural pressures in favour of a 'race to the bottom', the allocation of funding and regulation responsibilities would suggest that the German and Swedish schemes are more prone to this type of retrenchment.[131] The decentralized procedures of setting benefit rates in Germany, and even more so in the old Swedish system are expected to eventually deteriorate social assistance benefits. However, there are some institutional safeguards against this development in both countries. Benefit rates are recommended by agencies on the national level, but these agencies do not have any power of coercion themselves. This deficit is filled by specific procedural arrangements in both countries. In Sweden, the courts play a critical role in the enforcement of benefit rates. The possibility of a judicial review of social assistance benefit rates acts as a safeguard against a 'race to the bottom' in the municipalities. In the German case, the more or less uniform application of the recommended standard benefit rates is guaranteed by

---

counties have offered higher benefit rates during the last years (Bayerisches Staatsministerium für Arbeit und Sozialordnung, Familie, Frauen und Gesundheit, personal communication, 21 June 1999 and unpublished statistical material).

[130] The exact rules of financing and the burden-sharing among municipalities and federal states vary across the *Länder* (cf. Prinz, 1983).

[131] This does not mean, however, that the British social assistance scheme is immune to retrenchment, but the additional pressures stemming from decentralized financing and regulation responsibilities do not apply in this case.

Adequacy 113

the fact that the municipalities and the federal states are represented in the German Association for Public and Private Welfare itself and thus participate in the decision-making process. It appears that the corporatist decision-making process obligates them to comply with the standard benefit rates agreed upon. This procedure ensures that the level of benefits is relatively uniform throughout the country, yet it does not necessarily guarantee that benefit levels are adequate to alleviate poverty. This gap is filled by the enforcement of the principle of human dignity in the German Basic Law on the part of the Constitutional Court. These institutional mechanisms may thus help to effectively secure an adequate standard of provision.

Inflation, Wages or Political Deliberation? Indexation of Benefit Rates

Once social assistance benefit rates are defined, benefit rates must be regularly adapted to the development of prices or wages in order to guarantee an effective alleviation of poverty in the long run. Indexation procedures are thus an integral component for the adequacy of social assistance benefits, as they guarantee that benefit levels do not fall behind the general income level within a society. The adequacy of social assistance benefits may be at stake if setting of benefit rates is open to political deliberation rather than governed by regular indexation. The choice of the indexation mechanism is not arbitrary, however. Depending on the real growth rate of wages, the choice of the indexation mechanism may make a large difference. If wages are growing faster than prices, price-indexed social assistance rates will fall behind the general income growth in the long run. In all of the countries considered here, social assistance benefits are regularly adapted to prices as opposed to wages. The indexation procedure is not always institutionalized in the sense that benefits are quasi-automatically adapted in line with prices, so there is some room for political deliberation.

In the United Kingdom, income support benefits are usually adapted to inflation each April. Unlike for other social security benefits, this procedure uses the 'Rossi index' which is based on a basket of goods excluding housing costs. Therefore, the relative distance of social assistance benefits to other social security benefits is not constant due to the fact that indexation of non-means-tested benefits is based on another index (Eardley et al., 1996b: 397).

In Germany, social assistance rates are regularly adapted to inflation, but this mechanism has been frequently suspended. Notably during recent years, the government's policy curbed the increase of benefit rates and lead to a real curtailment of benefits in every year, since 1992. Between 1993 and 1995, the yearly adaptation of benefit rates has been limited to a politically defined ceiling. In 1996, the up-rating of benefit rates was again based on

114 *At the Margins of the Welfare State*

inflation rates, but based on a lower price index that excluded the cost of housing. The adaptation in the two following years paralleled the increase of old age pensions which in turn are based on the development of net wages (Oberbracht, 1993; Steffen, 1995: 77-82; Bundesministerium für Arbeit und Sozialordnung, 1997: 672-674).

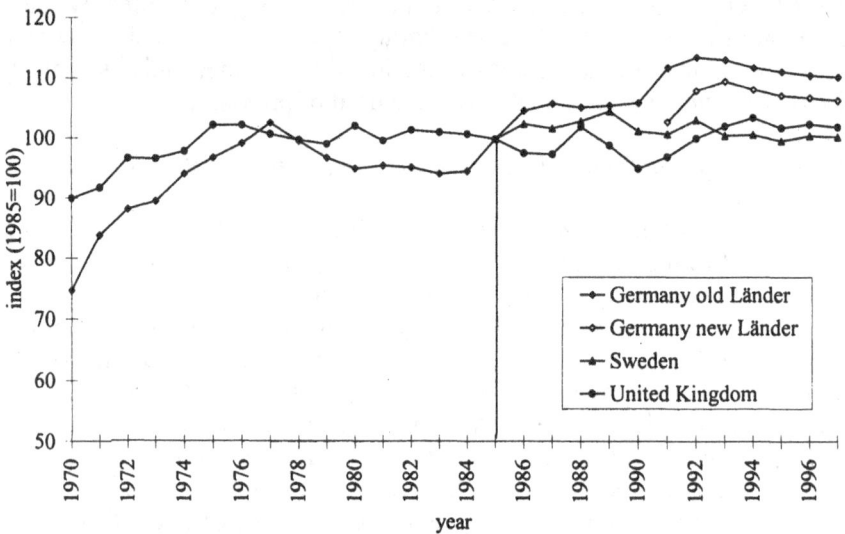

Figure 6.1 Development of real value of social assistance benefit rates in Germany, Sweden and the United Kingdom (1985=100)

Note: The standard benefit rates given for Germany refer to the average benefits paid in the old or new federal states respectively. For Sweden, the data presented reflect the recommendations of the National Board of Health and Welfare; the benefit rates actually paid by the municipalities may deviate from these levels.

Source: Germany: Federal Ministry of Labour and Social Security: Statistisches Taschenbuch, various volumes. Sweden: Statistiska Centralbyrån: Sveriges officiella statistik, various volumes, and information provided by the National Board of Health and Welfare. United Kingdom: Department of Social Security: Social Security Statistics, various volumes; Central Statistical Office/Office for National Statistics: Annual Abstract of Statistics.

In Sweden, the recommended *socialbidrag* rates are based on the development of the basic amount (*basbelopp*) in social insurance that is, in turn, annually adapted to prices. However, the full indexation of social assistance benefit rates was suspended between 1995 and 1997; during this period, only 60 per cent of the actual inflation rate was taken into account (OECD, 1998a: 173, 202). Moreover, since the Swedish municipalities are free to autonomously set local standard benefit rates, an overall assessment of the

Adequacy 115

development of real benefit rates cannot be presented. Several Swedish municipalities have suspended the indexation of social security benefits since the late 1980s (Elmer, 1989: 109-110, quoted in Schwarze, 1994: 53). They have argued that the index used by the National Board of Health and Welfare overestimated the actual cost of living of social assistance recipients, since it included the fast-rising housing costs that were not included in the standard benefits (Ditch et al., 1997: 52).

Figure 6.1 illustrates the development of the real value of social assistance benefit rates in Germany, Sweden and the United Kingdom. In order to allow the comparison of benefit rates across countries, benefit rates have been indexed with the base year of 1985.[132] The figure shows that standard benefit rates have developed differently in the three countries. While the real value of the British income support has proved to be relatively stable since the mid-1970s, the German benefit rates display a stronger variation over time, but with a clear upward tendency. While social assistance benefit rates were markedly augmented until 1977, the late 1970s saw a marked real decrease in benefit rates which came to a halt in the early 1980s. After the introduction of the new basket of goods in 1985, benefit rates again increased sharply. Only after 1992, benefit rates have suffered a real decrease, since a full indexation has been partly suspended for several years. After a strong initial growth, benefit rates in the new federal states have virtually paralleled the development in West Germany since 1993.[133]

For Sweden, data are only available since 1985 and only reflect the standard benefit rates for single people as recommended by the National Board of Health and Welfare.[134] An earlier analysis of benefit levels has shown that benefit rates were relatively stable during the early 1980s (Gustafsson, 1993: 254), and this trend seems to have continued for the second half of the 1980s and the 1990s. The real value of recommended benefit rates in Sweden increased until 1989, but has slightly decreased since then, largely due to the fact that the basic amount has not kept pace with inflation.

The development of real benefit rates does not necessarily indicate whether social assistance benefits have kept pace with the general develop-

---

[132] The year 1985 has been chosen because this is the first year data have been available for Sweden.

[133] Although the data presented here only refer to the development of benefit rates over time, but do not allow an interpretation of absolute levels, there is one exception for East Germany. Benefit rates for East Germany are indexed to the base year of 1985 in the former FRG. The average benefit level in East Germany is since 1993 constantly some 3-4 per cent lower than benefit rates in West Germany, due to still different price levels in the two parts of the country.

[134] The benefits actually paid by the municipalities may markedly deviate from these amounts.

116 *At the Margins of the Welfare State*

ment of incomes in a society. For this purpose, the relation to wages is much more relevant than the indexation to prices. Figure 6.2 shows the development of standard benefit rates as a percentage of the take-home pay of an average production worker.[135]

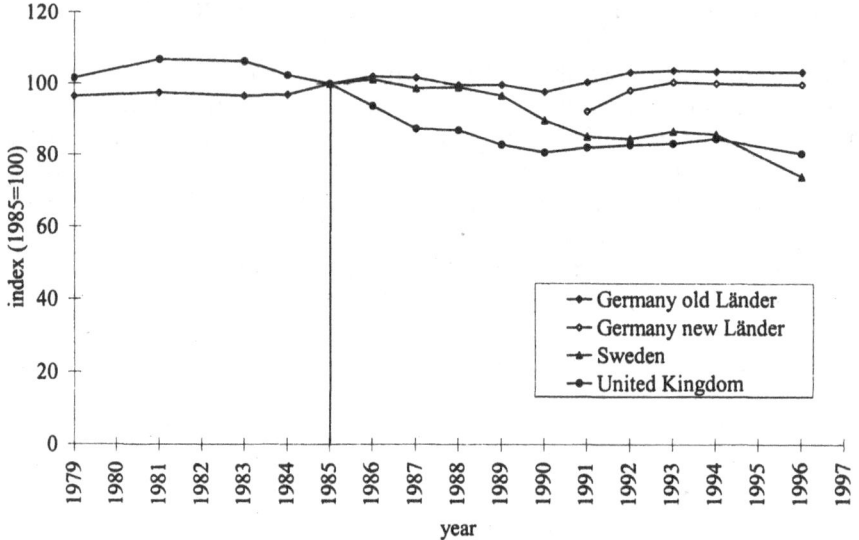

Figure 6.2 Development of standard benefit rates as a percentage of average production workers' take-home pay (1985 = 100)

Source: See Figure 6.1 (p. 114).

Figure 6.2 shows that social assistance standard benefit rates have kept pace with the development of net earnings of workers in Germany, but have fallen behind net wages in Sweden and the United Kingdom. The British income support rates fell during the mid-1980s, but display a more stable development in the 1990s. Recommended benefit rates in Sweden relatively declined between 1989 and 1991 and again between 1994 and 1996. In Germany, benefit rates paralleled the development of wages due to the relatively generous uprating of benefits and a low growth in real wages.

However, it must be emphasized that the ratios presented in Figure 6.2 only reflect standard benefit rates but do not include additional benefit payments. In addition, the relative weight given to additional household mem-

---

[135] These data are based on OECD data on average production worker's (APW) income. Take-home pay includes not only wages, but also takes into account taxation and government transfers (cf. OECD, 1997).

bers in the calculation of benefit rates may also be subject to change over time. A fully-fledged analysis of the development of social assistance rates should take into account that possible curtailments not only may affect the regular payment rates, but also these components of the total benefit package. A documentation of these changes is much more difficult, since official statistics often do not catch these changes that frequently occur only on the basis of administrative discretion rather than formal rules (cf. Schwarze, 1994: 91-92).[136]

Structure of the Benefit Package

The previous assessment of standard benefit rates did not reflect a large part of the actual benefit rates provided for by social assistance schemes. Claimants are not only entitled to the standard benefit rate intended to support the head of the household, but also to supplements for additional household members, to supplementary benefits in case of special needs, one-off payments for larger purchases, and to some kind of reimbursement for their housing costs. It is therefore necessary to assess the structure of social assistance benefit packages in order to allow a detailed comparison of social assistance benefit rates.

Standard Benefit Rates and Institutional Equivalence Scales Social assistance schemes typically provide a certain amount of money for the head of the household, as well as an additional allowance for each household member. These additional benefits are typically lower than the rates for the head of the household, since extra needs have to be balanced with economies of scale in larger households. For spouses, extra payments are 80 per cent of the single rate in Germany, 66 per cent in Sweden and 57 per cent in the United Kingdom (1993). Additions for children are typically differentiated by age, based on the assumption that older children have higher needs than younger ones. Curiously, the marginal need of additional household members is weighted very differently in the three countries. For all age groups, the relative level of benefit rates for children is markedly higher in Germany and Sweden than in the United Kingdom where there is a special family premium (see Figure 6.3).

The 1996 reform of the German social assistance law introduced a ceiling for larger households, responding to concerns that households with several children were better off with social assistance than with income from em-

---

[136] Social assistance payments granted on the basis of administrative discretion rather than formal entitlements may be used as a favourable veil to conceal curtailments from the public (cf. Pierson, 1994).

118 *At the Margins of the Welfare State*

ployment. This reform should have been effective from July 1999, but was preliminarily suspended by the incoming new government (Brühl, 1998). This regulation stipulated that standard benefit rates have to be designed in a way that families with three children receiving social assistance should be not better off than a comparable low-wage household with one full-employed earner. Similar measures have been taken by some Swedish municipalities (Schwarze, 1994: 54-55). With this regulation, the principle of 'less eligibility' over-rides the principle of need and potentially undermines an effective alleviation of poverty for larger households.

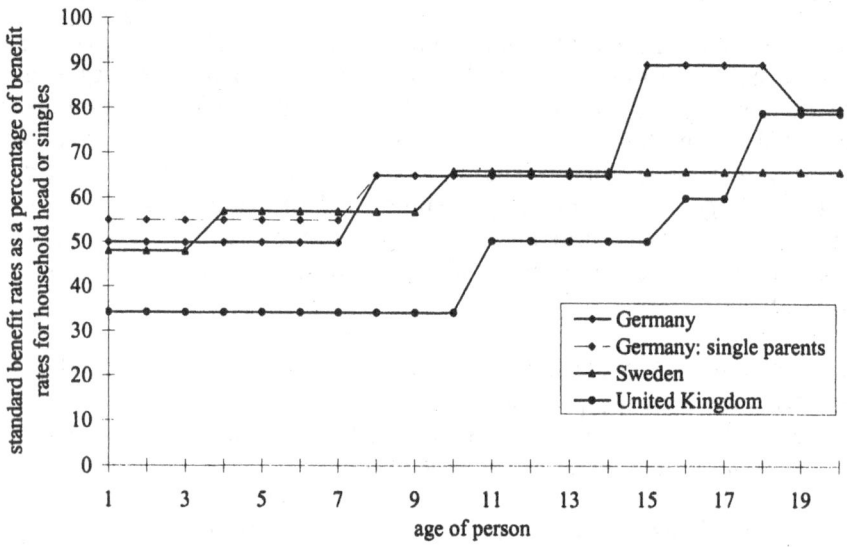

Figure 6.3 Standard benefit rates for additional household members

Note: For Sweden: Standard benefit rates as recommended by the National Board of Health and Welfare. Germany: children of single parents receive 55 per cent of the adult rate up to the age of 7.

Source: Own calculations based on national statistics and social assistance regulations.

The benefit structure for Sweden again only reflects the national recommendations. Municipalities have not only enjoyed a large degree of discretion in setting the level of benefit, but also in determining equivalence scales embodied in the benefits. For example, couples received between 52 and 73 per cent more than single people in 1992 in a sample of municipalities (Svensson, 1993: 44-45; own calculations).

Benefit Additions to Cover Special Needs (Premiums) To a varying extent, low-income households can receive extra payments to cover special needs or one-off costs. Special payments are supposed to meet extra needs of some groups of claimants, such as for example elderly or disabled claimants or single parents. They are usually paid on a regular basis as an addition to the standard benefit rate. A comparison of these benefits across countries faces a number of problems. Contingencies covered by special payments in one country may be covered by one-off payments in another.[137] Moreover, special needs may also trigger an entitlement to another social security benefit, bringing claimants entirely out of social assistance whereas people in another country may be entitled to social assistance and special additions. This makes a comparison of benefit additions across countries very difficult.

Table 6.1 gives an overview of additional benefits regularly paid to some groups of claimants in Germany and the United Kingdom. Since the determination of benefits covering special needs lies entirely in the discretion of municipalities in Sweden and may therefore vary considerably, no data are given for the Swedish case. In order to allow a cross-national comparison, premiums are shown as a percentage of standard benefit rates for a single adult. It becomes evident that eligibility for additional benefits and the level of additional payments vary strongly across countries.

In Germany, social assistance is split between general social assistance (*Hilfe zum Lebensunterhalt*) and 'aid in special circumstances' (*Hilfe in besonderen Lebenslagen*), as indicated above. The latter scheme provides categorical benefits for some groups of the population,[138] but this study only focuses on general social assistance that also provides some benefits in addition to the standard benefit rates. Special needs of certain groups of the population, such as pregnant women, single parents, handicapped people and the elderly (since 1996 only if handicapped), are granted premiums (*Mehrbedarfszuschläge*) in addition with the standard benefit rate within the general social assistance scheme. These benefits make up between 20 and 60 per cent of the standard benefit rate (see Table 6.1). Such additions may cumulate if a person is entitled to several supplements, yet the sum of the additions is limited to the amount of the standard benefit rate, i.e. claimants may

---

[137] For example, pregnant women receive an addition to the normal benefit rate in Germany, but are entitled to a lump-sum one-off payment in Britain.

[138] The aid in special circumstances covers the following schemes: aid for pregnant women and young mothers, aid for family planning, aid for the handicapped and the blind (care, rehabilitation and integration), aid in case of sickness and sickness prevention, aid for long-term care, aid for the establishment of a living (*Hilfe zum Aufbau oder zur Sicherung der Lebensgrundlage*), home helps, social work for marginalized groups such as the homeless or prisoners, aid for the elderly (*Altenhilfe*) (cf. Bundesministerium für Arbeit und Sozialordnung, 1997: 677-682).

120 *At the Margins of the Welfare State*

not receive more than the double amount of the social assistance rate in total (Brühl, 1998: 47).

Table 6.1 Provision of benefit additions (premiums) for specific groups of the population (benefit rates given as a proportion of standard benefit rates for a single adult), 1995

	Germany	United Kingdom
Family	– no specific premium[139]	– 22%
Lone parent	– 40% if one child younger than 7 or if two or three children younger than 16; 60% if four or more children	– 11% (in addition to family premium) (only for claims dating from before July 1998) (non-cumulative)
Pregnant woman	– 20% after 12th week of pregnancy	– Maternity grant in the social fund: lump sum of £100 per child, higher expenses can be covered by the discretionary social fund
Pensioner	– 20% for pensioners who claimed social assistance before July 1996; 20% if mobility impaired (for new claims since July 1996)	– 40% for pensioners aged 60-74; 45% for pensioners aged 75-79; 55% for pensioners aged 80 and over, or aged 60 and over, if receiving qualified disability benefit or registered blind (non-cumulative)
Invalidity	– 20% in case of invalidity if mobility impaired	– may receive incapacity benefit instead of income support
Disability	– 40% for handicapped people receiving disability benefit (*Eingliederungshilfe*); 'appropriate amount' for people who are blind, sick otherwise disabled, or threatened by disability if they need to have a special diet	– 43%-77%, depending on degree of disability (non-cumulative; except severe disability premium); 43% for disabled children

Note: Per cent values refer to a percentage of the standard benefit rate for a single adult.

Source: Bundesministerium für Arbeit und Sozialordnung (1997; 1998), Brühl (1992; 1998); CPAG (1997a; 1998).

For the time being, the introduction of the income support scheme in 1988 ended a history of ever more standardized benefit rates in British social assistance. Payment covering special needs were left to the discretion of welfare officials in the national assistance system of 1948; after the introduction of the supplementary benefit in 1966 informal guidelines have been used. A major review in 1980 has put these rules into law (cf. Atkinson, 1990). The introduction of income support in 1988 replaced this complex system of 'ordinary' and 'long-term' rates and manifold supplements for specific needs by a more transparent system of standard benefit rates. These benefits were based on 'typical' needs of specific family types and some 'premiums' for people with specific needs, such as single parents or the disabled. Any other

---

[139] The German social assistance scheme does not grant a specific premium on a household basis, yet benefit rates for children are higher than in Britain.

expenses are supposed to be covered by the social fund. The premiums available under the income support scheme include benefit supplements for families and single parents, pensioners and disabled people (Table 6.1; cf. Eardley et al., 1996b: 396-398).[140] Some of these benefits can be paid on top of other premiums, some cannot (these benefits are marked as 'non-cumulative' in Table 6.1; cf. CPAG, 1998: 360-372). Responding to concerns of poverty in old age, the British government decided to increase the income support benefit rates for pensioners in April 1999 (cf. Rake, 1999).

One-off Payments One-off benefits meet exceptional needs that do not occur on a weekly or monthly basis and are not covered by standard benefit rates. Payments may be made for the purchase of expensive consumer goods (e.g. furniture or special clothing) or other exceptional or unexpected needs. Unlike special payments, the payment of extra benefits is not necessarily connected to the regular receipt of social assistance, but can also be granted to non-claimants in all three countries considered.

If it is difficult to assess the level of standard benefit rates in a comparative perspective, it is almost impossible to evaluate the impact of these special payments. Since benefits are frequently granted on an irregular and discretionary basis, a direct comparison of these regulations is not feasible. Ditch (1995) illustrated the various difficulties in making cross-country comparison of discretionary payments. Nevertheless, it is possible to identify some general patterns in the treatment of special needs in social assistance.

One-off benefits embodied in the German *Sozialhilfe* (*einmalige Leistungen*) are supposed to cover the acquisition of larger items not covered by standard benefit rates, including clothing, bedding, furniture and other household equipment, repairs and renovations. Besides, these benefits also cover the costs of socio-cultural integration that do not occur on a day-to-day basis. They may include bicycles for children, radio sets, watches, school trips for children, birthday presents, etc. In addition, there is a Christmas premium in most federal states. These benefits are granted on a discretionary basis, either as one-off benefits or, in the case of clothing, as a lump sum payment every six months, but administrative practices vary (cf. Eichhorn and Fergen, 1998: 482-483).[141] Benefits are usually given as grants, although there is also the possibility to give loans. Although social security officials

---

[140] The premium for single parents has been eliminated for new claims after July 1998 (Bennett, 1998a: 101; 1998b: 399).
[141] Most social assistance offices actually have detailed regulations about which items should be covered by these special benefits and how frequently people can apply for a certain item (for example, a winter coat is normally paid for every 5 years, if the individual circumstances do not make an earlier acquisition necessary).

rely on detailed regulations laid down in administrative statutes, the administrative and judicial practice is far from uniform (cf. Brühl, 1992: 89-118).[142]

The British income support is supplemented by a discretionary scheme to meet one-off needs, the so-called social fund. Established in April 1987, the social fund is designed to meet special needs of claimants.[143] It is split into regulated and discretionary payments. On the basis of legal regulations, the social fund offers grants to cover costs accruing for maternity, funerals, cold weather and winter fuel payments to claimants on income support or other means-tested schemes.[144] In addition, special community care grants seek to support people who would otherwise be required to live in an institution (C. Walker, 1993: 129-130). Other needs of claimants are supposed to be dealt with through loans. Claimants may receive 'crisis loans' to cover emergencies and 'budgeting loans' for larger purchases. Only one third of the fund's expenditure is paid as a grant whereas two-thirds are given as loans (C. Walker, 1993: 131). In most cases, the loans will be recovered from claimants' future benefit payments or other incomes (OECD, 1998a: 32).[145] Repayments will take place at 5, 10 or 15 per cent of the benefit payments over a period of up to 72 or in exceptional cases 104 weeks, depending on the client's circumstances (C. Walker, 1993: 130). This implies that claimants have to live on an income below the income support level during the repayment of the loan (Huby, 1996: 10; Rahilly, 2000). For both the regulated and

---

[142] A number of municipalities, supported by the federal Minister, initiated an initiative to replace one-off benefits by lump-sum payments for claimants. Referring to experiences of a pilot project, they argue that claimants prefer this mode of payment because they have a greater sovereignty in using their budget without having the hassle of applying for each expense. Municipalities favour lump sum payments because of a simplification of administrative procedures and cost saving (cf. Klinger, 1998).

[143] The social fund replaced the payments for special needs in the supplementary benefit (exceptional circumstances additions and exceptional needs payments until 1979, from 1980 single payments, additional requirements and urgent needs payments) that have been heavily criticized for their complexity and the degree of discretion involved (Buck, 1996: 16-24). The social fund was designed to meet three main objectives: '(1) To concentrate attention and help on those claimants facing the greatest difficulties in managing their normal income. (2) To enable a more varied response to inescapable individual need that can be achieved under present rules. (3) To handle the arrangements in a way that does not prejudice the efficiency of the main Income Support scheme.' (Cmnd. 9518 (1985), para. 9.6, quoted in Buck, 1996: 26). For a more detailed evaluation of the social fund, cf. Buck (1996); Evans (1994); Huby and Dix (1992); Walker (1992); Social Security Advisory Committee (1992); Harris (2000a; 2000b); Rahilly (2000).

[144] Maternity grants are paid to claimants of income support and family credit, funeral grants also to claimants of housing benefit, whereas cold weather and winter fuel payments are limited to claimants of income support and income-based jobseeker's allowance (C. Walker, 1993: 129; CPAG, 1998: 410-420).

[145] Given that each social security office has a fixed annual budget for this kind of loans, they are eager to recover these advance payments from claimants (OECD, 1998a: 32).

Adequacy 123

the discretionary social fund payments, the capital limit is less generous than in the income support scheme (CPAG, 1998: 442-490).[146] Income support claimants who possess some financial assets are not eligible for benefits from the social fund unless they have liquidated their own funds.[147]

Decisions on discretionary social fund payments are supposed to take into account all circumstances of the case in question, in particular any other resources that could meet the need. Since this evaluation of the client situation includes the probability of the repayment of the loan, applications may be turned down if the claimant's circumstances do not allow the repayment of the loan in the future. This may lead to the paradoxical situation that the most needy claimants are refused help from the social fund because they are deemed not to be able to repay the loan.

The budget of each social fund district office is limited, so exceptional needs can only be covered at the expense of other claimants.[148] Social fund officials therefore seek to concentrate available means on the most pressing needs. Although the High Court has ruled that the evaluation of need shall be independent of budget constraints, budget considerations have a strong impact on the decisions taken in individual cases (CPAG, 1998: 460-462). However, at least during the first years of operation, the social fund was subject to massive problems of over- and underspending (C. Walker, 1993: 131). The fixed budget also implies that there might be regional inequalities and variations in the course of a fiscal year (C. Walker, 1993: 136-137; Evans, 1994; CPAG, 1998: 461). In addition, the welfare officials face strong incentives to recover the loans from claimants in order not to exceed the office budget.[149]

Earlier evaluations of the social fund have regularly raised the issue of unequal provision of benefits. There have been concerns that benefits are subject to massive creaming effects and do not reach the claimants most in need (Huby and Dix, 1992). The system is believed to discriminate against ethnic minorities, clients with insufficient knowledge of the English language and clients with low oral and written skills. Although the evidence on higher rejection rates of these client groups is ambiguous, there are concerns

---

[146] If claimants possess financial assets of more than £500 (£1,000 for people aged 60 and older), the excess capital is deducted at a rate of 100 per cent from social fund payments (CPAG, 1998: 443).

[147] Since these capital disregards have not been adapted to inflation, their real value has decreased by roughly one third since their introduction in 1988 (cf. Evans, 1994: 13); own calculations on the basis of Department of Social Security, 1998 and earlier volumes).

[148] Benefit Agencies establish a monthly expenditure profile according to their budget on the basis of the national guidelines issued by the Secretary of State (CPAG, 1998: 458-459).

[149] This assessment collides with an earlier description of the social fund scheme stating that the budget of the social fund offices was not dependent on the recovering of loans from claimants (C. Walker, 1993: 132).

that prospective claimants are turned away before even having submitted a formal application (cf. C. Walker, 1993: 128-142).[150] Consequently, the client structure does not reflect the structure of income support claimants, let alone differing need levels. Single parents appear to be overrepresented among social fund recipients whereas pensioners are clearly underrepresented (C. Walker, 1993: 137). Claimants' lobby groups and social scientists are seriously concerned that those most in need will not get any help from the social fund, especially if the officials deem the chance of loan repayment low.[151] Possibly, future evaluations may come to a different conclusion because of a growing standardization of the administration of social fund benefits (cf. CPAG, 1998: 457-458).

One-off benefits in Sweden are hard to monitor since there are no national regulations on the provision of this kind of benefits and there is a large degree of variation across municipalities. Yet there is some evidence that one-off payments have been handled more restrictively during recent years. Some social assistance offices have even discussed the provision of loans rather than grants for some types of one off-benefits (dental prostheses or household equipment) (Schwarze, 1994: 54-55).

Comparing Britain and Germany, we find marked differences in the prevalence of one-off payments. A rough comparison of expenditures shows that outlays for the social fund are much smaller than expenditure for one-off benefits in Germany. Gross expenditures for the social fund amounted to some 3 per cent of the combined expenditures for income support and the social fund during the 1990s, and only a minority of income support recipients apply for benefits from the social fund during a year.[152] In Germany, these benefits usually make up a non-negligible proportion of the total amount paid to claimants, on average around one-sixth of current benefit expenditure, and has been relatively stable over time and over different types of households.[153] For Sweden, comparable data are not available. The effect

---

[150] Huby (1996) summarized the research on the effects of the social fund as follows: 'Lowered levels of expectation, together with the erosion of notions of rights and entitlement to benefits in a scheme based on eligibility and discretion, lead to a blank despondency among claimants which does little to elicit feelings of empowerment' (Huby, 1996: 11).

[151] An evaluation of the social fund concluded that 'we cannot show that those who got awards were in greater need than those who did not; nor can we conclude that the social fund is meeting its objective "to concentrate attention and help on those applicants facing the greatest difficulties in managing their income".' (Huby and Dix, 1992: 127).

[152] According to a very rough estimate, around one in three recipients of income support also receive benefits from the social fund (own calculation based on Department of Social Security 1992: 93-95; 1997: 105-107; 1998: 103-105).

[153] Cf. Bechtold et al. (1993); Bundesministerium für Arbeit und Sozialordnung (1997: 676); own calculations on the basis of Statistisches Bundesamt (1998: 4). One-off-benefits for people who are not regular claimants of social assistance have not been considered. Total

Adequacy 125

of discretionary one-off benefits on an effective alleviation of poverty through social assistance is ambiguous, however. On the one hand, they can help to accommodate special needs and thus enhance adequacy, but on the other hand, discretionary schemes may be less effective in the take-up dimension, since some claimants may refrain from applying for benefits because of the additional application procedure involved (see Chapter 6).

Housing Costs Housing costs make up a considerable proportion of private households' budgets, and are thus an integral part of social assistance benefit packages. Most countries have not included housing costs in the standard benefit rates, but cover them separately (cf. Eardley et al., 1996a: 67-71); Germany, Sweden and the United Kingdom generally follow this pattern. In each of these countries, claimant households obtain full coverage of their housing costs if considered as 'reasonable'. Each country organizes its compensation for housing costs differently, however.

In the United Kingdom, income support claimants who live in rented flats or houses receive the full amount of housing benefit from the Benefits Agency in order to cover their rent.[154] However, a small amount of housing costs (other than rent) has to be born out of income support. Income support is considered as a passport benefit to housing benefit and to council tax benefit, which means that there is no separate means-test as long as claimants receive income support.[155] Owner-occupiers can obtain help with their mortgage from income support (CPAG, 1998: 27-46).

In Germany, the costs of housing are fully offset by the social assistance office if they do not exceed a certain 'reasonable' amount.[156] Housing costs are not covered by social assistance as such, but by the general housing allowance (*Wohngeld*) that non-claimants may also receive. Although housing allowance is generally administered by separate administrative units, claimants of social assistance usually receive their housing allowances through the social assistance offices. The housing allowance is not financed out of the same budget as social assistance; the federal government and the *Länder* share the cost. Therefore, municipalities use an internal compensation

---

expenditures for social assistance only include regular social assistance while excluding aid in special circumstances.

[154] Housing benefit is tapered off for higher incomes, but this usually does not apply to claimants of income support (Kemp, 1995).

[155] Department of Social Security, personal communication, 22 October 1998.

[156] Recipients of social assistance are normally granted a lump-sum housing benefit via the social assistance office, so they do not have to collect this benefit separately. The social assistance offices, however, internally recover their expenses for housing from the housing benefit scheme. There are different sources of funding: Housing benefit is funded jointly by the federal government and the federal states, whereas social assistance is financed by the municipalities.

mechanism to recover their expenditures for housing allowance for claimants of social assistance from these bodies (Bundesministerium für Arbeit und Sozialordnung, 1997: 639-661).

Claimants of *socialbidrag* in Sweden can usually have their full housing costs covered by social assistance up to an 'adequate' amount (Schwarze, 1994: 51), so claimants of social assistance do not have to claim housing benefits separately. They may claim housing allowance,[157] but this counts as income for the purpose of calculating their entitlement to social assistance (Eardley et al., 1996b: 361-362). The social assistance offices have increasingly applied restrictions on the payment of housing costs during recent yea₁ ₃. If the apartment is considered too expensive for the claimants' household, the social assistance office may ask recipients to move to a cheaper apartment if available. Besides, some cities have suspended the indexation of the upper limits for the payment of housing costs through the social assistance agency in recent years (cf. Schwarze, 1994: 54-55 for the city of Malmö). The National Board of Health and Welfare has issued a recommendation on the 'reasonable' costs of housing, but the actual policies of municipalities often deviate from this standard (cf. Byberg, 1998: 85).

Although full housing costs are in principle covered by social assistance, administrative practices and the distribution of housing costs on different components of the benefit package vary. In Germany and Sweden, recipients of social assistance have their full housing costs covered by the social assistance office, whereas claimants in the United Kingdom have to register for housing benefit (yet usually have their full housing costs covered). However, even if their rent is covered by social assistance, there may still be some costs associated with housing that are supposed to be paid out of the standard benefit rate (e.g. fuel or electricity), as this is the case in Sweden (cf. Eardley

---

[157] There are three kinds of housing allowances in Sweden: a general housing allowance funded by the central government (*bostadsbidrag*) for the working-age population, a special housing allowance for pensioners, and a supplementary housing allowance for pensioners. The latter two used to be administered and funded by the municipalities, but the central government has taken over the fiscal and administrative responsibilities in 1995. From January 1995, the reform of pensioners' housing allowances in Sweden replaced the *kommunalt bostadstillägg* (KBT) by the *bostadstillägg till pensionärer* (BTP), whereas the supplementary housing allowance for poor pensioners, the *särskilt kommunalt bostadstillägg* (SKBT) was substituted by the *särskilt bostadstillägg till pensionärer* (SBTP). The municipalities had the right to supplement these benefits by a further supplement (*kommunalt kompletteringsbelopp*; KKB) until 1998 (Riksförsäkringsverket, 1998a, 1998b). Housing allowances are means-tested, but with more generous rules than in the *socialbidrag* scheme. Because of concerns about benefit fraud, since 1997 claimants only receive a preliminary housing allowance. At the end of the year, the actual yearly income is used to set the final rate of the housing allowance, and the social insurance office (*försäkringskassan*) may now claim back overpaid benefits or pay out additional benefits (Riksförsäkringsverket, 1998a).

et al., 1996a: 118-119). This emphasizes the need to consider housing benefits as an integral component of the benefit package in cross-national comparisons.

Adequacy: Evidence from the Luxembourg Income Study

The preceding sections have laid out those institutional elements of social assistance schemes which may favour or hinder an effective alleviation of poverty. Yet, they have also shown that a comparative assessment of standard benefit rates alone can only sketch an incomplete or even misleading picture of social assistance levels. The composition of the income package available to claimants can strongly vary across countries. Some needs may be covered out of the standard benefit rate in one country, but by additional allowances in the other, thus making a direct comparison of benefit levels virtually impossible. These differences are most marked in respect to the coverage of housing costs. Less important but still not negligible are taxes, social security contributions, and health costs to be paid out of the benefits in some countries.[158] Only a comprehensive analysis of minimum income packages can answer the question of whether social assistance schemes can guarantee an adequate standard of living, and whether benefits are high enough as to keep recipients out of poverty.

This section will assess *entitlements* to social assistance, not the amount of money people actually have received. The notion of entitlement refers to the amount of money a specific household should receive as stipulated in the social assistance regulations. Whether households are eligible for social assistance has been discussed in Chapter 4, and whether they actually receive the full amount of benefit they are entitled to will be discussed in Chapter 6 below.

The assessment of social assistance entitlements must take into account that minimum income benefits are dependent on the specific needs of the individual household. Benefits are determined by the type and the composition of the household, the age of household members, entitlements to one-off benefits, the cost of housing as well as a bundle of other characteristics that may trigger eligibility for additional premiums or other social assistance benefits (as for example disability or pregnancy of household members). The analysis of the adequacy of social assistance entitlements is therefore not as

---

[158] Social assistance benefits are taxed in neither country, except for benefits for the unemployed in the United Kingdom. For the countries considered in this paper, only in Sweden there are some health care costs to be covered out of social assistance. Housing costs do not accrue in Germany, but to a large extent in Sweden and only marginally in the United Kingdom (Bradshaw, 1997: 242-244).

straightforward as it may seem. The possibility of large variations of social assistance entitlements across household types precludes a simple measurement of adequacy in the form of absolute levels or wage replacement rates. The evaluation of social assistance entitlements should therefore allow for different household need levels. A comparative analysis of social assistance entitlements can follow two strategies. A relatively easy and exact method of analysis is the use of model households. Social assistance entitlements are calculated on the basis of the legal regulations of each country for a number of pre-defined model families. This methodology produces a relatively easy and exact measure of adequacy, yet its results are not necessarily representative for the entire population. More comprehensive results are yielded by a simulation of social assistance entitlements on the basis of household microdata. This method allows to gain a thorough picture of social assistance entitlements among the sampled population. Each of these methods has its specific advantages and disadvantages, but they complement each other well.

In the following, the adequacy of social assistance will be explored in two steps. Social assistance entitlements are first assessed on the basis of the model family approach, using institutional information for the calculation of entitlements for selected household types. The information assembled in this analysis is used to assess the adequacy of social assistance entitlements to a relative poverty standard. The second section departs from the use of model households and presents a simulation of social assistance entitlements based on LIS micro-data. These data allow the comparison of social assistance entitlements to the amounts actually received and can shed some more light on the adequacy of benefit levels stipulated by the institutional regulations.

Assessment of Social Assistance Entitlements Based on Model Households

The evaluation of social assistance entitlements on the basis of model calculations allows one to keep the need level of the household constant and thus permits an informed comparison of social assistance entitlements across countries. Basically, this approach defines a number of model households with specified needs.[159] We can then assess the entitlements to social assistance the families would have in each of the countries considered. However, the choice of household types to be assessed invariably involves a certain degree of arbitrariness and is far from reflecting the actual variation of household types in the real world. The circumstances of these model house-

---

[159] This method has also been applied in the seminal study on social assistance in a comparative perspective (Eardley et al., 1996a). In order to secure comparability with the results of this study, the methods applied here closely follow their approach.

holds have to be specified in detail in order to enhance the precision of the comparison across countries.

Methodology In order to keep the household need level constant across countries, this method requires the definition of model households. The more detailed the definition of model households, the less representative are the chosen model households for the recipient population. Thus, the definition of model households inevitably has to balance precision and representativity.

Following Eardley et al. (1996a), thirteen model households have been chosen for this book. The following household types are used for the computation of social assistance entitlements.

A Single person (35 years)
B Single person (68 years)
C Couple (both 35)
D Couple (both 68)
E Couple (both 35) with child (1)
F Couple (both 35) with child (7)
G Couple (both 35) with two children (7, 14)
H Couple (both 35) with three children (4, 7, 14)
I Couple (both 35) with four children (4, 7, 10, 14)
J Single parent (35) with child (1)
K Single parent (35) with child (7)
L Single parent (35) with two children (1, 7)
M Single parent (35) with two children (4, 7)
N Single parent (35) with two children (7, 14)

The choice of model households closely sticks to the methodology of Eardley et al. (1996a) in order to ensure comparability with their results. Some small changes have been made, however. Their model families have been supplemented by four new household types because of their relevance for current discussions on poverty. Since large families with three or more children run a overproportionate risk to claim social assistance and to be poor in every one of the three countries, two additional households with three and four children have been added (household types H and I). Two more types of single parent families have been included in order to account for a peculiarity of the German social assistance scheme which permits a full income disregard of parent allowance (*Erziehungsgeld*) and thus considerably improves the income situation for many parents with young children under three years (Bundesministerium für Arbeit und Sozialordnung, 1997: 683; Brühl, 1998: 103).[160] The family types with a child aged 1 year (house-

---

[160] The *Erziehungsgeld* scheme grants a monthly payment of DEM 600 (€307, as of 1999) to parents of young children provided that one partner is working less than 19 hours per

hold types E, J and L) assume that the parent allowance adds to the total household budget. The level of social assistance without any claims for parent allowance is reflected in the model families with children aged 7 (household types F, K and M) who are entitled to exactly the same amount of social assistance except for the parent allowance.

Based on the institutional information on social assistance benefits laid out above, the following minimum income benefits are available for the model households chosen. Basically, all households are assumed to be eligible for the full amount of social assistance. Since benefit rates may considerably vary across municipalities in Sweden, the recommended rates are used here as a guideline, yet the benefits actually paid out may deviate from these values. The marginal regional variation of standard benefit rates in Germany are taken into account by using the average standard benefit rate of the 'old *Länder*'.[161] The 'new *Länder*' will not be considered here.[162]

Since the purpose of this analysis is the assessment of the adequacy of the minimum income level set by social assistance, all households are assumed to have no earnings or capital income, so no income disregards and special premiums for working claimants are to be considered. Likewise, it is assumed that these families do not have any entitlements to social insurance benefits that require previous contributions or the fulfilment of other conditions. Thus, unemployment benefits or minimum pensions are not taken into account. The calculation of social assistance entitlements should however consider universal social security benefits that are not dependent on previous contributions and are fully disregarded in the calculation of social assistance. This type of benefits therefore increases the amount of disposable income for a broad majority of the claimant population. The above mentioned German parent allowance fits into this category. This benefit is fully disregarded in the calculation of social assistance benefits and thus adds to the total social assistance claim. One could argue that the Swedish basic pension would also meet these criteria, but benefits are conditional upon previous long-standing residency in Sweden. Since many recipients of social assistance in Sweden are refugees, they cannot meet these criteria and thus have to fully rely on

---

week or not working at all in order to take care of the child. The national parent allowance is available for two years, but some federal states provide complementary schemes for up to one additional year. These state benefit schemes are also fully disregarded for the calculation of social assistance. After six months, the benefit is means-tested (cf. Bundesministerium für Arbeit und Sozialordnung, 1997: 610-616).

[161] Since social assistance standard benefit rates are usually updated in the middle of the year, the yearly average has been chosen as the reference amount (cf. Bundesministerium für Arbeit und Sozialordnung, 1997: 664).

[162] In Eastern Germany, benefit levels are slightly lower than in the West, but wages and prices (notably rents) have not reached yet the Western level either.

Adequacy 131

social assistance anyway. For the calculation of social assistance entitlements, the basic pension is therefore not considered.

In addition, the model families may be entitled to special premiums that are supposed to meet additional needs of specific claimant categories. The model calculations include family premiums (Britain), single parent premiums (Britain and Germany), as well as additions in case of old age (Britain and Germany). Other premiums, such as premiums in case of disability or pregnancy, were not taken into account, since this would unduly constrain the generalization of results. Since the Swedish recommended benefit rates lack any stipulated premiums for special needs, there are no premiums taken into account for Sweden.

Standard benefit rates have to be further complemented by the value of one-off benefits. One-off benefits can make up a considerable share of the total amount of social assistance benefits people receive, but it is difficult to gauge the exact amount of one-off benefits, since these benefits are – by definition – based on individual needs. The assessment of social assistance entitlements can therefore only be based on broad estimates of the value of one-off benefits. In the German case, the social assistance benefit level has been augmented by 16 per cent based on the evidence on average expenditure on one-off benefits. For the United Kingdom, the amount of one-off benefits from the social fund has assumed to be equal to the average net expenditure of the social fund per recipient of income support.[163] For Sweden, there is no systematic evidence available on the amount of one-off benefits actually paid, therefore this income component could not be considered in this calculation. However, since some of the items covered by one-off benefits in Germany and Britain are covered by the standard benefit rate in Sweden, the level of the social assistance package should be comparable.

The final major component of recipients' households total income is made up by benefits to cover the cost of housing.[164] Since housing costs are subject to large cross-country and regional variation, and strongly depend on the size and quality of the accommodation, actual social assistance levels after housing may markedly diverge from the levels reported in these model calculations. For Germany, the housing costs are gauged on the basis of the

---

[163] The average benefit per recipient of social assistance 1995 was £22.20, net of repayments of loans (own calculations on the basis of the DSS Social Security Statistics). Since the amount of social fund benefits paid vary with the size of the household, it was assumed that each member of the household received this amount in addition to the standard benefit rate. Variations in claiming behaviour and admission rates variations different household types could not be considered.

[164] The model calculations are based on the assumption that recipient households have their full rent paid by social assistance or related schemes, provided that the rent level is considered as reasonable by the social assistance authorities.

132 *At the Margins of the Welfare State*

official statistics on the average housing costs of recipients of social assistance differentiated according to household size.[165] The housing costs for social assistance households in Britain and Sweden have been approximated on the basis of rent levels for York and Stockholm.[166]

The addition of these four income components makes up the total benefit entitlement of recipients of social assistance. It thus constitutes an effective minimum income standard for the majority of the population, although there may be higher or lower standards for some categories of the population (cf. Veit-Wilson, 1998).

Absolute Level of Social Assistance Entitlements On the basis of the model calculations, we can assess the absolute level of social assistance entitlements for specific model households. Figure 6.4 shows entitlements for social assistance after housing, referring to the value of the monthly benefit package in ECU adjusted for differences in purchasing power.[167] Keeping in mind that the comparison of absolute income levels across countries faces a number of methodological problems, some conclusions can be drawn from Figure 6.4. The comparison of social assistance levels in the three countries shows a clear rank order of benefit levels for most family types: Sweden offers a very generous social assistance benefit level, Germany once more takes the middle rank, while the Britain offers a relatively stingy benefit level. This pattern is broken only for families with very young children and for the elderly. Families with young children receive the most generous benefit package in Germany if they are eligible for parent allowance in addition to their social assistance benefits. Without this entitlement, their benefit package is still higher than in Britain, but much lower than in Sweden. The second exceptions to the general pattern concerns elderly households. Britain

---

[165] Own calculations based on Bundesministerium für Arbeit und Sozialordnung (1994: 632; 1998: 676); Breuer and Engels (1994). Housing costs of larger households not available in these data (more than 5 persons) have been estimated by using the marginal housing costs of the last person in the largest household for which data were available as a proxy for the housing costs of each additional person.

[166] These calculations are based on Eardley et al. (1996a: 114) who reported the rent level in these two cities for 1992. In order to obtain the rent level for 1995, these data have been adjusted with the national retail price index for housing and household goods for each country. For larger households, a marginal rent of £17 per additional person has been assumed.

[167] Purchasing-power based comparisons of income level across countries are very sensitive towards variations in the measure of purchasing power. There may be large differences in the measured income level if the calculations are based on purchasing power parities from a different source or use a slightly modified definition (cf. Brunger, 1996). In addition, national purchasing power parities may not be able to catch the specific consuming patterns of low income groups, since they rely on an overall measurement of prices. These absolute measures should therefore be complemented by additional indicators of income levels based on relative measurement.

grants relatively generous benefits to elderly households as compared to the non-elderly, both for singles and for couples. For single people, benefits even exceed the German ones; couples can expect a benefit level that is higher than for non-elderly couples, yet benefits are higher in Germany than in Britain. The German benefit level is even higher than the Swedish one, so Germany takes the top rank for this household type.

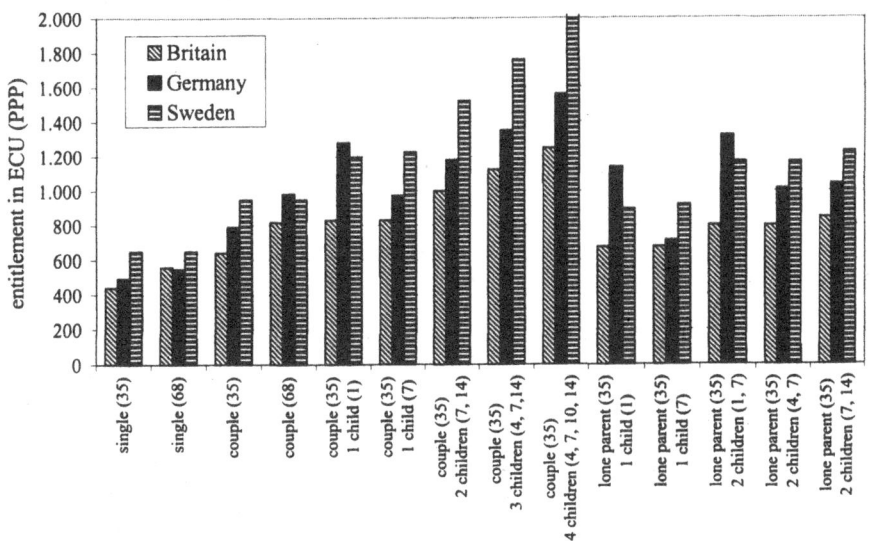

Figure 6.4 Level of social assistance entitlements for different family types, after housing costs (1995)

Note: Differences in purchasing power have been accounted for by using PPS conversion rates specific to private consumption provided by the European Union (Eurostat 1997: 107). Households are assumed to have their full rent paid by social assistance or related schemes.

Source: Own calculations based on institutional information presented above and LIS.

The overall ranking of social assistance levels appears to fit neatly to our expectations derived from the level of poverty in the three countries considered, with some reservation for Sweden. Britain is not only characterized by relatively low benefit rates, but also by high poverty rates, whereas Germany has higher benefit levels and lower poverty rates. For Sweden, the problems in measuring poverty do not allow an unambiguous judgment. However, absolute benefit levels are not sufficient for the evaluation of the adequacy of social assistance benefit levels, even if variation in purchasing power is taken into account. The absolute benefit levels do not offer any evidence on the relative income position of claimant households within the income dis-

134 At the Margins of the Welfare State

tribution of the country considered. The next section will explore this question in more detail.

Relationship of Social Assistance Levels to Relative Poverty Lines The poverty-alleviating power of social assistance benefits depends upon their relationship to a poverty line. For this purpose, the level of social assistance entitlements of these model households can be easily compared to the minimum income level as defined by a relative poverty line.

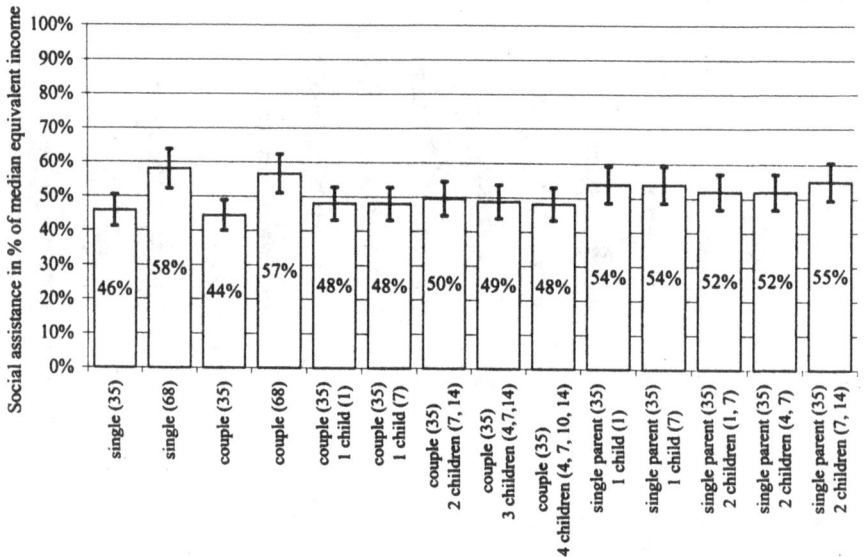

Figure 6.5 Level of social assistance entitlements as a proportion of median income, Britain 1995

Note: Median income calculated from LIS. Equivalence scale: head of household 1.0, other adults 0.5, children 0.3 ('modified OECD scale'). The lines at the top of the columns account for an error of 10 per cent in each direction.
Source: LIS, own calculations.

If poverty is defined as 50 per cent of median equivalence income, do minimum income benefits bring people out of poverty?[168] Which income level do

---

[168] Consistent with the data presented above, the calculations are based on a relative poverty line of 50% of median equivalence income; equivalence income of each model household is computed on the basis of the 'modified' OECD equivalence scale (see Chapter 2). The corresponding results for alternative equivalence scales can be found in Table 6.2 (p. 139). Whereas the model calculations presented above all referred to the year 1995 for reasons of

Adequacy 135

recipients of social assistance reach relative to the general income level in the society in which they live?

Figure 6.5 displays the level of social assistance entitlements after housing costs as a proportion of median income for Britain 1995, and illustrates the relationship of social assistance benefits after housing costs to the median income. This allows the evaluation of the question whether social assistance entitlements would bring the model households over a specific poverty line (50 per cent of median equivalent income being the most common measure of poverty, often supplemented by 40 and 60 per cent). Since the actual entitlement of households may vary depending to individual circumstances and divergent rent levels, the chart includes an error indicator that allows for a scope of 10 per cent in each direction.

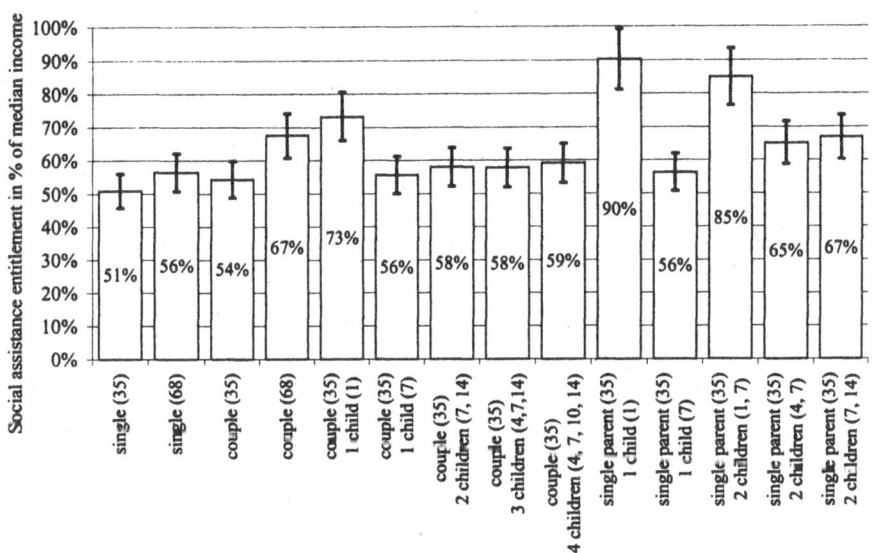

Figure 6.6 Level of social assistance entitlements in per cent of median income, Germany 1994

Note: See Figure 6.5.

Source: LIS, own calculations.

For the model households specified above, the British social assistance provides an income level of between 44 and 58 per cent of median income. Only the households of the elderly and single parents are brought above a

---

comparability, the German data in this section refer to 1994 because newer LIS data are not available.

poverty line of 50 per cent of median income, whereas childless working-age households and two-adult families with children have an income lower than the 50 per cent income standard, with the only exception of a two-parent family with two children exactly matching the 50 per cent level. None of these model households falls below the 40 per cent poverty line, though. Interestingly, the preferential treatment of the elderly and single parents exactly mirrors the liberal idea that the welfare state should comfort people whose earnings capacity is limited (by old age or caring responsibilities), while only providing a basic minimum income for less vulnerable groups.

For Germany 1994, social assistance entitlements provide an effective protection from poverty for each of the model households (Figure 6.6). The level of social assistance varies from 51 per cent of median income to 67 per cent of median income, or even to 90 per cent for families with young children receiving parent allowance.[169] The combination of parent allowance and social assistance offers a very generous level of support for families with young children, but their income would clearly exceed the poverty line even if they did not receive this additional benefit (corresponding household types with older children), yet their income position is relatively bad compared to the other family types. Relatively well-off are elderly couples, families with several children and single parents, whereas especially prime age single people and couples receive rather modest benefits, yet still above the poverty line.

Overall, the German social assistance scheme appears to provide for a fairly generous benefit level that would allow all model households to find their way out of poverty. Benefit levels are not particularly generous, so most model households reach an income level of shortly above 50 per cent of median equivalent income. As in the British situation, the elderly and single parents enjoy a more generous benefit level than prime-age households, and parents with small children receiving the parents' allowance will even reach a more comfortable income level well above the 60 per cent poverty line.

---

[169] Earlier calculations of the level of the German social assistance have described the level of social assistance as an income range between 40 and 60 per cent of average net incomes (Hauser and Hübinger, 1993a: 113; Hauser, 1995b: 18-19). On average, social assistance provided 48 per cent of average net incomes during the early 1990s (Hauser, 1995a: 7-8). A more recent study has gauged the level of the German social assistance benefits amounting to 56-71 per cent of average equivalent household income, depending on household size, in West Germany, and 48-59 per cent in East Germany (Andreß, 1999: 103, own calculations). The difference between these values and the level of social assistance calculated here can possibly be explained by the fact that these calculations have referred to the national mean rather than median income and the choice of the equivalence scale.

Adequacy 137

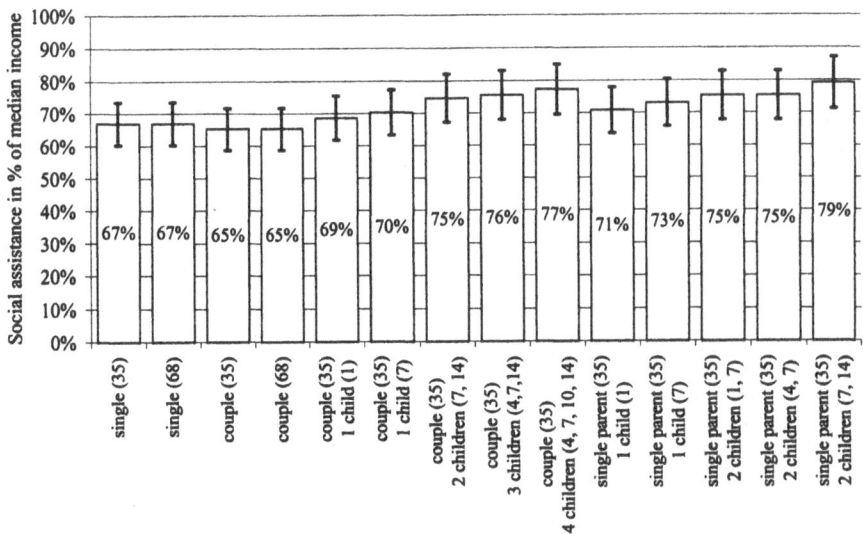

Figure 6.7 Level of social assistance entitlements as a proportion of median income, Sweden 1995

Note: See Figure 6.5 (p. 134).

Source: LIS, own calculations.

The Swedish social assistance offers a more uniform pattern of more generous benefits. Each of the model families is brought even above the 60 per cent poverty line, some even enjoy an income position of more than 70 per cent of median income. Moreover, there seems to be a strong relationship between the size of the household and the level of provision, the larger the family, the more generous are the benefits. This effect must be attributed to the fact that the institutional equivalence scales that are embodied in the social assistance scheme attach a larger weighting to children than does the modified OECD equivalence scale that has been used in Figure 6.7. Benefit rates may however be slightly overstated, since the rent level used in the calculations refers to the capital of Stockholm whereas the average rent level is somewhat lower. In addition, claimants are required to pay a higher share of housing costs other than the rent out of their standard benefit rate than in the other two countries (cf. Eardley et al., 1996a: 109-139). However, even if the rent level was markedly reduced, the Swedish social assistance scheme would still bring households over the poverty line. It should be remembered that the benefit rates shown in Figure 6.7 refer to the recommended benefit rates from which the actual benefit rates paid may considerably diverge. The recommended rates shown above can only provide some general guidance on the benefit level rather than an accurate reflection of reality.

Although even a sophisticated calculation of benefit packages based on model households cannot fully reflect the full complexity of social assistance payments, we can identify some patterns in the benefit structure in the three countries. Sweden provides for the most generous level of social assistance benefits which does not only lift the model households out of poverty, but offers a comfortable income position even above 60 per cent of median income. The second rank is taken by Germany which is characterized by a strong variation of benefit rates depending on the household circumstances, yet all model households are brought over the poverty line. Britain is the only country for which the model household approach testifies inadequacy. For some working-age households, benefits are not sufficient to bring them above the poverty line. Only the elderly, and to some degree also single parent households, can expect adequate social assistance benefits.

The Relevance of Equivalence Scales For the evaluation of adequacy of social assistance, one methodological issue has to be emphasized in particular at this point. The institutional equivalence scales embodied in the social assistance schemes do not only vary across countries, but do not necessarily conform with equivalence scales used in poverty research. The analysis of the effectiveness of poverty alleviation through social assistance must therefore pay attention to the relationship between equivalence scales used. Since equivalence scales attach a different weight to the needs of household members according to their age and the overall size of the household, measured adequacy of social assistance benefits necessarily will vary with the relationship between these scales. Figure 4.3 (p. 75) has demonstrated that equivalence scales used in poverty research deviate considerably from the institutional poverty lines.

Given that the choice of the equivalent scale influences poverty rates, we expect that they also have an effect on the measured adequacy of social assistance entitlements for the model household types. Table 6.2 shows the relation between the level of social assistance and the median income for selected household types in Britain, Germany and Sweden, using the three most common equivalent scales, the 'classical OECD scale' (E_{cl}), the 'modified OECD scale' (E_{mod}) and the 'square-root scale' (E_{sq}). The charts presented above (Figure 6.5, Figure 6.6, and Figure 6.7) were based on the 'modified OECD scale' (E_{mod}). Bold figures mark a below-poverty level of social assistance, i.e. social assistance benefits would not be able to alleviate poverty for these household types based on the equivalence scale used.

Adequacy 139

Table 6.2 Level of social assistance entitlement for different family types and poverty lines (as a percentage of median income)

Country and year	Germany 1994			Sweden 1995			UK 1995		
Equivalence scale	E_{cl}	E_{mod}	E_{sq}	E_{cl}	E_{mod}	E_{sq}	E_{cl}	E_{mod}	E_{sq}
Single person (35)	59	51	48	75	67	65	53	46	44
Single person (68)	65	56	53	75	67	65	66	58	55
Couple (35)	55	54	54	65	65	67	45	44	45
Couple (68)	69	67	67	65	65	67	58	56	57
Couple (35), child (1)	69	73	72	63	69	69	45	48	47
Couple (35), child (7)	52	56	54	64	70	71	45	48	47
Couple (35), 2 ch. (7, 14)	52	58	57	65	75	76	44	49	49
Couple (35), 3 ch. (4, 7, 14)	50	58	58	64	76	79	42	48	49
Couple (35), 4 ch. (4, 7, 10, 14)	50	59	61	63	77	83	40	48	50
Single parent (35), child (1)	90	90	78	69	71	63	54	54	47
Single parent (35), child (7)	56	56	49	71	73	65	54	54	47
Single parent (35), 2 ch. (1, 7)	79	85	74	68	76	68	48	52	45
Single parent (35), 2 ch. (4, 7)	60	65	57	68	76	68	48	52	45
Single parent (35), 2 ch. (7, 14)	62	67	58	71	79	71	51	55	48

Note: Families with children aged 1 are assumed to receive parent allowance in Germany. Shaded cells mark social assistance entitlements lower than a poverty line of 50 per cent of median equivalent income.

Source: LIS, own calculations.

A first glance at the distribution of shaded cells in the table demonstrates that the measured adequacy strongly varies with the equivalence scale chosen, but the effect is different for each country. Whereas the Swedish social assistance scheme does not let people's income fall below the social assistance level for any of the three equivalence scales, the picture is less coherent for the other two countries. The use of the square root equivalence scale (E_{sq}) would deem social assistance payments for all but three model families in Britain as inadequate, and also two of the German model families, whereas the other two scales would judge the level of social assistance as adequate to bring all German, and at least some of the British model families out of poverty. The application of the classical OECD (E_{cl}) scale results in a lower measured adequacy for larger households than the two other scales for all countries considered. The modified OECD scale (E_{mod}) and the square root scale (E_{sq}) provide relatively similar results, albeit with a slight systematic difference. Whereas the modified OECD scale attaches a slightly higher value to households with two adults than the square-root scale, this pattern is reversed for single parent households.[170]

---

[170] This pattern is due to the fact that the 'modified OECD scale' attaches a weight of 0.5 to the second (and further) adults in the household and 0.3 for children, whereas the 'square-root scale' judges every additional household member – adults and children – as increasing

The impact of these equivalence scales is not consistent across countries. If one attempts to mark the equivalence scale that provides the highest or lowest adequacy for each model family and country, the patterns markedly diverge. For example, whereas the highest level of measured adequacy of social assistance for single parents with one child in Britain is found by using the classical OECD equivalence scale, one would have to use the modified OECD scale in Germany and Sweden to obtain the maximum rate.

This methodological discussion has illustrated that the extent of the possible bias that originates from different equivalence scales in fact has a large impact on the empirical results. The following simulation of social assistance entitlements on the basis of the LIS data will therefore pay particular attention to these effects.

Limitations of the Model Family Approach As indicated above, the model family approach is not free from methodological problems. It keeps constant the needs level of the households in international comparison, but is necessarily limited to a small number of model households. Moreover, there is a trade-off between the exactness of the measurement and the representativity of results: the more exactly the needs of the model households are defined, the smaller is the share of the population covered. In addition, the family types used for these computations are not necessarily representative of recipients of social assistance. For example, larger families are not included at all in this and other studies, nor are families with several teenage children with typically higher needs than young children. Besides, the relative weight of family types within the recipient population varies across countries, so a summary measure of benefit levels across different household types is hardly interpretable (Eardley et al., 1996a: 129-131).[171]

Simulation of Social Assistance Entitlements

Whereas the use of model households has allowed to place the focus of the analysis of adequacy on a number of family types, its scope is necessarily limited on the set of pre-defined households. Another way of assessing the effectiveness of social assistance schemes is the simulation of social assistance entitlements on the basis of micro-data.[172] This simulation uses the

---

the household's need by a decreasing factor, starting at 0.41 ($\sqrt{2}$) for the second person in the household.

[171] Further limitations include the negligence of other income sources, such as income from employment and from other social security benefits, non-cash benefits (Eardley et al., 1996a: 109-129; Bradshaw, 1997; Krämer, 1997; 2000) and the treatment of one-off benefits.

[172] Imputation and simulation techniques have been increasingly used in social policy analysis in order to overcome limitations of the data or model policy reforms. Examples are

institutional information gathered in the previous sections to impute social assistance entitlements for each household in the sample. This approach allows us to complement the evidence from the model family approach by a more comprehensive evaluation of social assistance entitlements for the whole population.

The Luxembourg Income Study offers a rich basis for a simulation of social assistance entitlements, since it provides detailed information for each household in the sample. Thus, this approach circumvents some methodological problems present in the model family approach. The simulation reflects the actual life circumstances of households and does not require the – more or less arbitrary – definition of model families but represents 'real' families. The LIS micro-data also contain some information on actual housing costs that allow better estimates of housing costs than the rough estimates used in the model calculations above. Moreover, it also allows for variations in social structure across countries. Thus, the simulation of social assistance entitlements sketches a more realistic picture of the population than model calculations, yet it is not free from limitations. Due to the highly complex and incomplete information involved in the calculation of entitlements, the simulation of social assistance still has to operate with some rather crude estimates. Therefore, we expect to get a fairly detailed account of entitlements to social assistance, though it cannot fully mirror the actual situation.

The simulation of social assistance entitlements does not only isolate the dimension of adequacy from the dimensions of eligibility and take-up, but it also accounts for sampling and non-sampling errors in the data, at least to a certain degree. As the previous discussion in Chapter 4 has demonstrated, the use of survey data for the assessment of poverty and the effectiveness of social assistance is associated with a number of methodological problems that possibly bias measured poverty and the amount of social assistance received. For the measurement of adequacy, under-reporting of the amount of social assistance benefits has particularly fatal effects, since it leads to an underestimation of the actual level of provision. In addition, possible non-take-up adds to this problem and contributes to an even more marked underestimation of the adequacy of social assistance payments. These problems can be avoided by imputing the entitlement of social assistance for each household under the assumption that each household would receive the full amount of entitlement.

Andreß et al. (1995), Andreß (1999), Berntsen (1992), Rainwater and Smeeding (1998); Atkinson and Sutherland (1998), see also Harding (1996); and Bradshaw (1995).

142   *At the Margins of the Welfare State*

Methodology The simulation of social assistance entitlements on the basis of the LIS micro-data largely follows the methodology of the model calculations presented above. Using the information about the composition of the household and the age of its members, social assistance entitlements are calculated on the basis of the institutional regulations in each country. It is assumed that households do not have any income from employment or financial assets and do not receive any contributory social security benefits. For each household, social assistance entitlements are computed in the same way as in the model family approach, yet some additional explanations are necessary for each component of the benefit package.[173]

Since standard benefit rates have been uprated during the observation year in Britain and Germany, a weighted average of benefit rates has been used. Regional variations in the benefit rate could be considered for Germany (including East Germany), but not for Sweden. In the British case, the special rates for young people living on their own are neglected.

The simulation includes premiums for special needs for the elderly and single parents in Britain and Germany, as well as the British family premium.[174] All other premiums are not taken into account, since the information on life circumstances of the households available in the Luxembourg Income Study is not detailed enough to reflect entitlements in a satisfactory way. As for the model families, special premiums or income disregards for employed recipients of social assistance have not been considered for two reasons. First, the information on employment status in LIS does not allow us to monitor employment (and mobility in and out of employment) in enough detail to allow for a precise estimation of employment-related premiums and income disregards. Second, the inclusion of these benefits would also have required the inclusion of the British family credit, which would have gone far beyond the scope of this analysis. Since we focus on the adequacy of the minimum income level in the three countries, we can neglect special schemes for the working poor, since the combined income from employment and in-work benefits is supposed to provide for an income level that is slightly higher than for the non-working poor in order to not under-

---

[173] It is assumed that benefit units are equal to the households as defined in LIS.

[174] Indeed the social assistance legislation stipulated that no additions to cover special needs for the elderly and the disabled were payable in East Germany at this time, but pensions and unemployment benefits were automatically augmented to an equivalent lump sum amount (*Sozialzuschlag*) in order to provide a decent standard of living for these people without being formally dependent on social assistance. If the needs of the household were still higher than this amount, social assistance would step in. Since these regulations are very similar to those of West Germany, the simulation of social assistance entitlements for East Germany has not taken into account the Sozialzuschlag, but has calculated benefit entitlements as if the additions were payable according to the same rules as in West Germany.

mine work incentives. The calculation of the minimum income standards in social assistance can thus exclude special benefits for the employed. The estimation of one-off benefits follows the methodology of the family model approach. For housing costs, a more careful imputation could be made. However, the LIS data allowed to consider the actual housing costs only in the British case.[175] For Sweden, the relatively high Stockholm rent level used in the model calculations could be reduced for households living in more rural areas by 5 per cent.[176]

On the basis of these components, social assistance entitlements can be calculated for each household in the sample. We can also compute a simulated income distribution that assumes that each household has an income that is equal or higher than the minimum income level as stipulated in the social assistance regulations. Thus, the disposable income of households with an yearly income (before social assistance) of less than the social assistance level has been augmented to this minimum income level. Households with a higher income obviously do not have any entitlement to social assistance, so their actual disposable income remains unchanged. By this token, the simulation produces an income distribution that virtually cuts off the lower part of the income distribution.

Because of the complexity of social assistance regulations, a simulation can hardly ever reflect the exact social assistance entitlement of an individual household. The main sources for errors are different household definitions in the surveys and by the social assistance regulations, and payments that closely relate to the circumstances of an individual household. Generally speaking, the more discretionary the social assistance payments, the less exact are estimates of social assistance. By the same token, estimates are not able to exactly reflect social assistance payments (or the refusal of payments) if the underlying decisions relate to individual characteristics or behaviour that is not monitored in the LIS data (e.g. health problems or refused payments in the case of able-bodied claimants refusing to work).

Simulated Social Assistance Entitlements and the Level of Poverty The simulation of social assistance entitlements also allows to calculate poverty rates. This evaluation can show whether the minimum income standard provided by social assistance schemes is high enough as to alleviate poverty. Would there still be poverty if each household received a full social assistance entitlement? To be sure, the simulated results do not monitor the ade-

---

[175] Negative amounts of housing expenditure have been set to zero (N=2). The actual housing cost has been reduced by one fifth to account for the fact that expenditure for fuel etc. is not covered by housing benefit, but payable out of income support (CPAG, 1998: 242-262).

[176] Households are defined as living in rural areas if they do not live in Stockholm, Gothenburg, Malmö or any other big city as defined by LIS.

quacy of social assistance benefits that have actually been paid to claimants, but only reflect the normative level of social assistance according to the institutional rules stipulated by the legislatures. In other words, the simulation does not evaluate the social assistance scheme as it is, but as it ought to be according to its own standards. The adequacy of social assistance benefits can hardly be evaluated from actual poverty rates as such because these data may be biased due to the impact of ineffectiveness in the dimensions of eligibility and take-up, and also by methodological problems. By simulating the amount of social assistance that each household would receive according to the social assistance regulations of each country, we can isolate the adequacy of social assistance schemes from intervening effects. The simulation thus predominantly focuses on correct identification of social assistance entitlements by controlling for effects caused by the ineffectiveness of social assistance schemes in the dimensions of eligibility and take-up, and methodological problems associated with the surveys.

The following sections will present poverty rates for an income distribution with simulated social assistance entitlements. Poverty rates are calculated as a percentage of median equivalent income, as for the original data. The median income has been calculated from the original data, not from the simulated income distribution, so poverty lines are kept at the same nominal level in the comparison of original and simulated poverty rates.[177]

Figure 6.8 presents poverty rates for the original and the simulated income distribution in each of the three countries. The shading of the columns depicts different intensities of poverty (see Figure 2.1, p. 15).

The simulation demonstrates that if all households in the sample received the exact amount of social assistance entitlements as stipulated in the national social assistance regulations, poverty would be markedly reduced or even virtually eliminated. Although there are some methodological limitations, the simulated social assistance entitlements should provide a good approximation of the minimum income level people would receive according to the legislature in each country.

The most striking effect of the simulation of social assistance entitlements is that both extreme and severe poverty would be practically wiped out in each of the three countries. Moderate poverty is also markedly reduced in Britain and Germany, while the near poverty bracket is fairly stable. The simulation of the Swedish social assistance entitlements has also

---

[177] One could argue that poverty lines should be calculated from the simulated data itself in order to take into account the changes in the income distribution, and to follow more closely the logic of a relative definition of poverty asserting that poverty always should refer to the income level in the respective society. However, the primary purpose of this simulation is not the evaluation of the income position of the poor population as such, but the assessment of adequacy of minimum income benefits in the current setting.

eradicated moderate poverty, and even almost eliminated the near poverty bracket. Overall, poverty rates at the 50 per cent level would be reduced to some 2 per cent both in Germany and Britain. The Swedish example is even more notable: poverty is virtually eradicated at the 50 per cent level, and sharply reduced at the 60 per cent level, as could be expected from the model family calculations.

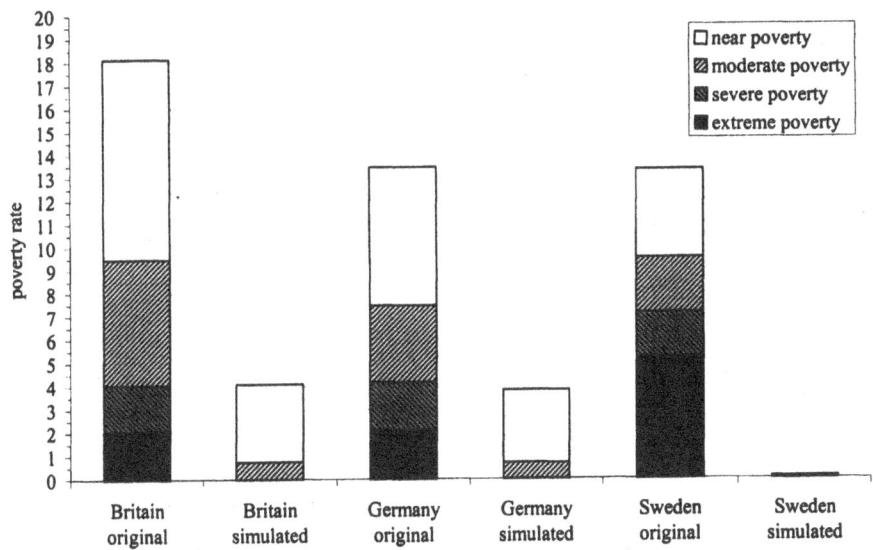

Figure 6.8 Poverty rates based on original and simulated social assistance benefits

Source: LIS; own calculations.

Both in Britain and Germany, simulated social assistance entitlements could not fully alleviate moderate poverty, but the more severe forms of poverty below the 40 per cent poverty line are virtually eradicated. At the 60 per cent level, the simulation of social assistance entitlements did have an effect, yet a considerable amount of poverty persists. Generally speaking, the poverty lines of 40 and 60 per cent of median equivalent household income seem to delimit the scattered social assistance entitlement levels quite well – higher or lower social assistance levels appear to be fairly rare.

Table 6.3 Poverty rates for an income distribution with simulated social assistance entitlements

	Germany 1994			Sweden 1995			United Kingdom 1995		
	E_{cl}	E_{mod}	E_{sq}	E_{cl}	E_{mod}	E_{sq}	E_{cl}	E_{mod}	E_{sq}
'Real World': Original (non-simulated) income distribution									
60%	12.1	13.5	14.1	11.9	13.3	14.2	17.2	18.1	19.8
50%	7.2	7.5	8.3	8.6	9.5	9.9	9.6	9.5	10.8
40%	3.8	4.2	4.9	6.3	7.1	7.3	4.3	4.1	4.5
Simulation: Income distribution with simulated social assistance entitlements									
60%	8.3	8.2	8.9	1.5	0.5	0.8	13.2	10.7	13.0
50%	2.5	2.0	4.2	0.3	0.0	0.1	4.3	2.1	2.9
40%	0.5	0.2	0.5	0.0	0.0	0.0	0.7	0.1	0.2
Difference between original and simulated poverty rates (in percentage points)									
60%	-3.9	-5.3	-5.2	-10.4	-12.8	-13.3	-4.0	-7.5	-6.8
50%	-4.7	-5.5	-4.1	-8.4	-9.5	-9.8	-5.2	-7.4	-7.9
40%	-3.3	-4.0	-4.4	-6.3	-7.1	-7.3	-3.7	-3.9	-4.4
Difference between original and simulated poverty rates (in percent)									
60%	-32%	-39%	-37%	-87%	-96%	-94%	-23%	-41%	-34%
50%	-66%	-74%	-49%	-97%	-100%	-99%	-55%	-78%	-73%
40%	-88%	-96%	-90%	-100%	-100%	-100%	-85%	-97%	-96%
N	5,829			16,212			6,750		

Note: Poverty lines are calculated from the original income distribution.

Source: LIS, own calculations.

The poverty rates from the simulated data largely support the evidence from the model family approach. The level of social assistance benefits is high enough as to alleviate poverty almost completely, at least for the more severe forms of poverty. The difference between the original and the simulated data is astonishingly high. Poverty rates at the 50 per cent level have been lowered from depressed from 9.5 per cent in Britain and 7.5 per cent in Germany to some 2 per cent in both countries. The effect of the simulation is thus a reduction of between 7.4 and 5.5 percentage points, that is a reduction by some three quarters of the original level. In Sweden, poverty is reduced at the 50 per cent level from 9.5 per cent to zero.

Again, the results strongly vary with the choice of the equivalence scale. Table 6.3 shows the results for three equivalence scales and demonstrates that results are strongly dependent on the equivalence scale used, yet the general direction is the same. This pattern can possibly be explained by the variation of institutional equivalence scales within the social assistance schemes. Since the classical OECD scale attaches a high weight to additional household members, it tends to produce higher poverty rates for large families than the other two equivalence scales. The British social assistance scheme, however, grants relatively modest benefits to additional household members as compared to Germany and Sweden (see Figure 6.3, p. 118). Given the marked difference in benefit levels produced by the model family approach, it is remarkable that the simulation of social assistance entitlements produces fairly similar results for these two countries in Figure 6.8. This pattern is only true for the modified OECD equivalence scale (E_{mod}), however. Both other equivalence scales show a different pattern, pointing in a different direction. On the basis of the classical OECD scale (E_{cl}), simulated poverty rates at the 50 per cent level are higher in Britain than in Germany (4.3 and 2.5 per cent respectively), whereas the square root scale (E_{sq}) almost exactly reverses this pattern (2.9 and 4.2 per cent respectively). This example again illustrates fairly well the significance of equivalence scales for the evaluation of the effectiveness of social assistance schemes.

Simulated Social Assistance Entitlements and the Structure of Poverty

The previous section has demonstrated that poverty could be considerably reduced if every household received its full entitlement to social assistance. Social assistance schemes appear to be able to alleviate poverty in a fairly complete way, at least for the more severe forms of poverty. However, the evidence from the model family approach has also shown that the level of social assistance benefits markedly varies across household types. In addition, the interaction of equivalence scales was also found to have a major impact on measured adequacy. If some groups of the population can only expect a relatively low level of social assistance, their poverty risks will be higher than for other groups.

In many industrialized countries, a high poverty risk is in particular associated with the following groups of the population: single parents, especially if they have young children; families with children, especially large families; and the elderly, especially single elderly women. For some of these groups, social assistance levels are relatively low in some countries, as for example for working-age single people without children and two-parent families in Britain. Other groups can rather expect a relatively high level of social assistance, as for example single parents with young children in Germany, or the elderly in Britain. The evidence from this analysis can now be used to assess benefit adequacy for specific risk groups of the population. A comparison of poverty rates based on actual and simulated social assistance entitlements can show whether the high poverty risk of this group is a consequence of an insufficient level of social assistance or whether this effect is rather caused by ineffectiveness of social assistance in the dimension of universality or take-up, or by methodological problems in the measurement of poverty.

Five groups have been chosen for this purpose and are defined as follows:

1. single parents: households with one adult and one or more children under 18 years
2. two-parent families: two adults in a household with children under 18 years
3. large families: two parent families with at least 3 children
4. elderly: households whose head is 65 or older
5. single elderly women: single elderly women (65 or older) living on their own.

The following paragraphs will compare original and simulated poverty risks for these five groups in order to test the robustness of the benefit levels assumed in the discussion of the model households above. The difference between the original and simulated poverty rates can be accounted to a combination of two factors, as discussed above. On the one hand, social assistance may not reach the poor because of lacking eligibility or non-take-up, but on the other hand, these discrepancies could also be caused by sampling and non-sampling errors in the data.

Single Parent Families In most industrial countries, single parent families run a relatively high risk of being poor (e.g. Hauser, 1987; Hauser and Fischer, 1990; Millar, 1989). Their earnings capacity is limited because of their child care obligations, since both work and family responsibilities cannot be shared between two partners (cf. Bradshaw and Björnberg, 1997; S. Duncan and Edwards, 1997; Ford and Millar, 1998). In countries with a poor provision of child care facilities, the poverty risk of single parents tends to be particularly high (Gornick et al., 1997; Ford, 1998; Scheiwe, 1994).

Based on the calculation of social assistance entitlements for model households above, we would assume that the level of provision for single parent families is relatively generous in Sweden and just about adequate in Britain.[178] Due to the special treatment of the parent allowance, the German case is somewhat ambiguous, providing a very comfortable level for recipients of this allowance, and a less generous but still adequate provision for those without any entitlement.[179] The British benefit level for single parents is supposed to be adequate, but it is still lower than the German level.

---

[178] In this study, single parent families have been defined as households with one adult living together with one or more children under 18 years. With this definition, measured poverty risks for single parents tend to be higher than in studies that identify single parents on the basis of their marital status (that possibly include incomes of cohabiting partners).

[179] It would have been interesting to evaluate single parents with children under 3 years separately in order to assess the impact of the German parent allowance, but the small number of cases in this group (N=23 for Germany) has rendered this impossible.

Adequacy 149

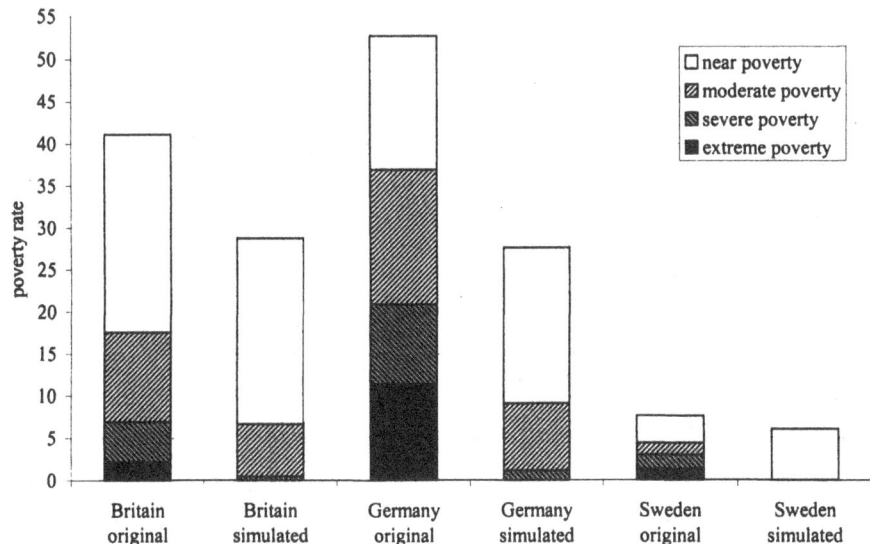

Figure 6.9 Poverty rates for single parents based on actual and simulated social assistance benefits

Note: Size of subsample: Britain: N=439; Germany: N=166; Sweden: N=557.

Source: LIS; own calculations.

When poverty rates are calculated on the basis of the simulated social assistance entitlements, poverty among single parents radically diminishes. The simulated income distribution leads to the complete eradication of poverty at the 50 per cent level in Sweden, but the majority of poor single parent households are not brought out of the near poverty bracket, although the evidence from the model family approach would have suggested so. For Germany and Britain, moderate and even some severe poverty persist, even though the evidence from the family model approach had implied that single parent families would reach a relatively comfortable income position well above the 50 per cent poverty line. The German performance is even slightly worse than the British one, in spite of the contradictory evidence from the model family approach.

Two-parent Families with Children Although two-parent families can share responsibilities for children, they have a relatively high poverty risk in many countries (cf. Smeeding et al., 1999; Cornia and Danziger, 1997; Rainwater, 1999). Whereas the income position of the elderly has been constantly improving, families with children do worse in many countries. Children increase the needs of the households while at the same time limiting the earning capacity of their parents. In addition, mass unemployment severely worsened the income position of many families with children, while other groups of the population, such as the elderly, are less exposed to these risks. Although two-parent families are better equipped to deal with these strains rather than single parent families, they still face a relatively high poverty risk in many countries.

The model calculations presented above would suggest that families with children enjoy the relatively best income position in Sweden, where the levels of minimum income benefits are so high as to catapult these families even out of the near-poverty bracket. In Germany, this family type is expected to be brought at least over the 50 per cent poverty line, whereas the British minimum income level leaves two-parent families in moderate poverty, yet the more severe forms of poverty should also be prevented.

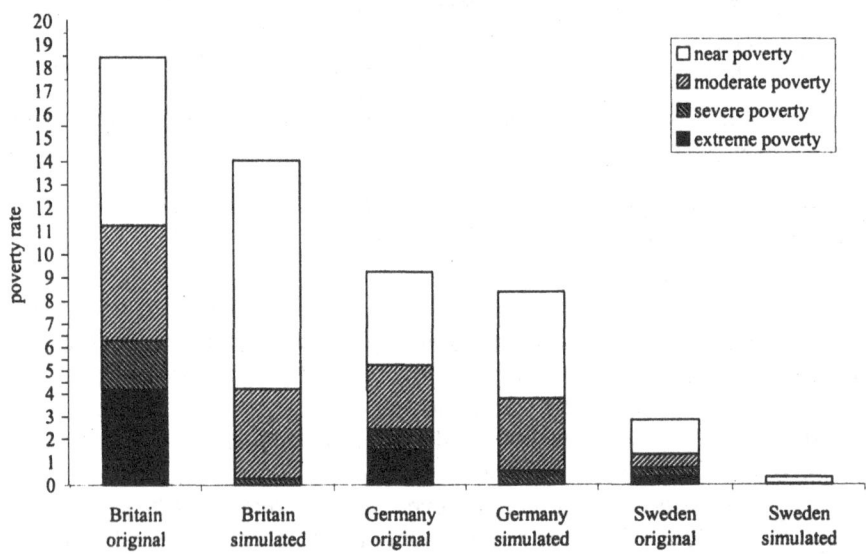

Figure 6.10 Poverty rates for two-parent families with children based on actual and simulated social assistance benefits

Note: Size of subsample: Britain: N=1,660; Germany: N=1,593; Sweden: N=9,425.

Source: LIS; own calculations.

For families with children, an interesting pattern emerges from the comparison of poverty rates based on original and simulated social assistance entitlements. Whereas the German poverty rates remain virtually unchanged both at the 50 and the 60 per cent level when moving from the actual to the

Adequacy 151

simulated data (yet with a more marked change for the lower poverty lines), poverty is almost eradicated in Sweden. This assessment fits well to the results from the model household approach that unveiled that Sweden provided a comparably generous benefit levels to two-parent families with children, whereas the other two countries offer rather meagre benefits compared to the other household types. For Britain, poverty rates based on the simulated income distribution are roughly comparable to the German ones, although the evidence based on the model families approach would have suggested that the British performance is markedly weaker than the German one. Still, both in Germany and Britain, simulated poverty rates of two-parent families with children are higher than the overall poverty rates. Social assistance benefits are thus not high enough to prevent this household type from an increased poverty risk.

Two-parent Families with Three and More Children If two-parent families with children in general are already prone to be poor, the poverty risk of large families should be even higher. In these families, increased need usually parallels even stronger child care obligations that often require that one partner is not in paid work at all or only works part-time.

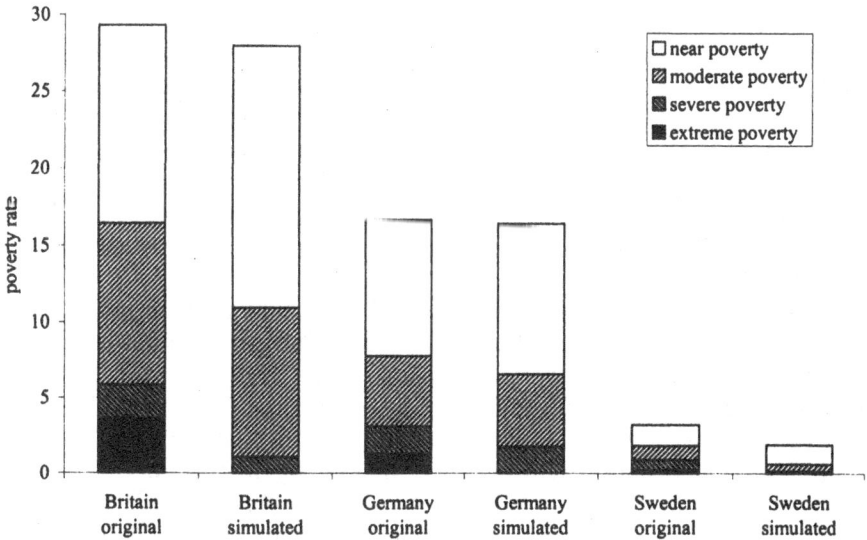

Figure 6.11 Poverty rates for two-parent families with three or more children based on actual and simulated social assistance benefits

Note: Size of subsample: Britain: N=346; Germany: N=228; Sweden: N=801.
Source: LIS; own calculations.

The evidence from the model family approach suggests that the level of protection is highest in Sweden and lowest in Britain, as for two-parent families with children in general. Interestingly, both Germany and Sweden grant slightly higher benefits to larger families whereas the benefit level in Britain is relatively stable when using the modified OECD equivalence scale, while benefit levels for large families are even relatively lower when using the square root equivalence scale (E_{sq}) (see Table 6.2, p. 139).

For two-parent families with three and more children in Sweden, the already low poverty risk is further reduced in the simulated income distribution to less than 1 per cent at the 50 per cent level. In Germany, simulated poverty rates are considerably higher, the simulated social assistance benefits leave 6.5 per cent of large families in poverty in Germany. As expected from the results of the model family approach, large families do indeed face a relatively high poverty risk in Britain; one in nine families is poor on the basis of the simulated social assistance benefits, yet this poverty rate is markedly smaller than in the original data. Both the British and the German social assistance schemes do not offer a sufficient minimum income level to large families, so many families would still be poor even under the simulated data. In contrast, the Swedish social assistance scheme can protect large families effectively from poverty.

The Elderly Although the income position of the elderly has considerably improved during the last decades in many countries, inequality among the elderly is still high, and some subgroups still face a very poor income position (Hedström and Ringen, 1990; Whiteford and Kennedy, 1995). In addition, the elderly tend to have strong reservations against claiming social assistance and other means-tested benefits, so it is interesting to see whether their poverty level markedly changes when their social assistance entitlements are simulated.

Both the British and the German social assistance scheme grant benefit additions to the elderly that should make their income position more comfortable than their prime-age counterparts.[180] The evidence from the model households presented above suggests that the income level of the elderly is very comfortable in Sweden, although curiously not as good as for the other family types with children. In contrast, the elderly in Britain enjoy a relatively good income level compared to younger families, but still much lower than in Sweden. For Germany, the evidence is ambiguous. Whereas the income position of single people is slightly worse than for their British counterparts, elderly couples are even better off than in Sweden.

---

[180] Similar evidence was not available for Sweden, but it may well be that some municipalities grant similar premiums.

Adequacy 153

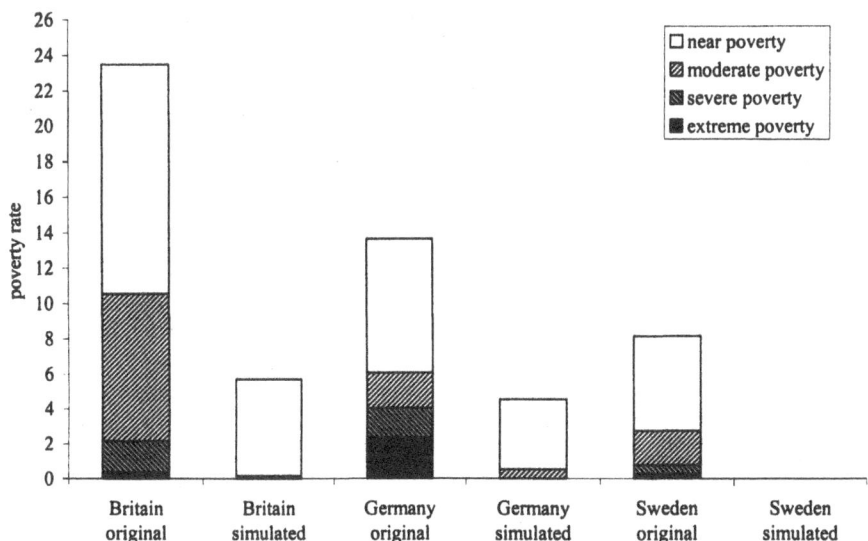

Figure 6.12 Poverty rates for the elderly based on actual and simulated social assistance benefits

Note: Size of subsample: Britain: N=1,771; Germany: N=1,095; Sweden: N=4,478.

In all three countries, the simulation of social assistance benefits produces a radical reduction of poverty rates for the elderly. Poverty at the 50 per cent level is virtually eradicated in all countries, and in Sweden also at the 60 per cent level. Whereas more than 6 per cent of the elderly in Germany are considered as poor according to the original data (50 per cent level), the simulated results suggests a poverty rate of less than 1 per cent with a complete elimination of severe and extreme poverty, and a reduction of the proportion of people living in the near-poverty bracket by more than half. The British pattern is very similar, with a slightly higher poverty rate at the 60 per cent level, but moderate poverty is virtually eliminated.

Single Elderly Women Whereas the elderly in general enjoy a relatively comfortable income position, single elderly women still run a high poverty risk (cf. Siegenthaler, 1996; Stapf, 1997; Rake, 1999).

Many single elderly women have had unstable employment histories and/or low earnings and could thus not accumulate abundant pension rights, especially in countries where pensions are closely linked to individual employment careers. Although pensions are not the only source of income for many elderly households because of occupational and private pensions, or other capital income, many single elderly women do not dispose of these assets to a sufficient degree (cf. Behrendt, 2000b). Depending on their marital status, single elderly women may also draw a considerable share of their total income from survivor's pensions and, if they are divorced, from pension rights of their former husband in some countries. Still, their income often is not sufficient as to guarantee a decent standard of living.

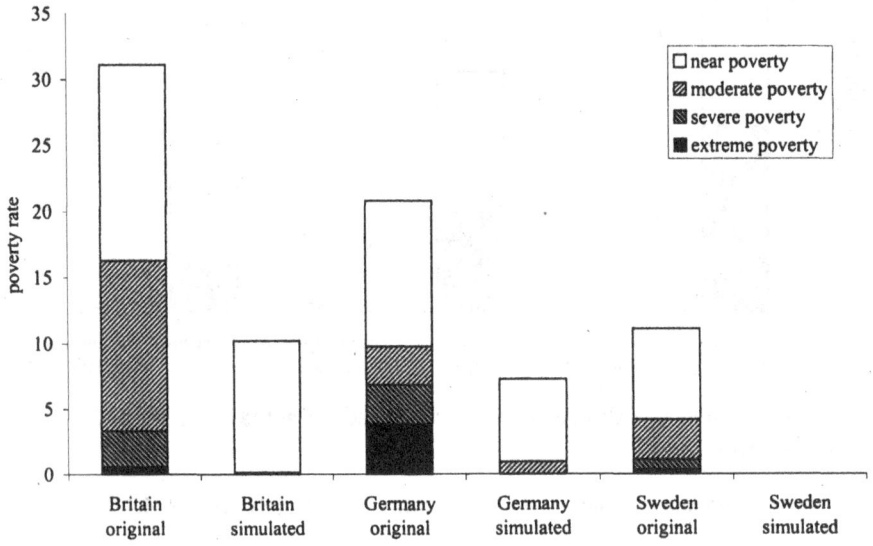

Figure 6.13 Poverty rates for single elderly women based on actual and simulated social assistance benefits

Note: Size of subsample: Britain: N=638; Germany: N=424; Sweden: N=1,697.

Social assistance entitlements for single persons are again highest in Sweden, and markedly lower in Britain and in Germany. Figure 6.13 shows the actual and simulated poverty rates of single elderly women.

Not surprisingly, poverty is again completely eliminated in Sweden, as for the elderly in general. In Britain, poverty has been radically eliminated at the 50 per cent level, but the near poverty bracket still includes more than one in ten single elderly women. In Germany, the poverty risk at the near poverty-level is slightly lower than in Britain, yet moderate poverty still persists at a very low level of 1 per cent. Overall, social assistance appears to provide a fairly effective level of provision for single elderly women that would almost completely eradicate poverty for this groups in each of the countries considered.

Adequacy 155

Adequacy and the Effectiveness of Social Assistance Schemes

The discussion of the adequacy of social assistance benefits in this chapter has shown that social assistance schemes by and large provide an adequate benefit level that would allow most claimants to enjoy a decent standard of living. Only a small minority of claimants would still live in poverty, even for subgroups of the populations with a high poverty risk in the original data. The results from the model family approach have shown that social assistance benefits are generous enough to almost completely eradicate poverty for all model families considered. Only Britain stands out with a benefit level below the 50 per cent poverty line for many family types according to our calculations, whereas Germany and Sweden provide an adequate standard of living in nominal terms. In fact, the simulation of social assistance benefit levels has largely confirmed that minimum income levels are in fact generous enough as to almost eliminate poverty in each of the selected countries, although with some flaws. Whereas the social assistance level in Sweden would be high enough to bring most households even out of near poverty, Britain and Germany are less successful. However, both countries succeeded at radically reducing poverty at the 50 per cent level for most households, although a small majority remains in severe poverty. Very good results have been achieved for the elderly, including single elderly women. Social assistance benefits are generous enough as to almost completely alleviate poverty for these groups. For prime-age households with children, the simulation of social assistance entitlements was able to markedly reduce poverty, yet poverty is still not completely eradicated in Britain and Germany. Notably families with three children and more face a substantial poverty risk in Germany and Britain even on the basis of the simulated data. Still, the simulation of social assistance benefit levels has considerably reduced their poverty rates.

According to these results, the evaluation of social assistance benefit levels leads to a fairly optimistic conclusion in respect to the adequacy of social assistance. In every one of the three countries – with some reservations for Britain and Germany – social assistance schemes are fairly effective in the dimension of adequacy. It appears that the ineffectiveness of social assistance schemes – as indicated by the persistence of poverty – is mainly caused by problems in the dimensions of eligibility and take-up.

This optimistic evaluation of social assistance schemes has to be qualified and put into a broader context, again considering the underlying methodological assumptions of this book. These assumptions in both the model family and the simulation approach necessarily limit the conclusions to be drawn from these data. In particular, it was not possible to treat premiums for special needs, one-off benefits and housing benefits in a way that would unambiguously reflect the adequacy of social assistance entitlements.

The Swedish case requires a special discussion. Sweden is the country with the highest benefit rates among the three countries, and the Swedish social assistance scheme provides a relatively generous standard of living. It has to be emphasized, however, that the simulation could only consider the recommended benefit rates for Sweden, whereas the benefits actually paid by the municipalities may in fact be markedly higher or lower. In addition, the strict means-tests set a high threshold for entering the social assistance scheme, and this may contribute to the fact that a low proportion of people that are deemed eligible for social assistance based on their disposable income actually claim social assistance. This point will be discussed in a more detailed way in the following chapter.

Nevertheless, the discussion of social assistance benefit standards in this chapter has shown that inadequacy of social assistance benefits contributes only a small share to the overall ineffectiveness of social assistance benefits. In other words, if the social assistance scheme in each country would work as it is supposed to do according to the social assistance regulations, poverty could be markedly reduced or even eliminated.

Chapter 7

Do Social Assistance Schemes Encourage Take-up?

Even if social assistance schemes provide benefits for the whole population living in a country, and even if the level of benefits guarantees a decent standard of living, poverty may still occur if social assistance benefits are not claimed by those who are entitled to receive them. The dimension of take-up thus constitutes the third and last precondition of an effective alleviation of poverty.
Unlike for the first two dimensions, eligibility and adequacy, public policies only have a limited influence on the question of take-up, as the process of claiming cannot entirely be controlled by the state. Ultimately, the question of take-up is largely governed by individual actions on the part of potential claimants, but individual perceptions and behaviour are strongly influenced by public policies. There is a broad array of possible causes of non-take-up that relate to a direct or indirect impact of public policies onto non-take-up. In order to disentangle these effects of public policies on the claiming process, we can distinguish demand side and supply side factors (Corden, 1995). Whereas demand side factors predominantly refer to people's perceptions and behaviour, supply side factors relate to programme structures and administrative processes. Public policies have an only indirect effect on demand side factors, but their impact on supply-side factors is more obvious. The following discussion of the impact of the institutional impact on non-take-up will therefore mainly focus on the supply-side effects of public policies on take-up, although there is close interaction with demand side factors.

Social Assistance Schemes and the Causes of Non-take-up

Possible Causes of Non-take-up

Following Deacon and Bradshaw (1983), the reasons for non-take up can be classified into three broad categories. First, people may not be aware of benefits available and their entitlement to these benefits (ignorance). Second, claimants may fear stigmatization when claiming benefits (stigma). Finally, social assistance regulations and the claiming process may be fashioned in a way that hampers a full take-up of benefits (complexity). Every one of these three factors touches upon the relation between claimants and administration. The reasons of non-take-up are thus not only to be searched at the client level, but also at the administrative level (cf. van Oorschot, 1998).

Knowledge and Information The knowledge about a benefit certainly poses an essential precondition to take-up. A necessary condition for claiming benefits is certainly the information that a benefit is existent at all. In addition, people have to be aware of the eligibility conditions, in other words, they must come to believe that they may be eligible for this benefit and that this benefit can meet their needs (cf. Kerr, 1982; van Oorschot, 1995: 42-45; Corden, 1995: 25-32). Knowledge about the benefits available and their eligibility conditions is thus an essential precondition for a full take-up of benefits. Public policies can encourage take-up by actively disseminating information among the population, as well as through more focused measures that actively encourage potential claimants to apply for the benefits they are entitled for.

Stigmatization The second bundle of possible causes is often summarized as stigmatization. This term usually describes a two-sided process, entailing both the 'labelling' as welfare recipient by others and the person's own low self-esteem because of the inability to secure one's living. Moreover, people perceive themselves (or are perceived by others) as being inferior or useless for society, because they receive benefits but they are unable to reciprocate this grant (cf. Simmel, 1908; Deacon and Bradshaw, 1983).

Means-tested benefits tend to be perceived as stigmatizing for two reasons. On the one hand, the receipt of benefit is usually not contingent upon contributions and is therefore often perceived as charity rather than being 'earned' by previous contributions. On the other hand, the procedure of means-testing is perceived as degrading or humiliating, since people have to prove that they are unable to support themselves by their own means in order to qualify for this benefit. Institutional arrangements and the programme structure may influence processes of stigmatization in a positive or in a negative direction. Stigmatization may be intensified by regulations that make the receipt of social assistance benefits visible to others and subject to social control.

The dimension of stigmatization is closely associated with the knowledge of claimants. There is some evidence that ill-informed claimants tend to be more concerned about stigmatization than claimants who actually know the basic regulations of social assistance (cf. Bujard and Lange, 1978b: 142-144). However, even when being told about their entitlement to social assistance, a considerable proportion of claimants still hesitate to submit a claim (cf. Taylor-Gooby, 1974, cited in van Oorschot, 1995: 39).

Complexity of the Claiming Process The third bundle of possible reasons for non-take-up relates to the claiming process itself.[181] People may face a broad variety of difficulties when claiming social assistance. First, the claiming process requires some effort that may deter people from claiming (Deacon and Bradshaw, 1983: 136). This problem can be well conceptualized in terms of (not necessarily monetary) costs associated with the claiming process (Coleman, 1982; Atkinson, 1989 [1984]). These costs may occur in terms of time, social prestige, individual freedom, and, although this sounds paradoxical, even money. Temporal costs of claiming benefits include the time necessary to submit a claim and to renew this claim in due course, if necessary (gaining knowledge about eligibility and entitlement conditions, filling in forms, spending time in the social welfare office, etc.). The procedure of the means-test may be perceived as particularly humiliating, since claimants have to uncover not only their economic resources, but also their social circumstances. They have to demonstrate that they are unable to support themselves and thus admit personal failure. In addition, the social assistance office may require some measures that restrict individual freedom. Claimants may be obliged to comply with work obligations, move into a cheaper flat, or seek to obtain support for their children from a former spouse. Some potential claimants may also consider the fact that they have to spend a lot of time at the social assistance office as a undue restriction of their personal freedom. Finally, the pecuniary cost of claiming may occur in terms of money spent for transport to the social welfare office etc. or, in some cases, in earned income forgone while spending time in the social assistance office. These costs of claiming reduce the value of the claimed benefit. By this token, non-claimants are not necessarily acting irrationally, although they could be better off in money terms (cf. Moffitt, 1983: 1023). If claimants behave as rational actors, they balance the pecuniary and non-

---

[181] For a more general discussion on the relationship between poverty and administrative practices, cf. Lipsky (1979; 1980).

pecuniary cost of claiming with the expected amount of benefit. Non-take-up will occur if these costs are higher than the anticipated return.[182] Whereas these costs of claiming can be deemed as to some extent functional because they deter unjustified claims or unavoidable because of temporal delays in claiming, very high costs of claiming can be considered as a failure of social assistance schemes, as the general mandate of the social assistance scheme is not fulfilled (cf. Kayser and Frick, 2000: 3-4).

Secondly, difficulties can occur if claimants are unable to comply with administrative requirements, e.g. if they do not succeed in obtaining or filling in the necessary forms, or in bringing the necessary documents to prove their need. Some groups of claimants may face particular difficulties in the claiming process because of a lack of some basic abilities necessary in the claiming process, if the administration is unable to deal with these difficulties in a satisfactory way. Barriers to claiming are for example information and application forms that require elaborate reading and writing abilities. Moreover, problems of communication between claimants and social welfare officers may add to these problems (van Oorschot, 1995: 49). These problems may be overcome by simplifying the claim process or by offering help through the social assistance officers themselves or charities, advice bureaus, claimants' organizations or others.

Third, non-take-up of benefits may be 'produced' by the administration itself by not granting benefits to claimants in spite of their entitlement (cf. Rowlingson and Whyley, 1998). This type of non-take-up may either affect the entire amount of benefit or only parts of it. Partial non-take-up in particular point to deficiencies in the administrative processing of cases, at least under the assumption that claimants receive sufficient information and support from the part of the administration (cf. Hartmann, 1981). The empirical evidence on partial non-take-up is sparse, but we can assume that this problem is particularly relevant for (possibly discretionary) payments to meet special needs and one-off needs, and discretionary benefits in general (cf. Berthoud, 1983; Ringeling, 1981).

In particular partial non-take-up tends to be nurtured by a discretionary organization of one-off benefits. Many people may hesitate to claim this kind of benefit if it is associated with additional administrative hassle, possibly intruding questions on the part of the social assistance officer as to whether the claimant actually needs the particular item he or she has applied for, especially if the benefit claimed for is relatively inexpensive (cf. Lipsky,

---

[182] From the perspective of the administration, high claiming costs can be functional in the sense that the non-poor are effectively deterred from entering the claiming process: '[I]n the presence of imperfect targeting, take-up costs can deter the non-poor from disguising themselves as poor and from claiming state support. They can thus provide a self-selection mechanism that can enhance the efficiency of state support.' (Duclos, 1995: 392).

1991). In this case, many claimants may prefer to live on a very low income rather than make full use of their legal entitlement. One-off benefits are typically subject to creaming effects, so benefits tend to be claimed by articulate and active people, whereas people with poorer communicative abilities or other problems often do not fully take up their entitlement. Elderly claimants appear to forego parts of their entitlement more often than younger claimants (cf. Bujard and Lange, 1978b: 40-44).

Temporal Patterns of Non-take-up

Many researchers have regarded the problem of non-take-up as a stable phenomenon. However, there is some evidence that a considerable portion of non-take-up observed is actually not of a permanent nature (cf. Hartmann, 1985; Corden and Craig, 1991).[183] Earlier research on the take-up of the British supplementary benefit has suggested that non-take-up often occurs for a limited time period, as there is considerable fluctuation that should be accounted for. Similar evidence exists for Germany. Bujard and Lange (1978b) have reported that an earlier study in Cologne has found that more than one in two elderly claimants of social assistance that would have been entitled to social assistance by the age of 65 did not receive benefits until much later; on average, temporal non-take-up amounted to more than five years (Bujard and Lange, 1978b: 139-40).

From a claimant perspective, frictional non-take-up may possibly be much less serious than permanent non-take-up, since claimants may possess some financial assets that can be liquidated. Delayed take-up may occur for different reasons. On the one hand, claimants may hesitate to claim if they believe that the lack of income will occur only for a short time or if they initially assume that they can make ends meet without having to claim benefits. On the other hand, delays may be caused by administrative ineffectiveness in determining and conferring payments. The empirical evidence on different time patterns of non-take-up is sparse, recent research has not systematically scrutinized the dynamics of non-take-up (van Oorschot, 1995: 2-4).

We can assume that the dynamics of take-up are most marked for people who are relatively well-off but still eligible, and only expect to receive a

---

[183] Richardson and Naidoo have put this point as follows: '[A] considerable amount of non-take-up [...] may be accounted for through temporary non-claiming. A given take-up rate can be interpreted as based on either on a stock of permanent non-claimers or on a regular flow of temporary non-claimers (or a combination of both). While much discussion of this issue tends to assume that non-take-up is a static phenomenon for those who do not claim, we would suggest that the "flow" interpretation should be given greater attention.' (Richardson and Naidoo, 1978: 45, cited in van Oorschot, 1995: 3).

relatively small amount of benefits. Another portion of frictional non-take-up is expected to be made up by people in volatile social and economic circumstances (cf. Blank and Ruggles, 1996; Corden and Craig, 1991).[184]

Moreover, frictional non-take-up is nurtured by complex administrative regulations that are not easy to comprehend. If a scheme operates with non-transparent eligibility conditions, many claimants will hesitate to apply for benefits, as long as they do not expect that they have a good chance of receiving the benefit. Not only claimants may have difficulties in keeping track of the entitlement, but the administrative treatment of cases must also reflect these changes. By this token, administrative errors may be more frequent for claimants in volatile circumstances than for claimants in more stable living conditions.

Since frictional take-up mainly concerns people who expect to receive small amounts of benefit and are moving in and out of eligibility, we would expect that frictional non-take-up generally does not result in severe hardship. Only when the income situation becomes unbearable, people will be forced to overcome certain difficulties and claim social assistance (cf. Marsh and McKay, 1993). Even though the income situation of temporal non-claimants is relatively good compared to others, frictional non-take-up may be an important factor in explaining the incidence of poverty.

Barriers to Claiming Social Assistance

The preceding paragraphs have demonstrated that the issue of non-take-up is a complex interaction between programme and administrative structures on one side, and individual attitudes and behaviour on the other. In examining the effectiveness of social assistance schemes in the alleviation of poverty, these bundles of possible causes for non-take-up discussed in the previous sections – knowledge, stigmatization, and complexity of the claiming process – alone remain unsatisfactory, since the effect of the institutional framework on take-up is not sufficiently reflected. More complex models of the claiming process may shed some more light on the process of claiming and the impact of the institutional framework.

---

[184] Corden and Craig have found marked patterns of take-up dynamics for the British family credit scheme and pointed to '[t]hose at the margins of eligibility, or going in and out, may find it especially difficult to recognize their own status at the appropriate time. People may find it hard to keep track of how they stand in relation to family credit, especially if their earnings vary or they have several children's birthdays to consider.' (Corden and Craig, 1991: 83)

Table 7.1 Possible effects of institutional structures on take-up

	Knowledge	Complexity	Stigmatization
General programme structure	– non-transparent programme structure – insufficient promotion of the scheme in the public	– weak organizational integration with other social security schemes – weak linkage with other social security benefits	– programme is aimed at groups in society which are associated with negative prejudices – negative attitudes towards dependency on society; programme challenges cultural norms or characteristics
Access to the scheme	– non-transparent application procedure and vague criteria of entitlement – application procedure requires elaborate communicative skills	– scheme leaves the initiative to start the claiming process fully to the claimants themselves – high costs in time and money associated with claiming – large scope of discretion for administration	– strict means-test or disability test – financial liability of family members – way of handling claims and claimants is experienced by claimants as humiliating and degrading
Processing of claims	– non-transparent administrative procedures in the claiming process	– frequent renewal of claim or applications for additional benefits required – poor quality of decision-making and technical administrative procedures – insufficient possibilities for legal appeals	– combination of a 'service' and a 'fraud control' function

Source: Partly based on van Oorschot and Kolkhuis Tancke (1989: 20), cit. from van Oorschot (1991; 1995); Corden (1995).

Explanations of non-take-up have frequently referred to sequential models of the claiming procedures, and have distinguished different stages in the claiming process (cf. Kerr, 1982; Leibfried, 1976; van Oorschot, 1995; Corden, 1995). Following van Oorschot (1995), the claiming process can be conceptualized as a three-stage model. In the first stage, claimants have to be aware of their need, of a benefit that possibly meets their needs and have to deem their situation as relatively stable in order to consider claiming at all (threshold stage). In the second stage, people are balancing costs and utility of claiming when assessing their need, the perceived utility of the benefit and their attitude towards claiming (trade-off stage). Finally, after having decided to claim, claimants may still decide to withdraw their claim (or not submit it at all) when confronted with administrative problems or new barriers, or change their attitude towards social assistance (application stage) (cf.

van Oorschot, 1995: 80-95). Taking this model as a starting point, Table 7.1 offers a tentative classification of the main arguments found in the literature on impact of institutional factors on the claiming process, re-arranged in a two-way table. The columns refer to the three main factors of non-take-up summarized above, knowledge, stigmatization and complexity. The rows describe three aspects of the institutional framework that can be associated with the three stages of the claiming process.

First, the programme structure lays out the general regulations of the social assistance scheme such as eligibility rules, conditions of entitlement, benefit levels, and responsibilities that may have a strong impact on the question of take-up even before the first direct contact between client and administration is established. At this stage, critical factors that may have an impact of take-up are the questions whether claimants are aware of the existence of a scheme and if they understand the entitlement criteria of the scheme to a sufficient degree as to believe that they may have a good chance to receive these benefits. In addition, a general negative attitude towards recipients of social assistance may have a detrimental effect on take-up rates.

Second, the access to the scheme marks a critical stage in the claiming process, since this is the first direct interaction between administration and claimant. Non-take-up is supposed to be fostered by an intransparent application procedure with vague entitlement criteria, especially if it requires elaborate communicative skills. Administrative practices may spur non-take-up if the initiative to start the claiming process is entirely left to the claimants themselves, if high pecuniary and non-pecuniary costs are associated with claiming, and the administration enjoys a large scope of discretion. In addition, this stage of the claiming process embodies strong stigmatizing effects if the programme operates a strict means-test, if social assistance may be recovered from family members, and if claimants experience the way of handling claims as humiliating and degrading.

Third, non-take-up may still occur once claimants have submitted their initial claim. The subsequent processing of claims involves the administration of one-off benefits, the regular renewal of claims, and any other interaction between administration and claimants after the initial application for benefits. Critical factors at this stage are again complicated administrative procedures that are not transparent for claimants and that possibly raise the probability of incorrect decisions on the part of the administration. The lack of an effective appeal procedure that can control the decisions of the administration and help to secure claimant rights may further contribute to non-take-up. Possible stigmatization effects add to these problems if the function of fraud control is overemphasized in the claiming process.

After having identified a number of factors that are commonly held as increasing the probability of non-take-up, the following sections will seek to identify these factors in the social assistance schemes of Britain, Germany and Sweden, in order to evaluate their effects on the take-up of social assistance benefits.

The Administration of Social Assistance and the Question of Take-up

On the basis of the factors outlined above, this section scrutinizes the institutional framework in Britain, Germany and Sweden and identifies elements that may favour or disfavour the take-up of benefits. Although it is not possible to establish a direct causal relationship between the institutional settings and the issue of take-up, the empirical evidence on take-up suggests that certain institutional features will encourage take-up whereas others will rather deter potential claims.

General Programme Structure

On the level of the general programme structure, two bundles of factors have been identified as having a potentially negative effect on take-up, an non-transparent programme structure and insufficient awareness on the availability of benefits among the public on the one side, and negative attitudes in respect to claiming social assistance and possibly stigmatizing effects on the other.

Stigmatization and the Salience of Social Assistance Stigmatizing effects in social assistance benefit schemes may be detrimental to take-up. Generally speaking, take-up is expected to be low where social assistance benefits aim at very marginalized groups of the population, while stigmatization effects are believed to be less severe where the receipt of social assistance is considered as being relatively normal (cf. Rainwater, 1982: 41). According to this argument, one could expect that take-up rates are higher in countries where a large share of the population receives social assistance than in countries where social assistance benefits are focused on a very small minority. Taking an extreme example, if everyone received social assistance benefits, most people would not feel stigmatized about the fact of receiving social assistance as such. Nevertheless, the process of claiming social assistance could still embody elements that could be perceived as stigmatizing by some recipients. One should therefore distinguish general stigmatization effects that relate to the condition of claiming social assistance at all from specific stigmatization effect that relate to certain components of the claim process. General stigmatization effects tend to be associated with general attitudes towards social assistance and individual feelings of failure (not being able to make one's living) whereas specific stigmatization effects rather refer to specific aspects of the administration of benefits.

If the receipt of social assistance is widespread and considered as fairly normal, general stigmatization is expected to be less problematic than in a country where recipiency is very unusual. For specific stigmatization effects, a large number of recipients may also have an indirect positive effect on take-up rates. It seems plausible to assume that programme structure and administrative procedures are adapted to the quantity of claims to be processed. In countries with a large number of claimants, the institutional framework is expected to be more standardized and based on pre-defined and clear entitlement rules rather than administrative discretion. For these reasons, the salience of social assistance is expected to reduce both general and specific stigmatization effects. In addition, the societal knowledge of entitlement conditions of social assistance is supposed to be higher if the receipt of social assistance is a wide-spread phenomenon within the population. In a strict sense, the salience of social assistance is not a feature of the institutional framework as such, but is an indirect effect of entitlement regulations.

Expenditure on Social Assistance One rough indicator of the salience of social assistance is the share of expenditure on this scheme within the welfare state. This indicator allows a direct comparison of the relative weight of social assistance schemes within the population on the basis of readily accessible data, yet results may be biased by structural effects.[185] Figure 7.1 shows the expenditure on social assistance given as a proportion of total social expenditure.

The expenditure on social assistance shares a rising tendency, but the level of expenditure varies considerably across the three countries. The United Kingdom stands out with a high percentage of social expenditure allocated towards social assistance – between one tenth and one fifth of social security expenditure was channelled into these schemes. The expenditure ratios in Germany and Sweden were much smaller, between 2 and 6 per cent in Germany and between 0.6 and 1.3 per cent in Sweden.[186]

---

[185] Expenditure on social assistance is not only dependent upon the number of people claiming, but also upon the amount of benefits actually paid out.

[186] At least in the Swedish case, the increase in expenditure is closely linked to rising unemployment and curtailments in other social security systems. Salonen (1997; 1998) has shown that curtailments in other social security schemes have led to a marked strain on the Swedish social assistance scheme. According to his calculations, some 10 per cent of expenditure on social assistance in 1997 have been caused by this shunting practice.

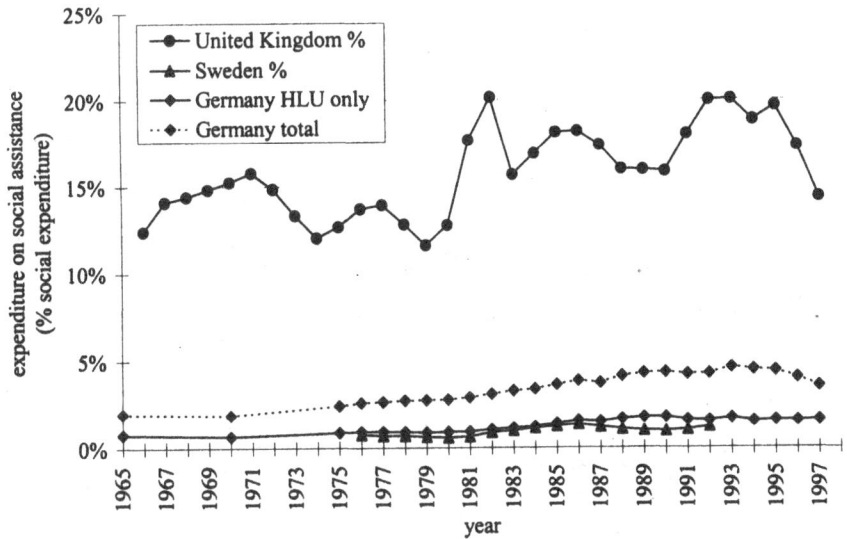

Figure 7.1 Expenditure on social assistance as a percentage of total social expenditure

Source: Britain: Department of Social Security: Social Security Statistics, various volumes. Germany: Statistisches Bundesamt, Fachserie 13, Reihe 2, various volumes, and unpublished material. Sweden: Statistisk årsbok för Sverige, various volumes.

The German case is not easy to assess because the aid for people in special circumstances (*Hilfe in besonderen Lebenslagen; HBL*) is integrated with the general social assistance scheme. Benefits paid under this scheme partly aim at needs that are covered by other schemes in the United Kingdom and Sweden. For example, a large proportion of these benefits is made up by payments to people in residential care or the disabled. This function is taken over by separate schemes in other countries. However, aid for people in special circumstances is always means-tested. One could thus argue that this scheme should be included here, yet some income limits are more generous. Since neither the inclusion of this expenditure nor their exclusion can be fully justified, the data presented here show both versions of expenditure where available.

One could argue that the relative high British shares of expenditure on social assistance are simply due to the fact that the United Kingdom is spending less on non-means-tested social security than Sweden and Germany and therefore allocates a large share of her social expenditure to social assistance. Yet, this is only partly true, as Figure 7.2 illustrates.

168 At the Margins of the Welfare State

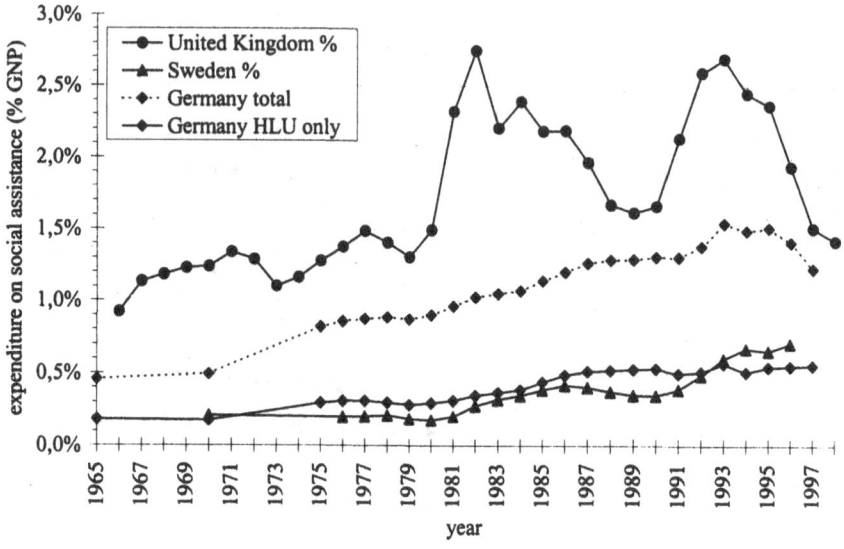

Figure 7.2 Expenditure on social assistance as a percentage of GNP

Source: See Figure 7.1 (p. 167).

Figure 7.2 shows the expenditure on social assistance as proportion of GNP and illustrates that expenditure has been notably higher in the United Kingdom than in the two other countries throughout the last thirty years, even if shown in relation to economic power. Social assistance made up between 1 and 1.5 per cent of GDP during the 1960s and 1970s, and oscillated between 1.5 and some 3 per cent of GDP thereafter. German and Swedish expenditure ratios are lower and appear to be much steadier, yet they are markedly rising. Expenditure on social assistance never touched 0.5 per cent of GDP in Sweden until 1992, but even at this relative maximum, this was only roughly a sixth of the British expenditure. In Germany, total social assistance expenditure rose from 0.5 per cent of GDP by the end of the 1960s to 1.5 per cent in the early 1990s. When excluding aid in special circumstances, the German level of expenditure is even quite similar to the Swedish.

The analysis of expenditure for social assistance illustrates that the relative weight of social assistance differs considerably across countries. Social assistance is more prevalent in the United Kingdom, both as a share of total social expenditure as in proportion to the GDP. In Sweden and Germany, social assistance comes closer to a residual scheme. The German case is fairly ambiguous: taking into account the total expenditure for general social assistance and for aid in special circumstances (*Hilfe in besonderen Lebenslagen*), Germany is positioned between Sweden and the United Kingdom (halfway in relation to GDP, somewhat biased towards Sweden in relation to social expenditure). However, considering only general social assistance, Germany is hardly discernible from Sweden.[187]

Recipients of Social Assistance The evidence on expenditure of social assistance can be supplemented by data on the number of claimants in each country. If social assistance schemes provide for a large proportion of the population, the receipt of social assistance is expected to be less stigmatizing than if social assistance is rather marginal. However, cross-national comparisons of claimant statistics are subject to some methodological reservations because of diverging time horizons. Some statistics refer to the number of recipients at one particular point in time, while others refer to the yearly total, either of persons or of cases. Unfortunately, each of the three countries considered here subscribes to a different method for the publication of their recipient rates, so the data are only partly comparable. The following charts will present the statistics in two steps in order to make them as comparable as possible. Figure 7.3 couples the British and German data on general social assistance (Hilfe zum Lebensunterhalt, HLU), each referring to one single day during a year. Figure 7.4 then shows recipient rates as yearly totals, presenting evidence for Sweden, and again Germany. Since the German statistical office recently switched their system of statistics on general social assistance, we can use the data on general social assistance (HLU) as a yardstick that appears in both charts. The data on aid in exceptional circumstances (Hilfe in besonderen Lebenslagen, HBL) keep to be reported as yearly totals.

The British social assistance has provided for a relatively high proportion of the population for decades, yet the proportion of recipients almost doubled during the Thatcher government in the eight years from 1979 to 1986. Eventually, some 17 per cent of the British population made up at least part of their income from social assistance between 1993 and 1996. Under the new jobseeker's allowance scheme, unemployed claimants are not included in the statistics any longer, so recipient rates are reduced to some 10-12 per cent of the population after 1992.

---

[187] Relating these expenditure ratios to Eardley et al.'s (1996a) social assistance typologies, we have to conclude these results stand in marked contrast to their classification. If one focused exclusively on expenditure on social assistance, Germany had to be classified together with Sweden, and definitely not together with the United Kingdom. However, in order to gain a wider picture, one has to consider other variables as well.

170   *At the Margins of the Welfare State*

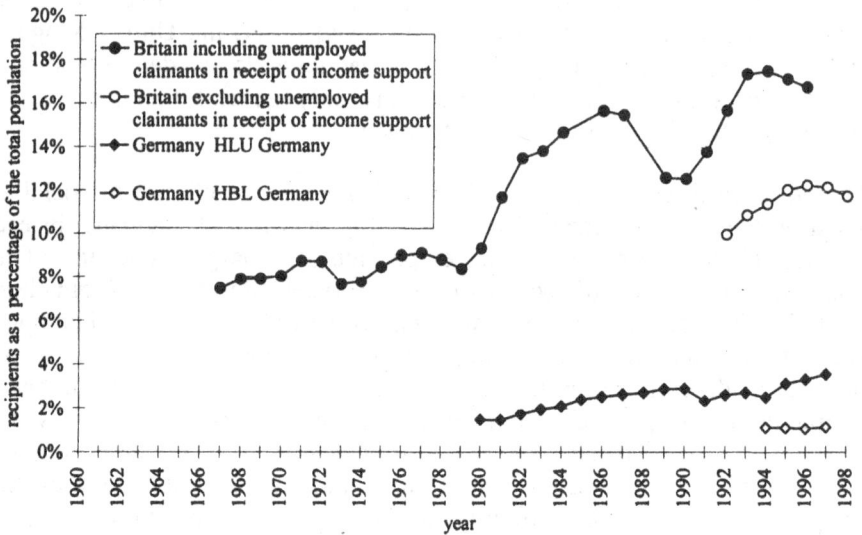

Figure 7.3 Recipients of social assistance as a proportion of the population in Britain and Germany (one day during a year)

Note: The data refer to the 31.12. of each year for Germany, and to one day in May for Britain. The definition of the British recipient rates has changed, as unemployed claimants in receipt of income support prior to the introduction of the Jobseeker's Allowance in October 1996 have been excluded. For the German data: HLU: general social assistance (*Hilfe zum Lebensunterhalt*), HBL: aid in special circumstances (*Hilfe in besonderen Lebenslagen*).

Source: Britain: Department of Social Security: Social Security Statistics, various volumes. Germany: Statistisches Bundesamt, Fachserie 13, Reihe 2, various volumes, and unpublished material.

Even compared to the narrower definition of recipient rates in Britain, social assistance is far less salient in Germany.[188] Not even 5 per cent of the population claimed social assistance in Germany, compared to one sixth of the population according to the broader definition, and one tenth according to the narrow definition of recipient rates in Britain.[189] Excluding people who

---

[188] However, the data may not be fully comparable because of seasonal variations: The German data have been collected at the end of the year, i.e. 31st December while the British data refer to 'one day in May'. Assuming that seasonal unemployment is typically higher in the winter than in spring, the British rates may slightly understate the number of recipients as compared to Germany. However, this variation does not fundamentally bias the quality of the data.

[189] The combined recipient rate of general social assistance and aid in exceptional circumstances amounts to 4.8 per cent. Given that between 30 and 40 per cent of recipients of

only have received aid in special circumstances (*Hilfe in besonaeren Lebenslagen*) and are not, in a strict sense the 'typical' social assistance clientele,[190] only 3.6 per cent of the population claimed in 1997. Interestingly, the recipient rate is significantly lower in East Germany, in spite of higher unemployment and a lower standard of living. This fact is due to the wide-spread entitlement to unemployment benefits and active labour market policies, as well as to a factual minimum pension in the new *Länder* ('*Sozialzuschlag*', terminated in 1996), but also to slightly lower benefit rates.

Figure 7.4 presents recipient rates for Sweden and Germany, now referring to the yearly total of claimants. Unfortunately, the German data are not fully comparable to the Swedish data, since the former refer to caseload rather than individuals. This implies that some recipients of social assistance may have been counted twice, if they stopped claiming social assistance and re-claimed it within the course of the year. Thus, the recipient rates reported here may lead to a slight overestimation of the share of the German population claiming, depending on the incidence of multiple spells. The Swedish data, in contrast, refer to individuals rather than cases and therefore correctly reflect the share of claimants within the population.

The caseload data on Germany show that up to 4.5 per cent of the population received general social assistance during 1992, and up to 6 per cent claimed either general social assistance (HLU) or assistance for special circumstances (HBL).[191] Since the data refer to caseload rather than individuals, the values of 4.5 and 6 per cent mark upper limits of recipient rates, while actual recipient rates may be lower in case of multiple spells of social assistance. For general social assistance, between 2.6 and 4.5 per cent of the population have claimed general social assistance at least once in 1992.[192] Recipient rates for general social assistance have experienced a sharp rise only during the 1980s, before then, they were relatively stable at some 1.5 per cent until the early 1970s and some 2 per cent during the late 1970s.

---

aid in exceptional circumstances also claim general social assistance (German Federal Statistical Office, 7 January 1999), the actual recipient rate is supposed to be somewhat lower.

[190] The 'aid in special circumstances' is overwhelmingly directed towards handicapped people and to people in need of long-term care. The introduction of the long-term care insurance in 1995 has significantly reduced the number of people in need of this kind of benefit, yet insurance benefits often are not high enough to cover all expenses, so many people still have to turn to social assistance.

[191] The data on general social assistance are only available until 1992.

[192] The lower limit of possible recipient rates is provided by the evidence on recipient rates on 31st December 1992 (see Figure 7.3). Comparable data are not available for more recent years and for social assistance for special circumstances (HBL), unfortunately.

172 *At the Margins of the Welfare State*

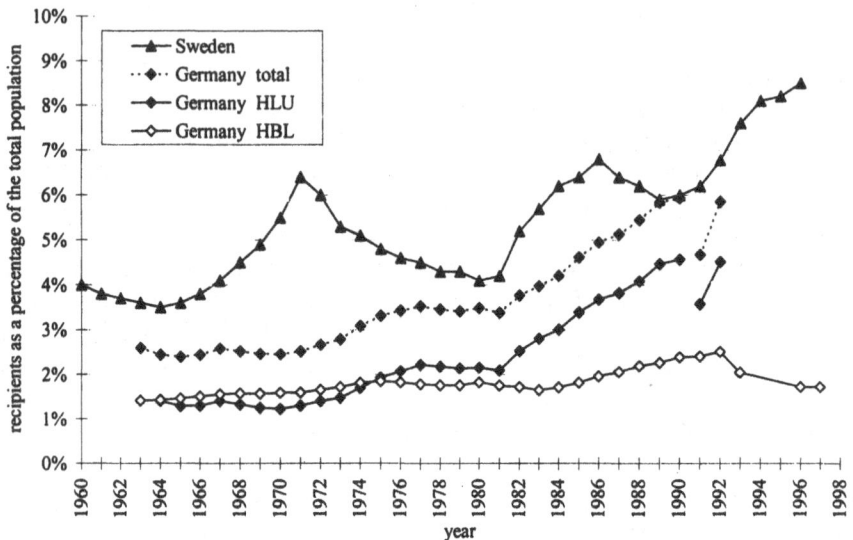

Figure 7.4 Recipients of social assistance as a proportion of the population in Germany and Sweden (yearly sum)

Note: For the German data: HLU: general social assistance (*Hilfe zum Lebensunterhalt*); HBL = aid in exceptional circumstances (*Hilfe in besonderen Lebenslagen*). The total given is to be understood as a maximum, while actual recipient rates may be lower because people may receive both types of social assistance at the same time. The HLU series and the total number of recipients have been discontinued after 1992.

Source: Germany: Statistisches Bundesamt, Fachserie 13, Reihe 2, various volumes, and unpublished material. Sweden: Statistisk Årsbok för Sverige, various volumes.

In Sweden, recipient rates are even higher than in the German case, and always have been from the early 1960s to the late 1980s. Only in 1990, recipient rates in Germany and Sweden were roughly equal, yet the German recipient rates probably overestimate actual recipient rates because of the double-counting of multiple spells. The relatively high recipient rates collide with the common portrayal of the Swedish social assistance as being 'residual' (Lødemel and Schulte, 1992; Eardley et al., 1996a). In fact, after a sharp decrease of recipient rates during the late 1930s and 1940s, the following decades were characterized by a stagnation at some 4 per cent of the population, before reaching a post-war minimum at 3.5 per cent in the first half of the 1960s (Olsson, 1986: 62; Korpi, 1975). After that, recipient rates rose to more than 6 per cent in 1971, declined again to 4 per cent in 1980. Since then, another sharp rise occurred up to nearly 7 per cent in the late 1980s, and by 1995, the recipient ratio has reached 8 per cent (cf. Salonen, 1993: 76). In cities strongly hit by economic crises and unemployment, as e. g. Malmö, more than one in ten inhabitants had to claim social assistance during the eighties (Schwarze, 1994: 57).[193] Thus, even the expansion of social insurance schemes in the heydays of the Swedish welfare state was paralleled by a growing number of claimants of social assistance.[194] This assessment fundamentally challenges the picture of a truly residual social assistance scheme in Sweden. Even if one takes into account that high recipient ratios might have been stimulated by generous social assistance benefits, there are still some reservations. The rigidity of means-tests and the intensive treatment by social workers clearly demarcate social assistance schemes from the non-means-tested social insurance schemes and tend to enhance barriers to claiming.

Using the German data as a common yardstick for the comparison of recipient rates in the three countries considered, it seems safe to conclude that recipient rates are highest in Britain, followed by Sweden and lowest in Germany.[195]

The Dynamics of Social Assistance The differences between yearly caseload data and the number of recipients at one particular point in time already pointed to the fact that there is a considerable fluctuation into and out of social assistance. Empirical evidence from dynamic social assistance research also provides some evidence for the assessment of the salience of social assistance within the population. Whereas cross-sectional data only reflect the salience of social assistance within the population at one particular point in time, dynamic analyses are able to give an answer to the question

---

[193] An historical overview on the development of claimant statistics is given in Salonen (1993: 72-73).

[194] However, rising recipient rates may not only indicate growing problems in terms of insufficient earnings or social security benefits, but might also be caused by improved benefits establishing entitlements for a larger share of the population. The Swedish social assistance has certainly become more generous over time, but not enough to fully explain the rise in recipient rates.

[195] I am grateful to Martin Schölkopf for drawing my attention to the danger of embarking on a circular argument at this point. Both expenditure on social assistance and recipient rates are dependent on non-take-up rates, so the incidence of non-take-up (stimulated by strong stigmatization effects) should not be explained by high recipient rates (or expenditure on social assistance) that are in turn spurred by high take-up rates. However, leaping ahead to the empirical non-take-up rates discussed below, the ranking of countries would remain fairly stable even if the German and Swedish expenditure and recipient rates were markedly increased. In addition, expenditure and recipient rates are dependent on a number of other factors beyond non-take-up rates.

of how many people have received social assistance during a period of several years.

Studies on the dynamics of social assistance agree on the fact that a considerably larger share of the population receives social assistance during a longer period of several years rather than a single-year analysis would suggest. Yet, the degree of incidence depends on the length of the period of observation; the share of the recipient population is expected to be greater the longer the period observed. Most single-country studies agree that many more people have been in contact with the social assistance scheme of their respective country during a period of several years than a snapshot analysis would suggest, albeit there is hardly any truly comparable evidence.[196] A comparison of social assistance dynamics in Bremen and Gothenburg has shown that social assistance spells are indeed shorter in Gothenburg than in Bremen, yet the total time on social assistance is shorter in Bremen than in Gothenburg (Buhr, 1999; Gustafsson, 1998). The data do not allow a detailed comparison across countries, since comparable data for Germany and the United Kingdom are not available.

Salience of Social Assistance and the Problem of Non-take-up Whereas the Swedish and the German social assistance schemes can be considered as rather marginal, both in terms of expenditure and coverage of the population, the British income support scheme plays a larger role within the welfare state. Claiming social assistance is a much more wide-spread phenomenon in the United Kingdom than in the two other countries. With recipient rates four times higher in Britain than in Germany – with Sweden situated between these two cases, but closer to Germany than to Britain – we can expect that it is considered as being much more 'normal' to claim social assistance in Britain than elsewhere. In this respect, claiming social assistance would be

---

[196] The dynamic aspects of social assistance receipt have been investigated in a growing number of studies since the late 1970s and 1980s. Most of the research work originated in the United States where there has been traditional concern about welfare dynamics. In most other countries, the research into the dynamics of social assistance was established much later. Whereas most American studies use longitudinal micro-data, many of the European studies rely on administrative data, since official statistics or panel surveys have not been available or do not offer data on social assistance in the necessary detail. For Germany, the establishment of a longitudinal database on social assistance in Bremen has initiated a large body of research based on administrative data (e.g. Buhr, 1995; Leisering and Leibfried, 1999) and panel data (Voges and Rohwer, 1991a, 1991b). The empirical evidence on Sweden is based on a single major study analyzing social assistance records in the four Swedish cities of Helsingborg, Landskrona, Lund, and Malmö (Salonen, 1993) and a comparative small scale study on long-term recipients (Fridberg, 1993). For the United Kingdom, there is also a growing number of studies based on the BHPS (e.g. Ashworth et al., 1997) and a claimant survey (Shaw et al., 1996).

considered as being less stigmatizing in Britain than in Germany and Sweden.

Societal Attitudes towards Recipients of Social Assistance Another factor that may contribute to low take-up rates are the general attitudes towards recipients of social assistance and the poor within the general public. Strictly spoken, this indicator is not an institutional factor, but it is closely associated to the broader institutional framework of the welfare state. Institutions may not only be regarded as some kind of 'frozen' product of the politically mediated public interest, but public attitudes also appear to parallel the actual institutional framework in a given country (cf. Roller, 1995b; Mau, 1997a).

It can be assumed that negative social attitudes towards recipients of social assistance or the poor tend to foster stigmatization and thus increase the probability of non-take-up. One indicator for negative attitudes within the population is the degree to which the incidence of poverty is associated with individual failure, such as idleness or a poor self-discipline, rather than with factors that lie beyond the control of the poor themselves, such as bad luck, or societal injustice. Comparative studies of attitudes towards recipients of social assistance and the poor suggest that negative attitudes are strongest in the United Kingdom, followed by Germany, and lowest in Sweden (van Oorschot and Halman, 1998).[197]

Although the extent of negative attitudes towards the poor seems less distinct in Sweden, there is a general negative image of public assistance in the population, too, as in many other European countries (Svallfors, 1997). Public support for expenditure on social assistance is weak, both compared to other social security programs and to other Scandinavian countries (Goul Andersen et al., 1999: 247-250). Hallcröd (1996b: 49) reports that a large proportion, or even the majority of the population agreed to the views that most recipients of social assistance did not really need the support (43 per cent), are cheating (58 per cent), or are lazy and lack willpower (47 per cent). Moreover, a broad majority (61 per cent) of the sampled population believed that many recipients of socialbidrag are outsiders in society

---

[197] This study is based on the data of the 1990 European Values Study. Distinguishing four possible causes for poverty – laziness or lack of willpower (individual blame), bad luck (individual fate), societal injustice (social blame) and consequences of the modern progress (social fate) –, they identified distinct national attitudinal patterns. In the United Kingdom, 45.9 per cent of the sampled population considered laziness or lack of willpower as the most or second most important reason for poverty, whereas 41.4 per cent of the sample supported this opinion in Germany, and 30.2 per cent in Sweden. Interestingly, countries formed clusters that closely represent common welfare state typologies, with the Anglo-saxon countries (except Ireland) scoring high on this item (the United Kingdom is however the most moderate of this group of countries), and the Nordic countries at the bottom of the list, and the others somewhere in between (van Oorschot and Halman, 1998: Table 3).

(Halleröd, 1996b: 49). Svallfors states that more than two thirds of the sampled population agreed to the statement that many recipients of social assistance were not really poor in 1986 and in 1992 (Svallfors, 1991: 615, Svallfors, 1995: 60).[198]

Attitudes towards recipients of social assistance can also be derived from the strength of meritocratic attitudes. One can hypothesize that the more hard work is considered as an instrument of social stratification within a society, the more negative are attitudes towards recipients of social assistance, who obviously cannot make ends meet on the basis of their own earnings. Meritocratic attitudes are strongest in the United Kingdom, where 84 per cent of the population agreed to the proposition that hard work is important for getting ahead in life, with surprisingly little variation between different socio-economic groups.[199] In Sweden, only two thirds of the population were of the same opinion, and only half in West Germany, while agreement in East Germany is stronger than in Sweden (71 per cent). This evidence suggests that recipients of social assistance have the lowest social prestige in Britain, followed by Sweden and Germany.

Another aspect are the general attitudes towards income redistribution within a society and variations between different socio-economic groups within a country. Differences in attitudes towards redistribution can serve as an indicator for the societal acceptance of redistribution. On the basis of the 1992 ISSP social attitudes survey, Mau (1997a) found the largest variations between different strata of the population in Sweden. Whereas only 29 per cent respondents in the highest income quartile agreed to the proposition that the government should reduce income differentials, 60-65 per cent of the remaining three quartiles did so. In the United Kingdom, 44 per cent agreed among the highest quartile, 66 per cent in the second, 72 per cent in the third and 74 per cent in the bottom income quartile. The least differentiation is found in Germany, where span of support reaches from 53 to 72 per cent in West Germany, and from 86 to 92 per cent in the East. Mau interprets the surprisingly low support of redistribution in Sweden as some kind of welfare backlash against an exceedingly inflated welfare state (Mau, 1997a: 23-24).

Interestingly, the evidence on the attitudes within the population appears to challenge the argumentation presented in the previous sections on the salience of social assistance. Negative societal attitudes towards recipients of

---

[198] The wording of the question was: 'How usual do you think it is that social benefits and services are used by people who do not really need them? – Many of those receiving social assistance are not really poor' (Svallfors, 1995: 60).

[199] The exact wording of the question was 'how important you think it is for getting ahead in life... hard work – how important is that? Essential – very important – fairly important – not very important – not important at all – can't choose'. For the percentages reported above, agreement includes 'essential' and 'very important' options (Mau, 1997a, 1997b).

social assistance are strongest in Britain, and somewhat weaker in Germany and Sweden. Nevertheless, these two indicators may not necessarily contradict each other. It may be possible that in a society with a large claimant population the receipt of social assistance is seen as a possible threat to the welfare of the society as a whole by a majority of the population. Though, the experience of claiming may be a less unpleasant experience for the individual if he or she is part of a large group within this society rather than a small minority.

Role of Social Assistance within the Welfare State The role of social assistance schemes within the welfare state may also have certain implications for the take-up of benefits. Stigmatization effects may be enhanced by a sharp differentiation between means-tested and non-means-tested benefits, or between contributory social insurance benefits and non-contributory minimum income benefits.

Within the German welfare state, the strong cleavage between contributory social insurance and means-tested social assistance may reinforce negative attitudes towards social assistance, especially for the elderly. Old people may be ashamed of claiming social assistance because they feel that they have not done enough during their working life to secure themselves a decent pension.[200] One could hypothesize that this attitude may possibly be less prevalent in countries with a less distinct link between earnings and public pensions, such as in Britain or Sweden.

For the United Kingdom, the income support scheme is well integrated within the general framework of the welfare state. Benefit levels of most social insurance schemes are not radically higher than in the income support scheme, and also offer a flat-rate benefit without a strong linkage to individual contributions. The cleavage between social insurance and social assistance schemes thus is much weaker than in Germany, while there is some evidence that the main division is to be found rather in the distinction between public and private provision of benefits.

In Sweden, social assistance schemes are clearly detached from most other social security benefits, for most of which the linkage between individual contributions and benefits is relatively strong. There is one important exception, however. The basic pension comes near to the idea of a universal benefit that is entirely financed out of general taxation and is available to the entire population, with some exceptions for migrants.

---

[200] This point is illustrated by a statement of a social assistance official that has been quoted in one of the earlier German studies on non-take-up: 'People think: I have my pension; it is small, but this is possibly my own fault. My earnings at the time have not been sufficient for a higher pension, whether it actually was my fault or not. But having only this small pension, I have to cope with that situation' (Bujard and Lange, 1978a: 120).

The role of social assistance benefits is thus most integrated in the general framework of the welfare state in Britain, while it constitutes somewhat more of a alien element in Sweden and in the Germany. As far as these aspects contribute to the stigmatization of recipients, take-up is most strongly deterred in Germany, and least in Britain.

Non-transparent Programme Structure and Insufficient Awareness The institutional framework of social assistance scheme is assumed to have an impact on the take-up of benefits. The construction of social assistance schemes may inhibit take-up if the programme structure is non-transparent and not easily understandable by claimants, and if the availability of benefits is poorly communicated in the public.

Generally, we can assume that a social assistance scheme tends to be more transparent if it is applied consistently rather than being subject to regional or local variations, and if the responsible bodies actively disseminate information among the population. The unitary organization of the British minimum income schemes facilitates the distribution of information on minimum income benefits among the population. Indeed, responding to concerns of non-take-up, the British government has sought to improve information on entitlements on social assistance within the population, by distributing information leaflets and encouraging reports in the media. Information usually is available at all post offices and in the offices of the Benefits Agency, as are the forms necessary to submit a claim. In Sweden, the availability of information is more difficult to assess, since the programme structure varies across municipalities, as do entitlement regulations. The dissemination of information is thus strongly dependent on the information policies on the local level, and may be expected to strongly vary across municipalities. In Germany, the eligibility rules are largely nationally fixed, yet the exact amounts of the standard benefit rate slightly vary across regions. The government has issued a number of leaflets on the availability of benefits, and some federal states and municipalities have also intensified the dissemination of information among the population, yet it is much less easily accessible than in Britain.

Weak Linkages with Other Social Security Benefits Closely linked to the previous point is the organizational and administrative integration of social assistance with other social security benefits. There is strong evidence that a pronounced integration of social assistance schemes with other social security schemes may be beneficial to take-up.

If the administration of social assistance schemes is done by the same bodies as for other social security benefits, claimants may not only feel less stigmatized about claiming benefits, but officials possibly also have a better knowledge on the availability of other benefits, and may refer claimants more easily to the appropriate office. To some degree, the British income support scheme is organized in this way, as social assistance benefits are administered by the Benefits Agencies that also administer most other social security benefits. In contrast, the German and Swedish social assistance schemes are organizationally separated from the administration of social security schemes, as the responsibility lies on the communal level.

The administration of social assistance schemes may also actively inform and encourage potential claimants. For example, the social security administration may notify claimants of low pensions on their payslip that they may be eligible for social assistance in addition to their pension (cf. Deacon and Bradshaw, 1983: 145; van Oorschot, 1995: 49-51). This kind of active encouragement has been practised in the United Kingdom, but there is no similar evidence for Germany and Sweden.

Another possibility which might actively improve take-up is the automatic payment of social assistance together with other social security benefits if those benefits are lower than a certain threshold. This method is applicable for categories of claimants whose living conditions are relatively stable, such as pensioners, as was the case in East Germany for some time after the reunification. Pensioners whose pensions were lower than the social assistance benefit level received those benefits with their pension, without any additional application procedure (cf. Wienand, 1997b; Alber and Schölkopf, 1999: 170).[201] In addition, passport benefits may also improve take-up, as claimants of one benefit may be automatically entitled to another, such as the provision of free school meals for children from claimant families in the United Kingdom. This method has a double effect on take-up, as it not only enhances take-up of the ancillary benefit, but also indirectly increases the incentives to claim the 'passport benefit'.

Access to Social Assistance

Access to social assistance basically involves both an informational and an organizational aspect. First, persons in need require information about social assistance and the conditions under which it is granted. Second, claimants must have the opportunity to contact the social assistance office and to find out whether they actually are eligible for social assistance, in order to eventually submit their claim.[202]

---

[201] This scheme (*Sozialzuschlag*) was discontinued after 1996 (cf. Alber and Schölkopf, 1999: 170, 179).

[202] The access to social security schemes may also actively be used by the government to prevent certain groups from claiming. For example, Rosenhek (1999) reports that the Israeli government has organized the administration of the child benefit scheme for large families in

The first contact with the social assistance office may constitute an important administrative filter for (potential) claimants. Consequently, the point of entry is considered as one of the critical points in the claiming process that can also have a decisive effect on take-up (Ringeling 1981).[203] In the application process, the interests of claimants may possibly counteract the interests of the social assistance officers themselves. The officers are interested in organizing the entry into social assistance as efficiently and effectively as possible. They seek to ensure that social assistance is given only to people who meet the legal entitlement criteria, and try to quickly establish the nature and the extent of their entitlement. Claimants typically are interested in minimal administrative requirements and in receiving their benefit fully and quickly.

The processing of first-time claims is organized differently in Britain, Sweden, and Germany. In the United Kingdom, all claims for income support have to be submitted by filling in the appropriate form available from the local Benefits Agencies or the local post offices. The application procedure may be made entirely by writing, but potential claimants may also ask for an interview at the Benefits Agency (CPAG, 1998: 128-140). Applications to income support have to be supported by evidence on the identity of the claimant, the financial situation, and the rent or mortgage to be paid. The entitlement to income support usually starts from the day of claim, yet claims may be backdated under certain circumstances. Benefits Agencies are obliged to decide on a claim within a fixed time limit. It is possible, however, to submit a claim to income support in advance, if it is clear that the claimant will be entitled to income support from a certain date.

Unemployed claimants are generally not entitled to income support but to the income-based jobseeker's allowance. The level of benefits is the same, but conditions and administrative routines are different. Jobseeker's allowance is administered at the JobCentres by employment service officials. Claimants are considered as unemployed if they meet a number of defined criteria, including capability and availability for work and a contract with the Employment Service on job search efforts (CPAG, 1998: 55-57). However, some claimants may have the right to choose whether they want to claim

---

such a way that effectively barred Arab families from claiming during the 1960s although they were formally entitled to these benefits. In particular, offices were placed far away from the main Arab settlements areas, so many families could not reach the offices in order to submit their claims.

[203] A early British study concluded that 'reception staff acted as a powerful "buffer" between field workers and their potential and as such exerted a considerable influence on the provision of primary agency services. Far from performing only a passive function within the organization, receptionists were frequently operating very much in the area of the professional judgement and discretion' (Hall, 1974, cited in Ringeling, 1981: 297).

income support or jobseeker's allowance. Most people of this group will claim income support rather than the income-based jobseeker's allowance, since the latter is conditional on a number of work-availability requirements. However, claimants of income support are not eligible for some services provided by the JobCentres. So far, there has not been any detailed evaluation of the transfer of claims of the unemployed to the JobCentres.[204]

In Germany, entitlement to social assistance does not start from the moment a formal claim is submitted at the social assistance office, but officers are obliged to provide social assistance to needy persons as soon as they are aware that somebody needs help, even if the person has not formally applied for social assistance (Brühl, 1998: ix-xi). Usually, people approach the social assistance office of their town or district and have an interview with a social assistance officer, but formal or informal applications to social assistance are also valid if they are handed in at a public office other than the social assistance office. Applying for social assistance usually involves a personal visit to the social assistance office, but procedures may vary across federal states and municipalities. The decision about the claim is normally provided in written form, but this is not obligatory. Yet, claimants have the right to require a written notice about the decision taken, the reasons for this decision and information about appeals against this decision (Brühl, 1998: 218-220).

Like some other continental welfare states, the German welfare state embodies the principle of subsidiarity in terms of a mutual support of the wider family. For social assistance, this principle of subsidiarity implies that benefits are only paid to individuals if their family cannot support them. This does not only apply to members of the immediate family like spouses or minor children as in Sweden and the United Kingdom, but all persons, irrespective of age, are supposed to be responsible for their spouses, children and parents.[205] If social assistance is paid to an individual, the social assistance office has the right to recover the payments from his or her partner or relatives (cf. Müller, 1998). There are, however, a number of exemptions and income disregards that limit the liability of related persons, referring to the person's own income situation, the number of children, the nature of relationship to the claimant and the type of social assistance benefits paid, and some *Länder* do not apply this regulation at all (cf. Brühl, 1998: 248-257). The actual expenditure recovered from partners and relatives thus is relatively small, amounting to 1.6 per cent of total expenditure in 1995.[206]

---

[204] Department of Social Security, personal communication, 22 October 1998.

[205] The liability of the wider family used to be even more extended, stipulating e.g. the mutual obligation for grandparents and grandchildren, but this has been changed in order to take into account the changing socio-demographic patterns.

[206] Own calculations based on Statistisches Bundesamt (1997: 116-117), referring only to the general social assistance (HLU).

However, there is some evidence that many people hesitate to claim social assistance because they fear that members of their family will be held liable for social assistance payments. Not only the actual check of the relative's income situation itself, but the mere possibility that relatives may be held liable for social assistance payments, as well as recurring myths about this issue, constitute an effective hindrance to claiming for many people. Old people in particular often hesitate to claim social assistance because they do not wish that their children be made responsible for their financial support and because they do not want to see their family relations negatively affected by this enforced liability (cf. Bujard and Lange, 1978b: 19-23, 26-37). A similar effect is seen with repayable social assistance benefits. Some people fear having to repay benefits in the future and thus renounce social assistance benefits altogether (cf. Hartmann, 1981).

A large variation across municipalities also characterizes access to social assistance in Sweden. Due to an increasing caseload and a different structure of the claimant population, many social assistance offices increasingly rely upon more standardized entry procedures than before. In Stockholm and Malmö, for example, applicants are first received by a social welfare officer who decides whether complex problems require the help of a social worker or whether financial assistance is enough to meet the individual needs (Julkunen, 1993b: 56).[207] If the need for social assistance is caused by insufficient transfer payments (predominantly in case of sickness or old age) and does not require an intensive involvement of social workers (*socionomer*), the case is managed by administrative staff in the so-called simplified administration (*förenklad socialbidragshandläggning*) or 'EGT-system' (*ekonomisk grundtrygghet*).[208] Some 50-80 per cent of the caseload is administered according to this simplified procedure in Malmö. This large share of cases accentuates gaps in the regular social security system

---

[207] The criteria on which this decision is taken are the following (for the city of Stockholm): (1) absence or insufficiency of unemployment benefits, (2) insufficient earned income, (3) insufficient sickness insurance allowance, (4) insufficient training/study grant, (5) delayed unemployment benefits, pension, or sickness daily allowance, (6) insufficient pension, (7) child in waiting line for day care placement or treated for psychic or medical reasons (reported in Julkunen, 1993b: 56).

[208] This administrative procedure took up an earlier reform concept that had not been realised. By the end of the 1970's, a working group commissioned by the government proposed the introduction of a guaranteed minimum income component for all social insurance schemes. A top-up payment (*socialförsäkringstillägg, 'SOFT'*) was supposed to replace social assistance payments paid in addition to low social insurance benefits in case of sickness, old age, unemployment and child care. The reform sought to facilitate the administration of benefits and abandon stigmatizing means-tests (*behovsprövning*) for this clientele. However, the realization of this reform was impeded by the deteriorating financial situation of social insurance funds during the 1980s (Schwarze, 1994: 62-65).

(Schwarze, 1994: 62-67). Nevertheless, the application procedure is not very formalised. This is, for example, illustrated in the fact that clients do not get any written notice about the disapproval of an application in some municipalities (Schwarze, 1994: 81-92; Byberg, 1998: 106-108). Byberg (1998) has also found that municipalities that administer social assistance in a specialized and formalized way not only spend relatively less on social assistance, but also receive fewer appeals against their decisions. Municipalities where social assistance is more strongly integrated with other social services and where decisions are more discretionary tend to have higher expenditures but also have to deal with a larger number of appeals against these decisions (Byberg, 1998: 141-147).

Many Swedish municipalities regulate the entry into the social assistance system through a telephone access system. First-time clients have to pass a telephone interview with a social assistance officer, where household needs and financial means are checked. Only if clients are deemed to be possibly eligible for social assistance, they get an appointment within the social assistance office; if they also have non-financial problems, they may be referred to specialized social services. The proportion of potential claimants admitted to a personal appointment widely varies across municipalities. In a survey conducted in seven social assistance offices in four Swedish cities, Minas and Stenberg (2000) found that a large proportion of potential claims were turned down after the initial telephone interview. Admission rates tend to be high where the telephone interviews are conducted by less experienced social assistance officers, whereas more experienced staff were less reluctant to finally decide about claims on the basis of the telephone interview.

Information about eligibility rules tend to be more readily available in the uniform British social assistance system than in Germany and Sweden, and regulations are more transparent given the lower degree of regional or local variation and administrative discretion. For the initial application procedure, the German scheme appears to offer relatively easy access to the social assistance office, since formal requirements are reduced to a minimum. There is, however, another feature of the German social assistance scheme that may effectively prevent people from approaching the social assistance offices at all – the possible recovery of benefits from partners and relatives although this regulation is relatively seldom applied. Based on this ambiguous information, in a very tentative attempt to rank the social assistance schemes of the three countries in terms of accessibility, we would consider the German assistance scheme to be less easily accessible than the British one, but probably still more than in Sweden. However, since the access to social assistance is subject to local variations, especially in Sweden, this classification should be treated with caution.

184 *At the Margins of the Welfare State*

Processing of Claims

The administration of social assistance benefits does not only involve the initial award of benefits, but also a continuous processing of claims during the whole claiming process. This entails the regular payment of social assistance benefits, the regular adaptation of benefits to the income situation of claimants, control of claimants' compliance, and possibly a review process. Problems of non-take up are assumed to be small if the processing of claims is relatively easy, transparent and non-stigmatizing for claimants, and if claimants enjoy strong entitlements. In contrast, non-take-up tends to occur more frequently if claimants have to go through several application procedures and means-tests, if these tests strongly intrude into a claimant's living situation, if discretion on the part of the administration is high, and if their rights position towards the administration is weak.

Administration of Claims In the United Kingdom, the administration of income support is very formalized and strongly resembles the administration of non-means-tested benefits. Income support can be paid into a bank account, by giro, a benefit order book or in cash. It is paid in arrears unless claimants are pensioners, receive widows' benefit or are returning to work after a trade dispute (CPAG, 1998: 144-147). Claimants have to give their National Insurance number when claiming benefits as a proof of identity and to cross-check their entitlement; the National Insurance number of the partner is also required since October 1998 (CPAG, 1998: 130). The administrative integration of social security and social assistance in the United Kingdom enables the Benefit Agencies to easily verify the information of claimants. Claimants may ask to have their benefit payments reduced in order to cover social fund loans or regularly occurring bills (direct payments) (cf. Mannion et al., 1994). They are required to immediately notify the Benefits Agency if their circumstances change in any way relevant to their entitlement to income support (CPAG, 1998: 136). The contact between claimants and the benefit office is relatively infrequent, since the income support scheme does not provide for any one-off payments and thus does not require recurrent contact between the claimants and the officers. Claimants only have to contact the benefit office in case of a change of circumstances.

Unlike income support, payments of the social fund are subject to a higher degree of administrative discretion (see Chapter 6). For this type of benefits, the frequency of contacts between claimants and the administration is much higher. There is some evidence that many potential claimants hesitate to apply for payments from the social fund for the following reasons. First, claimants may hesitate to apply for social fund benefits if they perceive the regulations as complicated and obscure, and the decisions of the social fund officers as unpredictable and arbitrary (Huby and Dix, 1992). Second, obtaining a loan rather than a grant is certainly less attractive to many claimants, given that they have to live on an income below the regular income support levels while repaying the loan if they continue to claim. Third, if the probability of refusal is high, some claimants may not even try to obtain benefits from the social fund. These factors may lead some claimants to the assessment that applying to the social fund was 'not worth the effort' (Huby, 1996: 11; Huby and Whyley, 1996). Indeed, a very rough estimate suggests that usually no more than 4 per cent of claimants apply for a social fund loan or grant during a given year.[209]

The German social assistance scheme combines standardization and discretion (cf. Schulte and Trenk-Hinterberger, 1986; André, 1994). The national framework legislation and the detailed recommendations by the German Association of Public and Private Welfare foster a relatively uniform application, albeit there is still some degree of regional and local variation, notably concerning one-off benefits and other special payments. Benefits normally are paid into a bank account, but payments can also be made in cash (Brühl, 1998: 202-203). Social assistance offices in Germany are allowed to cross-check the information given by claimants with other social security offices and in the car register. Claims are not regularly reviewed, but clients are required to give notice of any change in their circumstances (Ditch et al., 1997). However, due to the sharp differentiation between standard benefit rates and one-off benefits, claimants tend to have more frequent contact with the social assistance benefit office, and experience more means-tests than in Britain. In addition, the discretionary elements of social assistance tend to be more often subject to non-take-up than the more standardized elements. Because of time and budget pressures, social assistance officers may fail to inform claimants about their entitlement to one-off benefits (cf. Stumpfögger and Wiethoff, 1989: 196-198), and the administration of claims may be more sensitive to administrative errors than more standardized procedures. However, the empirical evidence on take-up for one-off benefits is ambiguous. On the one hand, many recipients of social assistance do not claim one-off benefits because of a lack of knowledge, reluctance on the part of social assistance officers or because they are discouraged by yet another application procedure and means-test (cf. Bujard

---

[209] Own calculations based on Department of Social Security (1997) and earlier volumes. The actual application rate is possibly even lower because this estimate is based on the assumption that every client submits no more than one application for a social fund loan or grant during one given year. In practice, however, claimants may apply several times. However, the number of applications may also include some applications from people who are not claiming income support, since recipients of family credit and disability working allowance are also entitled to payments from the social fund.

and Lange, 1978b: 82). On the other hand, there is some evidence that some types of one-off benefits even had higher take-up rates than the standard benefit rate, such as the Christmas allowance and the heating allowance. Apparently, some people claim these benefits even if they are reluctant to claim the standard benefit, possibly in the belief that these one-off benefits do not constitute a part of the social assistance scheme, thus attributing less stigmatizing effects (Bujard and Lange, 1978b: 82).[210]

The processing of claims in the Swedish social assistance has been traditionally closely integrated with social services. However, the increasing caseload in some Swedish cities during the 1980s has lead to the reform of administrative procedures in many municipalities. By now, claiming social assistance often does not necessarily involve an intensive treatment by social workers. Some observers have criticized that the increasing organizational separation of material support and social services undermines the principle of integrity (*helhet*) in the social assistance system. Curtailments in preventive measures and additional services in recent years have intensified this development (Schwarze, 1994: 91-92). However, a more formalized processing of claims may be welcomed by those claimants who perceive the social work treatment as intrusion into their personal lives.

Even though the degree of administrative discretion has diminished with rising recipient rates, these characteristics fully have not disappeared. Clients are required to renew their claim in writing each month, at least in some municipalities (cf. Buhr, 1999: 227), and the degree of discretion is still high. This may even lead to stark inconsistencies in the treatment of the cases. Similar cases may be treated differently, not only subject to variations between municipalities, but also depending on the local office and the social worker involved (Gustafsson et al., 1990). Yet, there seems to be a trend towards more precise standards due to an increasing number of legal appeals since the late 1980s (Schwarze, 1994: 89).[211] In addition, administrative rules and recent attempts to rationalize the administration of benefits limit the discretion of individual social welfare officers.

---

[210] This assessment corresponds to a more recent opinion asserting that the discretionary elements in the German social assistance as such are not responsible for low take-up rates: 'The cause of stigma associated with *Sozialhilfe* does not lie with total administration or discretionary decisions. Far more important, according to respondents, is the application of the means-test, including the recourse to relatives obliged to pay maintenance (about which there is little firm evidence). It is the needs orientation of *Sozialhilfe* which is contrary to the tradition of German social security, dominated by social insurance and based on the principles of reciprocity and restitution which causes the greatest offence. Stigmatization, it could be argued, applies to those who previously have not contributed to their support.' (Ditch et al., 1997: 22, emphasis original).

[211] During the 1980s, the chance for having a decision cancelled by the jurisdiction used to be rather small (Gustafsson, 1993: 254).

A survey among long-term recipients of social assistance in Sweden reveals some discontent about the provision of help. The most serious problems expressed are 'difficulty in approaching the agency' (62 per cent of the sample) and 'weak participation in decisions about oneself' (64 per cent). Discontent about the actual help was less prominent, yet some 40 per cent of the sample indicated that they were dissatisfied with the help received or that they did not receive the requested help at all (Julkunen, 1993a: 186). However, this high degree of discontent is seldom transformed into a formal appeal against a decision. Only one in ten long-term recipients of the sample is reported to have ever formally challenged a decision (Julkunen, 1993a: 197).

Faced with rising claimant numbers and concerns about benefit fraud, social assistance offices in each of the three countries have sought to intensify the degree of control in recent years. Although claimants are usually not required to regularly renew their claim, they are obliged to notify the social assistance office when their circumstances change. The administration of benefits in each of the countries varies, however. The more discretionary way of granting social assistance in Germany, and even more markedly in Sweden, involves more frequent and more intensive contacts with claimants than in Britain. The effect of a high intensity of contact is ambiguous, however. On the one hand, some claimants may hesitate to claim the full benefit they are entitled to if they perceive administrative procedures as unduly time-consuming and stigmatizing. On the other hand, regular contact with the social assistance office may be used to tailor benefits and other help to the needs of claimants, and thus improve the effectiveness of social assistance benefits.

Rights of Appeal Entitlements to social assistance have to be supplemented by strong rights of appeal for claimants, especially if these involve a strong discretionary element. Only if claimants are granted the right to appeal against a decision before a judicial court, the right to social assistance is effectively secured. Non-take-up may be effectively prevented by strong rights of appeal, in case non-take-up is caused by flawed decisions on the part of the administration. If social assistance officers have refused benefits to people who would be entitled for social assistance, or if claimants do not receive the full amount they are entitled to, strong rights of appeal can provide an effective safeguard against non-take-up. These rights do not only secure the rights of individual claimants who decide to appeal against a decision, but also have a more general effect, since the mere possibility of appeals contributes to a uniform and possibly more accurate application of social assistance regulations.

In the United Kingdom, claimants can first turn to the adjudication officer to have their decision reviewed, or submit an appeal to their local social security office. For the review decision taken by an independent tribunal, the adjudication officer submits a written justification of the decision taken. After the hearing of the case, the tribunal decides on the case in question. Both claimants and social security offices are allowed to appeal against this decision to a social security commissioner if the decision of the tribunal is not legally correct. Only if also this decision is believed to be incorrect in legal terms, claimants may turn to a Court of Appeal, and finally to the High Court. On all three levels, plaintiffs are required to obtain a 'leave' from the agency that issued the decision to be invoked in order to gain access to the higher level. If this 'leave' is withheld, plaintiffs are allowed to turn directly to the higher level in order to be admitted to submit an appeal. The costs associated with the appeal of a decision can be met by legal aid for low-income claimants, but only for costs associated with an application to the Court of Appeal and the High Court, not in the early stages of an appeal (CPAG, 1998: 167-185; R. Sainsbury, 2000: 212-214).

Appeal rights in relation to the social fund are dependent on the type of payment claimed for. Appeals related to the regulated social fund are subject to the same review procedure as for other social security benefits. After having their claim reviewed by an adjudication officer at the Benefit Agency, claimants may turn to the social security appeal tribunals, and eventually to the Social Security Commissioners. For discretionary benefits, a different procedure applies. Unlike for regulated social fund payments, there is no possibility of an individual appeal against a decision taken concerning these loans (CPAG, 1998: 492-298; R. Sainsbury, 2000: 214-215). Applicants may only ask for a review of the decision, normally to be handed within 28 days after the decision was taken. After having re-considered the decision by the staff of the local office and then by a senior officer, the client may turn to the Social Fund Inspectorate (cf. Buck, 1996: 1-2, 77-94). The number of reviews brought before the Inspectorate has markedly grown, since the introduction of the social fund in 1988, while the number of staff involved in the review process has more than doubled between 1988/89 and 1993/94 (Buck, 1996: 116). There is some evidence that creaming effects also bias this review procedure, at least in the early years of the social fund (C. Walker, 1993: 140-142).

If claimants are unhappy with a decision in Germany, they have to demand a formal re-examination of the decision before they can turn to the Administrative Court for judicial review (*Widerspruchsverfahren*) (cf. Schoch, 1998; Eichhorn and Fergen, 1998). Claimants have to submit their objection against a decision in writing within one month at the social assistance office. The decision is then reviewed by the administration. Generally, social policy experts (e.g. from charities or claimant associations) have to be consulted in a hearing. The claimant may, but does not have to attend the hearing. If the social assistance office does not agree to revise the decision in question, the claimant may turn to an administrative court, and eventually to appeal courts at the regional and national level. If urgent action has to be taken, the plaintiff may obtain a preliminary ruling in order to avoid hardship. Claimants may apply for legal aid in order to meet the cost of the legal review. This normally applies only to the costs of a lawyer, since claims to invoke a decision on social assistance are normally exempted from court fees (Brühl, 1992: 220-233).

In Sweden, the decisions of the local social welfare office are subject to appeal before the Lower Court, the Country Court and finally the Supreme Administrative Court. The jurisdiction of the courts is based on the recommendations of the National Board for the Social Services regarding the level of benefits (Halvorsen, 1993: 40; Fry and Stark, 1993: 91-99). With the 1998 reform, the rights of appeal of claimants were considerably restricted. Since then, a legal review of benefits is only possible for the portion of benefits that is compulsory for the municipalities, but the municipalities cannot be held responsible for non-compulsory payments.[212] The municipalities had long pressed against having their legal responsibilities restrained.[213]

Every one of the three countries provides the possibility to have the decision of the social assistance benefit offices reviewed. Generally, we can assume that the judicial review of administrative decisions is imperative for claimants' entitlements to social assistance especially in countries where the scope of administrative discretion is large. The Swedish example illustrates this point, given the jurisdiction's role in limiting the municipal discretion in order to safeguard the adequacy of social assistance benefits.

The available empirical evidence on these rights does not allow to clearly discriminate between these countries. Each country protects claimant rights to a certain degree, yet we cannot tell which review procedure is the most effective. We come to believe that the rights of appeal have a similar effect on non-take-up in each of these countries.

Impact of Institutional Structures on Non-take-up

From the evaluation of institutional features of social assistance schemes that are relevant for the issue of non-take-up, certain conclusions could be derived. Table 7.2 summarizes the expected effects of institutional features on take-up rates from the previous sections, as far as the available evidence has allowed to discriminate between countries. A '+' denotes that the institutional framework encourages take-up more strongly than in the two other

---

[212] Socialstyrelsen, personal communication, 20 August 1998.
[213] Svenska Kommunförbundet, personal communication, 18 August 1998.

190 *At the Margins of the Welfare State*

countries, whereas a '-' indicates that the country tends to deter potential claims more strongly than the others. A 'o' is used where the effect has not been sufficiently clear as to establish a tentative rank order of countries.

Table 7.2 Elements of the institutional framework and their effects on non-take-up

Programme Characteristics	Germany	Sweden	UK
General programme structure			
– intransparent programme structure	o	-	+
– insufficient promotion of the scheme in the public	o	o	+
– weak organizational integration with other social security schemes	-	-	+
– weak linkage with other social security benefits	o	-	+
– marginal role within the welfare state	-	-	+
– negative attitudes within the population	+	+	-
Access to the social assistance scheme			
– intransparent application procedure and vague criteria of entitlement	o	-	+
– scheme leaves the initiative to start the claiming process fully to the claimant	(+)	o	o
– strict means-test	o	-	+
– financial liability of family members	-	+	+
Process of claiming			
– claims must often be renewed	o	-	o
– administrative decisions are characterized by a strong degree of discretion	o	-	+
– poor rights of appeal	o	o	o

Source: Own compilation based on the discussion in the text.

From the overview on the effects of institutional structures on take-up summarized in Table 7.2, we can conclude that the British social assistance scheme embodies clearly less obstacles against claiming compared to Germany and Sweden. Most relevant are the close integration of social assistance with other social security schemes, the strong standardization of benefits and income disregards. In contrast, the Swedish social assistance scheme tends to discourage claims much more strongly than in the United Kingdom, largely due to the fragmented nature of the social assistance scheme, the strong emphasis on administrative discretion, the strict means-tests and the frequent renewal of claims. The German social assistance schemes appears to incorporate slightly fewer obstacles to claiming than the Swedish one, as the claiming process is more standardized and less subject to administrative discretion, even though the family liability regulations are assumed to have a detrimental effect on take-up rates.

From this overview of the institutional conditions of take-up, we can conclude that the institutional design of social assistance schemes seems to be most favourable to take-up – and thus most effective in terms of poverty alleviation – in Britain, while the German and possibly even more the Swedish schemes must be considered as less effective.

Empirical Evidence on the Take-up of Social Assistance Benefits

After having formulated expectations for the extent of non-take-up based on the institutional framework of social assistance schemes in the three countries, we can now turn to confront these assumptions with empirical evidence on non-take-up. The following sections will therefore gather and review existing studies of non-take-up in Britain, Germany and Sweden. Their notion of non-take-up is not fully compatible with our understanding of ineffectiveness, however. In order to clarify the relationship between take-up and the effectiveness of social assistance schemes, some methodological issues have to be discussed before turning to the empirical evidence on the extent of non-take-up.

Non-take-up and the Effectiveness of Social Assistance Schemes

The relationship between the effective alleviation of poverty and the problem of non-take-up is not as straightforward as it may seem. Non-take-up of social assistance benefits may lead to an ineffective alleviation of poverty through social assistance schemes, yet it is not necessarily an indicator of ineffectiveness, as the following discussion will show.

Under the assumption that the social assistance benefit level is equal to the poverty line, any non-take-up of benefits can be considered as ineffectiveness, provided that non-take-up can be considered as being directly or indirectly produced by the social assistance scheme (cf. van Oorschot, 1995: 5-9). However, on refuting the assumption that social assistance level and the poverty line coincide, the relationship between non-take-up and ineffectiveness becomes blurred. If the – however defined – poverty line does not exactly match the institutional poverty line, the status of poverty does not necessarily go with an entitlement to social assistance benefits. In other words, the poor are not necessarily eligible for social assistance benefits, and some people may be eligible for social assistance although they are not poor.

Along these two dimensions, the relationship between take-up and an effective alleviation of poverty is illustrated in Figure 7.5. Dependent on whether people are poor and whether they are eligible for social assistance, four possible configurations can be distinguished, two of which demarcate different types of non-take-up (cells A and B, marked by a bold frame).[214] These forms of non-take-up only partly coincide with configurations that are considered as ineffectiveness of the social assistance scheme (cells A and C, marked by shading).

		Need	
		Poor	Non-poor
Eligibility	Yes	A Non-take-up Ineffective	B Non-take-up Effective
	No	C Ineffective (eligibility dimension)	D Effective (but possibly inefficient)

Figure 7.5 Overlapping of non-take-up and an ineffective alleviation of poverty

Source: Based on van Oorschot (*1995*: 2-9).

Non-take-up and an ineffective alleviation of poverty only coincide in the case of a person (or household) who does not receive social assistance benefits in spite of being poor and being eligible for social assistance (cell A). For persons who are eligible for social assistance but not living in poverty, non-take-up may occur (cell B), but we would not interpret this type of non-take-up as ineffectiveness of the social assistance scheme, as people are not poor.[215] A third configuration refers to people who are poor but for some reason not eligible for social assistance (cell C). Most studies on take-up would not include these people in their notion of non-take-up. However, whether this group should be included in an assessment of non-take-up, is debatable and depends on the understanding of targeting in the case in question. If non-take-up within one particular scheme is to be assessed in legal terms, one would certainly not consider these cases as non-take-up, as this

---

[214] Van Oorschot's (1995) introduces an even more detailed classification of non-take-up, as he considers the question of whether people have claimed benefits as one additional dimension. However, as this distinction is not relevant for our argumentation at this point, this peculiarity has been omitted from Figure 7.5.

[215] From an individual perspective, non-take-up of social assistance benefits may be a product of a fully rational decision of individuals in these cases. If people are not poor (or, if they do not perceive themselves as poor), submitting a claim for social assistance may not be attractive because of the associated costs in terms of time and social prestige. In this sense, non-take-up of benefits is not associated with a 'failure' of the social assistance schemes, but must be rather regarded as a consequence of imperfect eligibility rules. The costs associated with claiming can thus be considered as institutional safeguards that complement the formalized means-tests in deterring unjustified claims from people who are not in true need.

group is not formally targeted by the scheme. If the analysis is based on a broader understanding of targeting, relating to the initial aim of the scheme rather than its formal regulations, this group would have to be included, since the programme fails to cover the population it has been targeted upon. In any case, the failure to grant benefits to this group of the population would be considered as ineffectiveness of social assistance schemes, since people are excluded from entitlement because of imperfect eligibility rules within the scheme (Corden, 1995: 5-6).[216] Since the incomplete eligibility of the population as one dimension of ineffectiveness has been already discussed in Chapter 5, this point will not be further discussed here.

Figure 7.5 has illustrated that the problem of non-take-up and an effective alleviation of poverty through social assistance schemes are not necessarily congruent. For the evaluation of effectiveness of social assistance schemes, the concept of take-up thus is both too broad and too narrow. On the one hand, non-take-up can occur without being a problem for an effective alleviation of poverty; this is the case if benefits are targeted onto the non-poor. On the other hand, the *a priori* exclusion of parts of the population from entitlement to social assistance adds to the problem of non-take-up. However, as it is not possible to exactly disentangle these issues in the empirical evidence, the usual indicators for non-take-up are taken as a proxy.

Quantitative Evidence on the Extent of Non-take-up

The empirical evidence on non-take-up of social assistance benefits in European countries is rather limited. Genuinely comparative research in take-up rates is virtually non-existent (cf. van Oorschot, 1995), yet there is a growing number of national studies. Among the countries chosen for this study, Britain stands out with a considerable body of research on non-take-up that has also been officially institutionalised. Evidence on Germany and Sweden is much less readily available, yet we would assume that the problem of non-take-up is much more serious, given that the institutional design of social assistance schemes in these countries seems to encourage non-take-up more strongly than the British scheme. Yet, the programme structure of social assistance in these two countries makes it more difficult to gauge the degree of non-take-up, since benefits are highly dependent on the personal circumstances of potential claimants and also subject to administrative discretion.

---

[216] Studies of non-take-up are not always explicit about this point; some tacitly operate with a broader concept of targeting for methodological reasons (e.g. Neumann and Hertz, 1998), whereas others explicitly use a narrower concept of targeting. The choice of the concept of targeting is often determined by the availability of data for the analysis of take-up: administrative data usually do not allow the application of a broader concept of targeting, whereas survey data often cannot exactly reflect eligibility.

Entitlements thus vary greatly, and this makes the analysis of non-take-up even more difficult. Studies of non-take-up in Germany have often recurred to a lump-sum estimation of additions for special needs, one-off payments and housing costs without being able to assess the actual entitlement of the individual household. The quality of these estimations is however decisive for the extent of non-take-up measured, as the salience of non-take-up may be critically over- or under-estimated (cf. Riphahn, 2000).

It would have been interesting to estimate the extent of non-take-up on the basis of the LIS datasets used for the analyses above, and the calculation of the social assistance entitlements used in the simulation above would have provided a solid basis for these estimations, but this exercise cannot be done for methodological reasons. In order to allow any safe conclusions, take-up estimates have to be calculated from monthly data, as this usually is the time frame that is considered for the determination of claims. Unfortunately, the LIS data only offer yearly data, so any calculation of non-take-up rates based on these data would be seriously flawed. For this reason, the following overview of quantitative evidence on take-up relies on the available empirical evidence in the literature.

United Kingdom The most extensive body of literature on take-up rates has been accumulated for the United Kingdom. Research started in the 1960s and has been based on two main types of sources (cf. Deacon and Bradshaw, 1983; F. Falkingham, 1985). Most large-scale studies relied on the Family Expenditure Survey (FES), but there is also a number of local studies that tend to produce slightly higher non-take-up rates, probably due to a slight underrepresentation of low-income families in the FES (Duclos, 1992: 104-105; 1995: 19-20). The official government statistics produced since the 1970s also use the FES as their database for their estimations of claimant non-take-up, but supplement these figures by administrative data on the amount of expenditure foregone by non-take-up (van Oorschot, 1995: 18).

The available quantitative evidence suggests that the non-take-up rates have been fairly stable since the last 1970s, even through the major reform of 1988 (Fry and Stark, 1993: 38-39). In 1994/1995, some 17-24 per cent of eligible households did not claim social assistance benefits although they were entitled to do so (see Table 7.3). Yet, only 8-12 per cent of expenditure went unclaimed, since the average amount of benefit foregone is considerably smaller than the average amount of benefit collected. This pattern fits well to the general assessment that large amounts of benefits are claimed more readily than small amounts (Fry and Stark, 1993). Thus, there is some evidence that claimants tend to deem small amounts of benefits as being 'not worth' claiming or being too 'costly' in terms of time and effort associated with the procedure of claiming.

Table 7.3 Empirical evidence on non-take-up of supplementary benefit and income support in Britain

Year	1983	1985	1987	1992	1993/94	1994/95	Source
Non-take-up (% of eligible households; claimant count)	24	16 9 37	19 9	13-23	12-21	17-24	A B C
Non-take-up (% of expenditure)	11	9 16	10	7-16	5-11	8-12	A C
Average amount unclaimed (% of average amount claimed)		49	46		48		A

Source: Own compilation based on the following statistics and studies: (A) DSS (various years); (B) Fry and Stark (1993), based on FES data; (C) Duclos (1992: 57) based on DSS data.

Regarding different means-tested benefits, some general patterns emerged: During the second half of the 1980s, supplementary benefit was taken up more frequently than housing benefits, but this pattern has changed since then. By now, housing benefit is now claimed more readily than before, with higher take-up rates than income support.[217] The highest take-up rates were recorded for council tenants, single parents and the long-term unemployed (Fry and Stark, 1993). Groups that are prone to fully claim their entitlement to social assistance are families with children (both single parents and couples), whereas low take-up rates are recorded for the elderly and the self-employed (Duclos, 1992: 66). There is no official evaluation of take-up of the discretionary elements of the Social Fund.[218]

Nevertheless, as the following sections will show, the problem of non-take-up is significantly less marked in Britain than elsewhere, as far as we know. The meagre empirical evidence on non-take-up in other countries suggests that the British situation in non-take-up is still relatively bright when compared to Germany and Sweden.

Germany For Germany, the empirical evidence of non-take-up is much less readily available than for the United Kingdom. It is noteworthy that there are no regular official statistics of non-take-up. However, a number of pioneering studies have assessed the problem of non-take-up of social assistance in the 1970s, spurred by concerns about a large problem of non-take-up for the elderly. Estimates of non-take-up in the whole population for the 1970s were largely based on EVS data (*Einkommens- und Verbrauchsstichprobe*), yet

---

[217] Official statistics of the Department of Social Security based on the Family Resources Survey for 1992-1995, own calculations.
[218] Department of Social Security, personal communication, 22 October 1998.

there are some methodological reservations.[219] On this basis, Klanberg (1979) estimated non-take-up rates of 36 per cent (1969) and 40 per cent (1973); similar calculations of Hauser and his collaborators resulted in slightly higher non-take up rates of 45 per cent (1969) and 49 per cent (1973).[220] With a different methodological design, Hartmann (1981) estimated that only half of all potential claims for social assistance were actually realized, and thereby confirmed some of the earlier estimations. Hartmann's account was based on a large-scale survey with a sample size of 25,000 that also included standardized interviews with some 1,000 people living in low-income households and some 70 in-depth interviews (Hartmann, 1981: 47-54, 155-180). However, not all methodological problems could be resolved.[221]

More recent estimations on the basis of income data and social assistance statistics reckoned the non-take-up rate to be between one third and half of all entitled households during the 1980s on the basis of the EVS data (Hauser and Hübinger, 1993a: 53-54), or even as much as 63 per cent for the early 1990s (Riphahn, 2000). Based on the SOEP, recent estimates reported that less than half of all claims for social assistance have been realized in West Germany during the early 1990s, and even less in East Germany (Neumann, 1999; Neumann and Hertz, 1998).[222] Using micro-simulation techniques in order to account for alleged under-reporting of social assis-

---

[219] The methodological critique of these studies focuses on the fact that large parts of the poverty-prone population were not represented in this study (the homeless, foreigners, persons living in institutions) or are underrepresented due to the methodological design of the survey. People are asked to exactly monitor their household income and expenditure during three months, a demand that many people cannot or do not want to comply with. In response to the fact that 69 per cent of a random sample of the population refused to participate in the first EVS survey in 1961, subsequent surveys have been based on a quota sample of volunteer households. Notably workers and older people had high non-response rates. Nevertheless, EVS data closely correspond to other statistics (Euler, 1992: 467), but it is not clear whether income data for low-income households are of an equally good quality, given these concerns. Besides, considerable delays in the processing of the EVS data preclude up-to-date information on non-take-up (cf. Hartmann, 1981: 40-46; Hauser et al., 1981: 67-70; Schulz, 1989: 192-196).

[220] Cf. Klanberg (1979: 129); Hauser (1981: 73); own calculations.

[221] Hartmann's study also suffered from the impossibility of including homeless and institutionalized people into his sample. People aged 70 or older have also been generally excluded from his sample. By this token, he could not fully resolve the problems of under-representation of low-income households that he had criticized in earlier studies, yet his method allowed him to explore the issue of non-take-up in more detail than the accounts based on EVS data (cf. Hartmann, 1981: 155-180).

[222] The exact figures for West Germany are reported in Table 7.4; for East Germany: the estimates were 80 per cent for 1991 and 70 per cent for 1995. Added together, the respective non-take-up rates for the whole of Germany amount to 59 per cent in 1991 and 52 per cent in 1995 (Neumann, 1999: 29).

tance in the SOEP, Berntsen estimated the extent of non-take-up amounted to 40 per cent of all potential claims or one third of expenditure during the mid-1980s (Berntsen, 1992: 81-82). In addition, Hauser and Hübinger (1993a; 1993b) have analyzed the socio-economic situation of a sample of clients of the Caritas, a church-based charity. In contrast to analyses based on large surveys, this method allowed them to include some groups of the population that are normally not included in surveys, such as the homeless. For the Caritas subsample, non-take-up rates of 38-44 per cent have been found for 1991 (Hauser and Hübinger, 1993a: 110-113; own calculations). Table 7.4 summarizes the evidence on non-take-up of social assistance in Germany.

Table 7.4 Empirical evidence on non-take-up of social assistance in West Germany

Year	~1970	~1975	~1980	1983	1986	1989	1991	1993	1995	1996	Source
Non-take-up (% of eligible households)	55	50	43	38							A
								63			B
			59								C
					~40						D
					70	55	55	53	49		E
										63	F
							38-44				G
		50									H
Non-take-up (% of expenditure)									14		B
					~33						D
							29		25		E
										45	F

Note: All data refer to West Germany.
Source: Own compilation from the following studies: (A) Hauser et al. (1981: 73); Hauser and Hübinger (1993a: 53-55), based on EVS; (B) Riphahn (2000), based on EVS, own calculations; (C) Hartmann (1981: 62), own survey; (D) Berntsen (1992: 81-82), microsimulation based on GSOEP; (E) Neumann and Hertz (1998); Neumann (1999: 29), based on GSOEP; (F) Kayser and Frick (2000: 18, 35), based on GSOEP; (G) Hauser and Hübinger (1993a: 109-113); own calculations (Caritas clients only); (H) Bujard and Lange (1978a; 1978b), own survey; only elderly.

The evidence on non-take-up of social assistance given in Table 7.4 sketches a remarkably stable pattern, although the data do not allow for identifying any trend over time because of different underlying databases and methods. However, all studies agree that there is a substantial degree of non-take-up in Germany. Roughly speaking, only between half and two thirds of eligible households actually realize their entitlement. As in the United Kingdom, the amount unclaimed is smaller than the average amount claimed (Kayser and Frick, 2000).

Most studies agree that non-take-up is most prominent among older people, especially among older women (Hauser et al., 1981: 75-84; Bujard and Lange, 1978a, 1978b). Larger households and families with children (including single parents) tend to take-up social assistance benefits more fully (Riphahn, 2000: 16-17).[223] Hartmann's large-scale study (1981) did produce different results, though. He showed that although older people felt more strongly about stigmatization, the actual salience of non-take-up among the elderly hardly differed from younger age groups (Hartmann, 1981: 94; 128). Riphahn's (2000: 16-17) more recent results do not support this claim, however, as non-take up rates clearly rise with the age of household heads. Only very young households (head under 30) also tend to have low take-up rates, possibly a product of restrictions in eligibility for this age group (see Chapter 5).

Although systematic research on take-up in Germany is still underdeveloped, it seems to be safe to conclude that the salience of non-take up of social assistance is larger than in Britain.

Sweden The empirical evidence about take-up rates of social assistance in Sweden is sparse, at best. The lack of empirical evidence can partly be explained by the characteristics of the social assistance scheme in Sweden. Since benefit rates vary greatly between municipalities, and entitlements strongly depend on the individual circumstances of the household, take-up is much more difficult to assess than in a more standardized system. This fact also precludes a micro-data analysis on the basis of the LIS data.

In a survey conducted in 1985, one tenth of the respondents considered themselves as eligible for social assistance, but only 2 per cent actually claimed (Gustafsson, 1987). Although one has to account for the fact that this type of survey may be distorted for a number of reasons, it is astonishing that only one in five Swedes believing themselves to be eligible for social assistance make use of their right.[224] These survey results are not comparable to the figures reported above, yet their magnitude may constitute a kind of maximum limit of non-take-up rates.

Take-up rates appeared to vary with age, with the lowest rates for the very young and the very old (Gustafsson, 1987). However, there is some evidence that increased information on social assistance in the schools has

---

[223] In addition, non-take-up is more frequent in rural than in urban areas (Riphahn, 2000: 16-17; Hartmann, 1985).

[224] A number of factors may account for overestimation or underestimation of these take-up rates when measured in surveys. On the one hand, people may be reluctant to admit that they believed themselves to be eligible for social assistance, but on the other, people may overestimate the actual level of social assistance and thus wrongly assume themselves to be eligible.

increased take-up rates among young people.[225] Halleröd's finding that being poor and receiving social assistance only overlapped to a small degree has also been interpreted as an indicator for low take-up rates (cf. Halleröd, 1991: 94-102). Non-take-up appears to still constitute a major problem during the 1990s (Sunesson et al., 1998: 24-25).[226] Recent estimates assert that one third of the poor in Sweden do not claim social assistance although being entitled to (Socialstyrelsen, 1997b: 20).[227] Table 7.5 summarizes the thin evidence available on non-take-up of social assistance in Sweden.

Table 7.5 Empirical evidence on non-take-up of social assistance in Sweden

Year	1985	1990s	Sources
Non-take-up (% of eligible households)	(~80)	~33	A B

Source: Own compilation based on the following studies: (A) Gustafsson (1987), based on survey; (B) Socialstyrelsen (1997b: 20).

The empirical evidence on non-take up in Sweden assembled in Table 7.5 precludes any definite interpretation because of very divergent methods and results. All we can conclude from these data is that there seems to be a relatively serious problem of non-take-up in Sweden, but its dimension is fairly obscure. Under the assumption that non-take-up has been fairly stable during the 1980s and 1990s, actual non-take-up rates probably will lie somewhere between these two values, but the exact extent cannot be established on the basis of the available evidence.

Similar to the German case, the thin empirical evidence available seems to confirm our expectation that non-take-up would be more wide-spread in Sweden than in the United Kingdom, but the available data do not allow a direct comparison of Germany and Sweden. The institutional setting of the Swedish social assistance has some characteristics that possibly discourage take-up even more than in the German scheme. It does not only grant social assistance on a largely discretionary basis, but the lack of any income disregards possibly has a further detrimental effect on take-up rates. However,

---

[225] Socialstyrelsen, personal communication, 20 August 1998.

[226] Halleröd (1996b: 49) reports for 1992 that a broad majority of the population (70 per cent) believed that many of those who are eligible for social assistance do not claim.

[227] These data are based on calculations of the Swedish Ministry of Finance. The take-up rate is calculated by substituting the number of people who would not be eligible for social assistance for some reason, e.g. owners of capital assets, students, self-employed, people working part-time or only part of the year or people who did not apply for housing benefit. However, these calculations tend to underestimate the non-take-up of social assistance, since they do not take into account that people may fall into more categories than just one (Socialstyrelsen, personal communication, 20 August 1998).

since we do not have any firm empirical evidence, this point still waits to be verified.

Non-take-up and the Effectiveness of Social Assistance Schemes

Although the empirical evidence on take-up rates is far from perfect, we can safely conclude that non-take-up is much less prevalent in the United Kingdom than in Germany and Sweden. Britain is not only the country with the strongest concern about non-take-up and the best empirical evidence on this issue, but also seems to have the least problem of non-take-up.

What does account for this fact? Can variations in institutional settings, as the general programme structure and the administration of social assistance, explain these outcomes? The discussion of these factors above has identified the following aspects as particularly relevant:

First, the British social assistance scheme is organized in a more standardized way than in Germany and Sweden, with several implications for the take-up of benefits. As the programme structure is rather simple, based on national regulations without regional variations in benefit rates and administered at the national level, information on the availability of benefits and eligibility conditions is more easily disseminated than in the fragmented and more complex benefit schemes in Germany and Sweden. As leaflets and claiming forms for social assistance are accessible at every post office and at every branch of the Benefit Agency, potential claimants can easily obtain the necessary information about their entitlement. In addition, the administrative integration of income support with other social security benefits possibly leads to a higher familiarity with eligibility conditions on the part of social security officers, and makes it easier to complement insufficient incomes by income support.

Second, take-up is expected to be high where social assistance is considered as an individual right rather than something to be granted on a discretionary or charity basis. Entitlements are very strong in Britain; social assistance is highly regulated and the administration of social assistance largely parallels the administration of non-means-tested social security benefits. In terms of administrative procedures, it does not make much difference to claim a pension or social assistance in Britain while the gap is much larger in Germany and Sweden. There, the administration of social assistance benefits lies with a different type of office at the municipal level, and administrative procedures differ more markedly from that of non-means-tested pensions than in Britain. In terms of administrative routines, notably the scope of administrative discretion is assumed to have a negative effect on take-up rates, since it often involves time-consuming application procedures and intensive checks of the claimant's situation that may be perceived as stigmatizing. In addition, discretionary decisions of social assistance officers may be more strongly subject to flawed results than more standardized routines. In Britain, only the social fund provides a discretionary element, yet the significance of this scheme is relatively small. Discretion at the local level is much stronger in Sweden, where municipalities have a say in benefit rates, yet limited by jurisdiction. The German social assistance scheme is governed by national framework legislation, and benefit rates hardly vary across federal states. Yet, there is some degree of administrative discretion in granting one-off benefits.

Third, the rights-based character of the British social assistance is also supported by the relatively generous exemptions for earned income and assets, whereas means-tests in Sweden are much stricter, not allowing for any income disregards. In a way, the design of the Swedish social assistance requires claimants to be 'poorer' than in Britain before granting any benefits. Therefore, the Swedish social assistance is much more strongly grounded in a poor law tradition than the British scheme, and the internal division of the welfare state into social insurance and social assistance is much more pronounced. Germany appears to be situated once again in a middle position, with relatively strong institutionalization of individual rights, yet with some degree of administrative discretion.

Fourth, the rules about liability of the extended family in the German social assistance schemes are assumed to have a detrimental effect on take-up. There is strong evidence that some people abstain from claiming social assistance because they fear that their relatives will be made liable for any social assistance payment. Although this rule is hardly ever applied because of generous income disregards and the general suspension of this rule in some federal states, many people seem to refrain from claiming because they are not aware of these exemptions or because they do not want the test of their relatives' income situation to reveal their own financial situation to their relatives, even if those relatives would not have to pay. Only the German social assistance scheme entails such a regulation of family liability, whereas the British and the Swedish schemes do not require contributions by members of the extended family.

Chapter 8

Conclusion

The starting point of this book was the question of why there is still income poverty in industrial welfare states, despite extensive systems for income redistribution. I argued that it is helpful to take a closer look at the margins of the welfare state, in particular at social assistance and related programmes. The basic safety net they form plays a critical role in shaping the mechanisms of poverty alleviation. In this book, the comparison of three countries – Germany, Sweden and the United Kingdom – helped to identify differences in institutional frameworks and to correlate these differences to the level and structure of income poverty.

Towards an Explanation of Poverty in Industrialized Welfare States

Why is there still income poverty in highly-developed welfare states when the level of social expenditure would suggest otherwise? The evaluation of social assistance schemes has demonstrated that the institutional design of these schemes is a crucial factor to understand the persistence of income poverty. Previous studies on the redistributional impact of the welfare state based on the comparison of pre-transfer and post-transfer income could only provide an incomplete or even flawed picture of the redistributional impact of the welfare state. But a closer look at institutional frameworks offers a more instructive picture of the mechanisms for poverty alleviation. The combination of micro-data and institutional information proposes a new perspective on the incidence of poverty in highly-developed welfare states. This approach is particularly useful for investigating the effectiveness of social security schemes and the outcomes of social policies in general. It illustrates that blending insights from comparative welfare state research with micro-data makes an essential contribution to the deeper understanding of the impact of specific social policy arrangements. Effective poverty alleviation strategies do not depend only on the amount of money that is redistributed, but also on the mechanisms by which this redistribution process is achieved.

Institutional Conditions for an Effective Alleviation of Poverty This book has developed three dimensions by which the effectiveness of social assistance schemes can be measured. These three dimensions reflect preconditions for an effective alleviation of poverty. First, benefits must be available to all persons with insufficient means (eligibility); second, benefits must be generous enough to meet the need of claimants (adequacy); finally, benefits must actually be claimed by the needy (take-up). Social assistance schemes in Germany, Sweden and the United Kingdom have been compared along these dimensions.

As the first precondition for an effective alleviation of poverty, the dimension of eligibility determines access to social assistance. As the above discussion has shown, social assistance is not fully universal in any of the countries examined, as some groups of the population are excluded on the grounds of age, residency or employment status, but cross-national variations in coverage are relatively small. As excluded groups of the population tend to have a lower probability of being included in surveys to measurement of poverty, it is not possible to precisely quantify the impact of the ineligibility of groups of the population on the alleviation of poverty.

The adequacy of social assistance benefits is identified as the second essential precondition for the prevention of poverty. Only when social assistance benefits are generous enough and meet the needs of claimants can poverty effectively be alleviated. The assessment of recipients' benefit packages shows that social assistance benefits do not always guarantee a benefit level that is sufficient to bring claimant households over the poverty line. Especially in the United Kingdom, the income packages available for claimants do not provide for an adequate standard of living for all families. In contrast, the recommended social assistance benefit levels in Sweden offer an adequate benefit level for most households, as do the German social assistance rates.

The effectiveness of the third precondition, take-up, is the most difficult to assess, since we are not only dealing with programme structures and regulations, but with the knowledge, perceptions and expectations of individuals. However, there is strong evidence that institutional structures have considerable direct and indirect effects on take-up. Whereas the unitary organization and standardized administration of social assistance in the United Kingdom are found to spur relatively high take-up rates, the more fragmented and discretionary social assistance schemes in Germany and Sweden are less successful in this respect.

Given the variations in the institutional design of the basic safety nets, we expect to find different patterns of poverty in the three countries considered. We can assume that the relatively high benefit rates of the Swedish social assistance scheme will catapult claimants higher up the income scale than their counterparts in the United Kingdom. However, a relatively large proportion of the Swedish poor will remain in poverty, as the strict procedure of means-testing and the more intrusive administration of social assistance provoke higher non-take-up rates than in the United Kingdom. British social assistance will therefore be more effective in alleviating more severe forms of poverty, while being relatively less effective in improving the income position of claimants in moderate poverty. Sweden and the United Kingdom thus pursue two markedly different strategies in the alleviation of poverty; the latter more effective among the lowest income ranks, but less far-reaching in terms of improving the income position of recipients. The track record of the German system appears to be less clear. Take-up is expected to be significantly lower than in Britain, yet possibly somewhat higher than in Sweden. Benefits are expected to be more adequate than in Britain, but still less generous than in Sweden. The dimension of eligibility has been omitted from this tentative classification, since we cannot derive an unambiguous pattern from the eligibility rules in social assistance schemes that would allow us to discriminate between the three countries.

Strategies of Poverty Alleviation The strategies embodied in the social assistance schemes are expected to produce a characteristic pattern of poverty alleviation in each of the three countries. We expect that the United Kingdom succeeds in protecting people from the harsher forms of poverty, although not all households receive a sufficient level of benefits to pass the poverty line. These expectations confirm earlier accounts of poverty rates and the redistributional impact of the welfare state (Mitchell, 1991; see also Chapter 2 above). In contrast, households that receive social assistance benefits in Sweden should enjoy an income level well above the poverty line. However, we expect that as a relatively large proportion of the population do not file claims in the first place many live below the poverty line. The observation of a large proportion of households living in extreme or severe poverty (Figure 2.1, p. 15) supports this interpretation, yet it should be recalled that this pattern is at least partly due to the differing household definition used in the Swedish data. In the German case, the institutional framework suggests that social assistance benefits are generous enough to bring most households over the poverty line, yet high non-take-up rates contribute to the persistence of poverty. Again, however, methodical flaws in the available data preclude an unequivocal interpretation.

206 *At the Margins of the Welfare State*

Mending the Holes in the Social Safety Net

By and large, the empirical results presented in this book reveal a relatively optimistic picture of the effectiveness of social assistance schemes. In each of the three countries, social assistance schemes provide a fairly good safety net for low income citizens. However, the safety net of each country embodies some specific 'holes' that thwart totally effective alleviation of poverty. If welfare states endorse the goal of poverty alleviation, social assistance schemes should provide universally effective protection from poverty. The mechanisms of poverty alleviation through social assistance schemes that are discussed in this book can provide guidance for future reforms to help to mend the holes in the social safety net.

Setting Benefit Levels In respect to benefit levels, the results of this study reached a fairly positive conclusion about the adequacy of social assistance benefits. Following common practice in comparative poverty research, a relative poverty line of 50 per cent of median equivalent income has been chosen as a yardstick. In Germany and Sweden, the level of the minimum income package is sufficient to bring most claimants out of poverty. The British benefit rates, however, leave some categories of claimants at an income level below the poverty line, and thus are not fully effective at alleviating poverty. If the effectiveness of social assistance schemes is to be improved in this regard, an augmentation of benefit rates for some categories of claimants should have a positive effect. By contrast, the Swedish recommended benefit rates are significantly above the poverty line and thus guarantee an adequate benefit level. Here, some observers are concerned about an overly munificent benefit level rather than an inadequate one, assuming municipalities abide by this standard (e.g. OECD, 1998a). In order to target benefits at the poorest strata of the population, the Swedish strategy uses strict means-tests and the lack of disregards for income and assets. However, this strategy tends to deter many justified claims, as indicated by the extent of non-take-up. Future reforms should consider whether this strategy truly functions to provide effective protection from poverty, or whether benefit levels could be slightly lowered while at the same time introducing income disregards. This is the aim of the recent social assistance reform in Sweden, yet it remains to be seen how effective it will be. In the German case, social assistance benefit rates almost exactly match the relative poverty line, and are thus not only effective, but also efficient in alleviating poverty, as far as benefit rates are concerned. It should however be remembered that findings can vary significantly depending on methodological choices.

Nevertheless, the scope of this study has left some questions unanswered. As some categories of the population are not covered by general social assistance schemes, their level of protection could not be assessed. In addition, the benefit levels in specialized social assistance schemes for some categories of recent migrants remain well below the benefit level for the general population, so these groups often do not enjoy a sufficient protection from income poverty. The effectiveness record of the basic safety net possibly would have been less optimistic if these groups had been better incorporated in the analysis.

Facilitating Access to Social Assistance Schemes The extent of non-take-up suggests that many potential claimants face barriers to claiming, especially in Germany and Sweden. Future reforms should ensure that the population is well informed about the availability of social assistance benefits, that eligibility rules and the rights positions of claimants are transparent, and that application procedures are designed in a way that does not present insurmountable hurdles to potential claimants. A closer integration of social assistance benefits with other programmes is helpful to reduce stigmatization effects.

In the German case, one element of such a reform is the formal abolition of liability of extended family, as it has detrimental effects on take-up. As this regulation has been practically invalidated in some federal states, and only generates a small amount of resources given generous income disregards for liable relatives, the elimination of this regulation will not deprive the social assistance offices of a major source of funds. However, it can markedly improve the living standards of those people who hesitate to claim under this regulation.

In addition, decision-makers could consider reducing the scope of administrative discretion, and such attempts have recently been made in Germany and Sweden. In the German scheme, these reforms focused mainly on the administration of one-off payments. A number of municipalities have experimented with granting lump sums for frequently-claimed goods instead of requiring separate application procedures for each item (Adamaschek, 1998). The Swedish social assistance reform has also reduced the scope of administrative discretion (Socialstyrelsen, 1997a). Although these reforms seem inspired by concerns about high administrative cost rather than low take-up rates, these measures should help to facilitate access to social assistance and thus improve the effectiveness of social assistance schemes.

Balancing Standardization and Discretion In the context of high recipient rates, minimum income policies can follow one of two strategies (cf. Bradshaw and Terum, 1997). The first strategy implies a standardization of benefits, a centralization of the administration and a strengthening of incentives instead of the personal control of recipients. This strategy is similar to the 'liberal type' of social assistance seen in the United Kingdom. The second strategy strengthens local discretion in terms of benefit levels and administration, which resembles the 'communitarian' model of social assistance found in Sweden and Norway (Bradshaw and Terum, 1997). These two strategies not only seem to form the basis of the 'social assistance regimes' found in these countries, but also to drive policy reform in the context of increasing financial burdens by the social assistance schemes (Bradshaw and Terum, 1997: 249, 255; Lødemel, 1997). Yet, a closer look at strategic reform shows a more ambiguous picture. Although the level of administrative discretion of the Swedish municipalities seems to have increased before the recent reform, as Bradshaw and Terum (1997) suggest, there has been a simultaneous trend towards standardization, as in other Scandinavian countries. Administrative procedures were rationalized for 'easy' cases, reserving the more intensive attention of social workers to a small sub-group of recipients with severe non-monetary problems such as drug addiction or mental illness. This suggests that the two strategies can also be pursued simultaneously.

From the perspective of poverty alleviation, both strategies have specific strengths and weaknesses. Whereas a strategy of high administrative discretion may help to customize the benefit package to the needs of claimants, it may also deter many other potential claims because of non-transparent entitlement rules, complicated or time-consuming application procedures and fears of stigmatization. In contrast, a strategy of standardization usually involves relatively easy access to social assistance and grants strong rights positions to claimants, but tends to offer lower levels of benefits that may be insufficient for special needs.

Accounting for the Dynamics of Poverty and Social Assistance Receipt
These prospects for reform fit well in the recommendations for reform that have been derived from research into the temporal patterns of poverty and social assistance. Dynamic research into poverty and social assistance has established firm evidence that there is a considerable degree of mobility in and out of both social assistance and poverty in many industrialized countries. Only a minority of claimants receive continuous social assistance benefits over years, while many people claim social assistance for a short time and quickly leave the system. The high migration in and out of the social assistance scheme also implies that a much larger proportion of the population comes in contact with social assistance offices than the case load numbers at any single point in time would suggest. Consequently, minimum income schemes should be designed to accommodate mobility in and out of need.

Conclusion 209

If poverty spells strike broadly but usually just briefly, then social welfare policies to alleviate poverty look much less like unidirectional transfers between ossified classes and much more like 'insurance' policies which any of us, rich or poor, might someday need. (Goodin et al., 1999: 8).

Thus, minimum income schemes should meet two criteria. On the one hand, they should provide effective protection from poverty when it is needed, without unduly deterring justified claims. This requires strong rights positions for potential claimants, transparent eligibility rules and easily accessible application procedures. On the other hand, minimum income schemes should actively support the tendency to quickly leave the scheme. One major element of social assistance schemes that governs exit is income disregards, in particular disregards for earned income. The existence of this type of disregard may be a beneficial instrument to accelerate exit from the scheme by allowing for a smooth (re-)integration of claimants into the labour market. It is, however, necessary to carefully balance the level of these income disregards, as both too high and too low disregards can have adverse effects. On the one hand, income disregards should offer strong incentives for claimants to take up employment or to stay in low-paid employment rather than being inactive. On the other hand, if income disregards exceed certain limits, wage structures may be distorted by de-facto subsidies of low wages that crowd out regularly paid work or undermine productivity.

Flawed Policies or a Flawed Measurement of Poverty?

The evaluation of the institutional conditions for the alleviation of poverty has exemplified that the ineffectiveness of social assistance schemes is part of the explanation of the persistence of poverty in highly-developed welfare states. Another part of the explanation, however, is provided by the methodological problems in measuring poverty. There is strong evidence of flawed measurement of poverty in common income surveys. Reasons include sampling and non-sampling errors in the available data and limitations in the comparability of results across countries. Social research should devote even more time and attention to the evaluation of the size and direction of these errors, and to minimizing their effects.

The approach chosen in this book may help side-step some of the problems present in income surveys and contribute to their rectification. Confronting micro-data with information about the institutional framework of social assistance schemes has yielded instructive results that could serve as indicators when estimating the specific shortcomings of the available income surveys. This can contribute to their improvement, in particular deepening the understanding of the coverage of lower income strata and the quality of the income data collected. This may require a number of refinements including: more detailed analyses of the coverage of the upper and lower margins of the income scale; a more careful handling of the sampling and interviewing process in order to cover lower and upper income strata more completely; and a more exact representation of income sources in the survey. Indeed, a more fundamental reconsideration of the survey design may be required. Reforms should be made with a view to enhancing cross-national comparability of survey data to enable research based on comparative data collection projects, such as the Luxembourg Income Study, to yield even better and more useful results. Most reforms of income surveys cannot be accomplished, however, without additional cost. Nonetheless, many suppliers and consumers of quantitative data on income agree that it is preferable to have truly reliable data at slightly higher cost rather than cheaper but flawed information. As that these survey data often form the bases for policy decisions, it may be that operating with imperfect information is ultimately more expensive.

In the field of poverty research, the sensitivity of measured results to the choice of household definitions, equivalence scales and the poverty line calls for more cautious interpretations of the results and a renewed interest in the development of alternative instruments for measuring poverty. Again, this is most important for comparative research, as small methodological variations may cause large effects, especially when rank orders are used. As far as poverty rates are used as indicators to evaluate welfare state outcomes, the analyses presented in this book show that an evaluation of welfare state outcomes in terms of poverty alleviation should look beyond easily accessible aggregate data, such as social expenditure ratios and Beckerman ratios, which often have serious methodological limitations. Instead, confronting this evidence with information about the institutional framework in each country can yield much more satisfactory and stimulating results.

Optimizing our knowledge about social reality is one, if not the most important precondition for its improvement. The recent initiatives at the European and the international level to install a system of indicators to monitor and compare national social policies and their outcomes are important steps in this direction. A consistent system of indicators will help to analyze and compare quality of life across countries, and also will contribute to the identification if successful and less successful social policy strategies and their preconditions. It is important to emphasize, however, that any policy conclusions derived from the system of indicators remain dependent on the quality of the indicators. It is evident that the better the system of social indicators, the more focused and ultimately effective the policy response will be.

Appendix

Table A.1 Construction of LIS datasets

Country	Year	Source	Sample Size
Australia	1994	Australian Income and Housing Survey	6,892
Canada	1994	Survey of Consumer Finances	20,826
Denmark	1992	Income Tax Survey	12,798
Finland	1995	Income Distribution Survey	9,249
France	1994	Family Budget Survey	11,286
Germany	1994	Socio-Economic Panel (GSOEP)	6,037
Italy	1995	The Bank of Italy Survey (Indagine Campionaria sui Bilanci Delle Famiglie)	8,070
Luxembourg	1994	The Luxembourg Social Economic Panel Study 'Liewen zu Letzebuerg'	1,809
Netherlands	1994	Socio-Economic Panel (SEP)	5,134
Norway	1995	Income and Property Distribution Survey (Inntekts-og Formuesundersokelsen)	10,101
Sweden	1995	Income Distribution Survey (Inkomstfördelningsundersokningen)	16,221
United Kingdom	1995	The Family Expenditure Survey	6,750
United States	1994	March Current Population Survey	61,041

Note: The sample size refers to households/families in the sample and has been adjusted for the double-counting of households (by excluding multifamily households).
Source: LIS documentation.

Table A.2 Trends in effectiveness of redistribution during early 1990s: full population

country (ranked by poverty rate after redistribution)	poverty rate (rank order)		poverty rate reduction (rank order)	
	before taxes and transfers	after taxes and transfers	absolute (percentage points)	relative (percent)
Belgium 1992	37.5 (4)	4.8 (1)	-32.7 (4)	-87% (2)
Finland 1995	44.3 (10)	5.0 (2)	-39.3 (1)	-89% (1)
Denmark 1992	39.1 (7)	6.8 (3)	-32.3 (5)	-83% (3)
Germany 1994	37.7 (5)	7.4 (4)	-30.3 (7)	-80% (4)
Netherlands 1994	39.4 (8)	7.9 (5)	-31.5 (6)	-80% (4)
Sweden 1995	45.9 (11)	9.6 (6)	-36.3 (2)	-79% (6)
United Kingdom 1995	43.7 (9)	10.0 (7)	-33.7 (3)	-77% (7)
Norway 1995	38.3 (6)	10.2 (8)	-28.1 (8)	-73% (8)
Canada 1994	35.1 (3)	10.3 (9)	-24.8 (9)	-71% (9)
Australia 1994	34.5 (2)	12.5 (10)	-22.0 (10)	-64% (10)
United States 1994	33.7 (1)	18.4 (11)	-15.3 (11)	-45% (11)

Note: Poverty rates are based on a poverty line of 50 per cent of national median income, adjusted for household size according to the modified OECD scale (weights of 1.0 for head of household, 0.5 for each additional adult and 0.3 for each child). Italy and Luxembourg could not be considered because LIS includes only data on net incomes for these two countries.
Source: LIS; own calculations.

Appendix 213

Table A.3 Income poverty and social assistance in Germany, Sweden and the United Kingdom

	social assistance			any means-tested benefit		
	received	not received	total	received	not received	total
Germany 1994						
poor	1.4	6.3	7.7	2.8	4.9	7.7
non-poor	2.1	90.2	92.3	10.5	81.9	92.4
total	3.5	96.5	100.0	13.2	86.8	100.0
Sweden 1995						
poor	1.4	8.1	9.5	2.7	6.8	9.5
non-poor	5.6	84.8	90.5	26.8	63.6	90.5
total	7.0	93.0	100.0	29.6	70.4	100.0
United Kingdom 1995						
poor	3.6	5.9	9.5	4.3	5.2	9.5
non-poor	20.3	70.2	90.5	21.6	68.8	90.5
total	23.9	76.1	100.0	26.0	74.0	100.0

Note: Based on a poverty line of 50 per cent of national medial equivalent disposable income and the modified OECD equivalence scale. Social assistance includes cash social assistance payments (LIS variable v25S1); any means-tested benefits encompasses cash and near cash benefits (LIS variables v25 and v26; see Table 3.2, p. 36).
Source: LIS; own calculations.

Table A.4 Sampling methods for the LIS datasets used in this study

	Britain 1995	Germany 1994	Sweden 1995
Sampling frame	Post Office's Postcode Address File	ADM (Study Group of German Market Research Institutions), based on list of registered voters, plus a subsample of immigrant households	Total Population Register
Sampling method	Multi-stage stratified random sample	Multi-stage random sample with regional clusters	Stratified sample
Sample size	~ 6,500 households	~ 4,600 households	12,532 family units
Type of data	Survey	(Panel) Survey	Tax files plus telephone interviews
Response rate	60%-70%	62% (1984)	Administrative files: near 100% (1996) Interviews: 77% (1996)

Source: LIS Documentation; Harris (1998); Foster (1996) for Britain; Hanefeld (1987); GSOEP (1996) for Germany; Jansson (1994, 1998) for Sweden.

214 *At the Margins of the Welfare State*

Table A.5 Definition of poverty lines for alternative equivalence scales (based on disposable income)

% of median	Germany 1994		Sweden 1995		United Kingdom 1995	
	E_{cl}	E_{sq}	E_{cl}	E_{sq}	E_{cl}	E_{sq}
median	22,720.83	27,909.50	110,985.40	127,827.60	6,861.68	8,330.30
60%	13,632.50	13,632.50	66,591.24	66,591.24	4,117.01	4,117.01
50%	11,360.42	11,360.42	55,492.70	55,492.70	3,430.84	3,430.84
40%	9,088.33	9,088.33	44,394.16	44,394.16	2,744.67	2,744.67
30%	6,816.25	6,816.25	33,295.62	33,295.62	2,058.51	2,058.51

Note: The median and the poverty lines for each country are reported in national currency units and refer to yearly income. Y = disposable household income adjusted for household size, based on alternative equivalence scales (E_{cl} = classical OECD equivalence scale; E_{sq} = aquare root scale). This analysis uses household weights as provided by LIS.
Source: Own calculations from LIS.

Table A.6 Distribution of means-tested benefits on households (percentage of households receiving means-tested benefits in each poverty bracket)

Poverty lines (% of median)	Germany 1994		Sweden 1995		United Kingdom 1995	
	E_{cl}	E_{sq}	E_{cl}	E_{sq}	E_{cl}	E_{sq}
extreme poverty	67	65	52	51	86	86
severe poverty	54	36	55	52	65	74
moderate poverty	37	44	48	49	69	63
near poverty	40	29	53	56	47	42
no poverty	7	7	25	24	8	7

Note: Y = disposable household income adjusted for household size, based on alternative equivalence scales (E_{cl} = classical OECD equivalence scale; E_{sq} = square root scale). The results for the modified OECD equivalence scale are provided in the text.
Example: Among all households living in extreme poverty before means-tested transfers in Germany 1994, 67 per cent received some kind of means-tested transfers according to the classical OECD equivalence scale, and 65 per cent according to the square root scale.
Source: Own calculations from LIS.

Appendix 215

Table A.7 Distribution of means-tested benefits on households (percentage of households receiving means-tested benefits in each poverty bracket)

Poverty lines (% of median)	Germany 1994		Sweden 1995		UK 1995	
	E_{cl}	E_{sq}	E_{cl}	E_{sq}	E_{cl}	E_{sq}
Poverty Status BEFORE means-tested benefits						
extreme poverty	5,1	5,5	8,3	8,9	12,1	12,3
severe poverty	1,8	2,2	2,1	2,5	2,7	4,8
moderate poverty	2,9	3,3	2,8	3,1	7,0	7,3
near poverty	4,7	5,0	4,1	5,1	7,2	6,2
50% poverty (cumul.)	*9,8*	*10,9*	*13,2*	*14,4*	*21,8*	*24,4*
Poverty Status AFTER means-tested benefits						
extreme poverty	2,3	2,5	4,9	5,4	2,1	2,2
severe poverty	1,7	2,5	1,5	2,0	2,3	2,3
moderate poverty	3,4	3,4	2,3	2,6	5,2	6,3
near poverty	5,0	5,8	3,3	4,3	7,6	8,9
50% poverty (cumul.)	*7,4*	*8,5*	*8,7*	*9,9*	*9,6*	*10,8*
Impact of means-tested benefits in absolute terms (Percentage Points)						
extreme poverty	-2,8	-3,0	-3,4	-3,5	-10,0	-10,0
severe poverty	-0,1	+0,4	-0,6	-0,5	-0,4	-2,5
moderate poverty	+0,5	+0,2	-0,5	-0,5	-1,8	-1,0
near poverty	+0,2	+0,8	-0,7	-0,8	+0,4	+2,6
50% poverty (cumul.)	*-2,5*	*-2,4*	*-4,5*	*-4,5*	*-12,2*	*-13,6*
Impact of means-tested benefits in relative terms (Percent)						
extreme poverty	-55%	-54%	-41%	-39%	-83%	-82%
severe poverty	-8%	+17%	-29%	-20%	-16%	-52%
moderate poverty	+17%	+5%	-18%	-17%	-25%	-14%
near poverty	+5%	+16%	-18%	-16%	+5%	+42%
50% poverty (cumul.)	*-25%*	*-22%*	*-34%*	*-31%*	*-56%*	*-56%*

Note: Y = disposable household income adjusted for household size, based on alternative equivalence scales (E_{cl} = classical OECD equivalence scale; E_{sq} = square root scale).
Example: For the United Kingdom 1995, 12.1 per cent (12.3 per cent) of the population were extremely poor before having received some kind of means-tested transfers and 2.1 per cent (2.2 per cent) after having received some transfers. Poverty rates for this poverty bracket were thus reduced by 10.0 percentage points or by 83 per cent (82 per cent) compared to the pre-transfer poverty rate, based on the classical OECD equivalence scale (square root scale in brackets).
Source: Own calculations from LIS.

216 *At the Margins of the Welfare State*

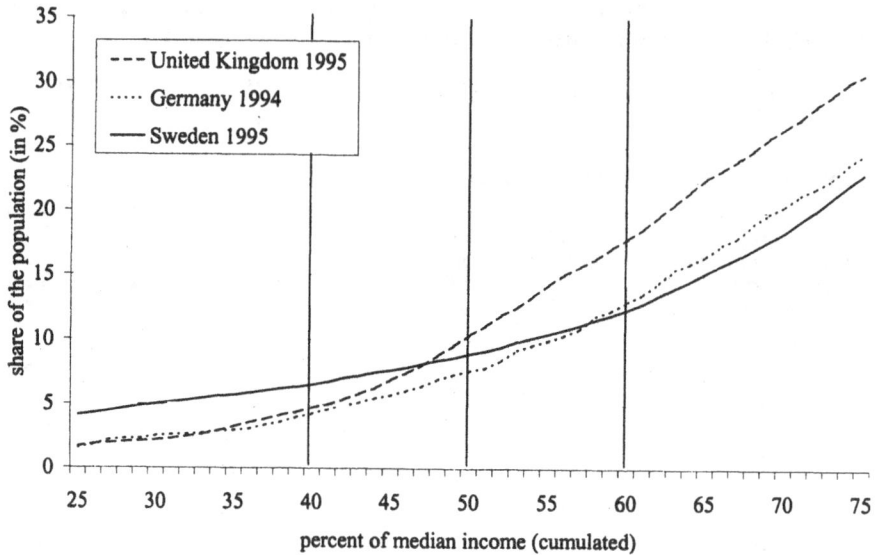

Figure A.1 Low Income Profiles for different equivalence scales for Britain, Germany and Sweden; classical OECD equivalence scale

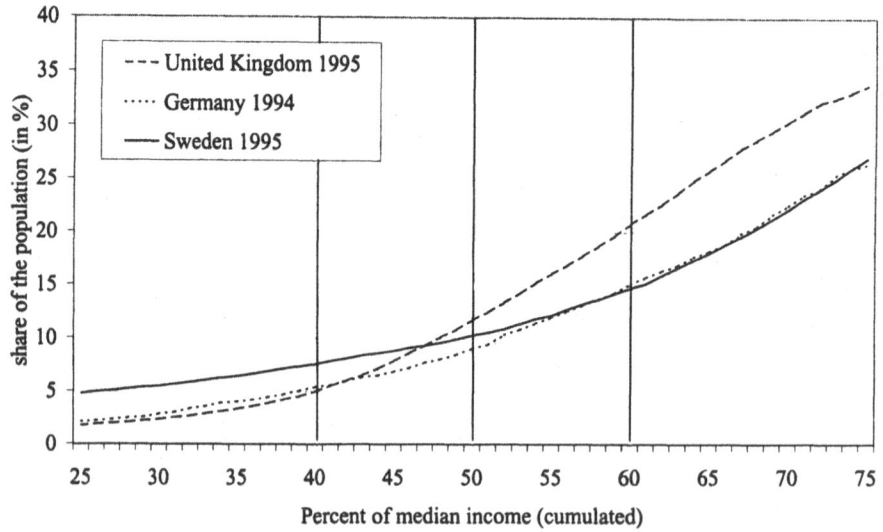

Figure A.2 Low Income Profiles for different equivalence scales (cumulated) for Britain, Germany and Sweden; square root scale

Appendix 217

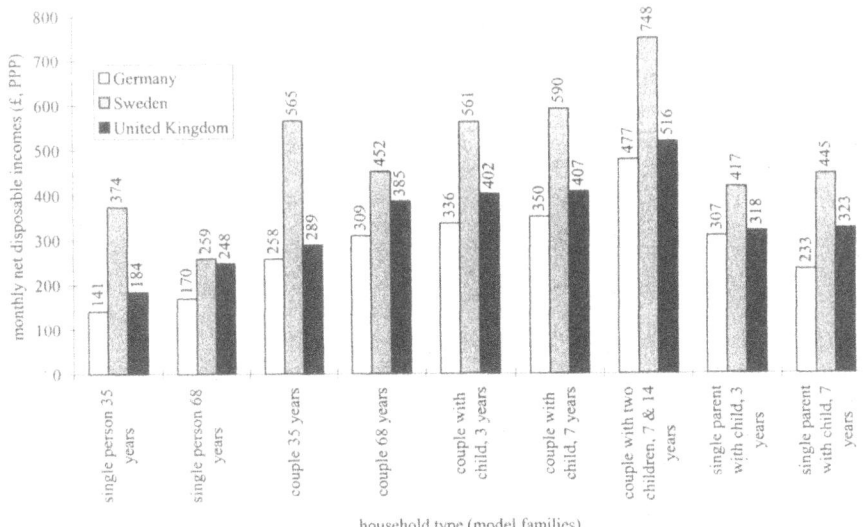

Figure A.3 Benefit package of social assistance recipients in Germany, Sweden and the United Kingdom (before housing costs), 1992

Source: Eardley et al. (1996a: 125). Social assistance rates and housing costs refer to the cities of Bremen, Stockholm and York.

218   *At the Margins of the Welfare State*

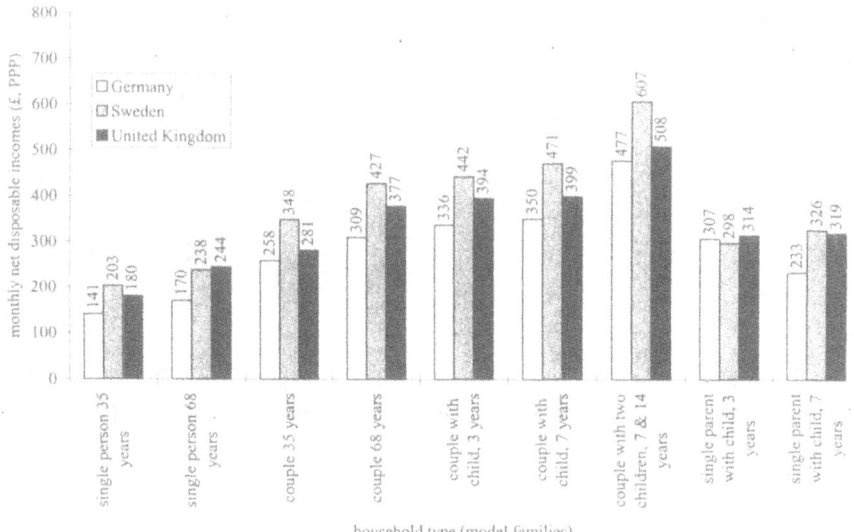

Figure A.4 Benefit package of social assistance recipients in Germany, Sweden and the United Kingdom (after housing costs), 1992

Source: Eardley et al. (1996a: 126). Social assistance rates and housing costs refer to the cities of Bremen, Stockholm and York.

Bibliography

Aaberge, R. and I. Melby (1998), The Sensitivity of Income Inequality to the Choice of Equivalence Scales, *Review of Income and Wealth* 44 (4): 565-569.
Adamaschek, B. (ed.) (1998), *Interkommunaler Leistungsvergleich: Sozialwesen*, Gütersloh: Bertelsmann Foundation.
Adler, M. (1997), The 'Habitual Residence Test' for Social Assistance in the United Kingdom and Its Implications for Migrants, in E. Eichenhofer (Ed.) *Social Security of Migrants in the European Union of Tomorrow*, Osnabrück: Universitätsverlag Rasch: 53-62.
Aguilar, R. and B. A. Gustafsson (1989), *Social Assistance and Public Expenditures*, Working Paper of the Department of Economics, Göteborg: Göteborgs universitet.
Alber, J. (1982), *Vom Armenhaus zum Wohlfahrtsstaat: Analysen zur Entwicklung der Sozialversicherung in Westeuropa*, Frankfurt (Main)/New York: Campus.
—— (1996), *Selectivity, Universalism, and the Politics of Welfare State Retrenchment in Germany and the United States*, presented at the 92nd Annual Meeting of the American Political Science Association, San Francisco (USA), 31 August 1996.
—— (1997), Il ripensamento del welfare state in Germania e negli Stati Uniti, *Rivista Italiana di Scienza Politica* XXVII (1): 49-100.
Alber, J. and M. Schölkopf (1999), *Seniorenpolitik: Die soziale Lage älterer Menschen in Deutschland und Europa*, Amsterdam: G+B Fakultas.
Alessie, R., A. Lusardi and T. Aldershof (1997), Income and Wealth over the Life Cycle: Evidence from Panel Data, *Review of Income and Wealth* 43 (1): 1-32.
André, G. (1994), *Sozialamt: Eine historisch-systematische Einführung in seine Entwicklung*, Weinheim/Basel: Beltz.
Andreß, H.-J. (1999), *Leben in Armut: Analysen der Verhaltensweise Armer Haushalte mit Umfragedaten*, Opladen: Westdeutscher Verlag.
Andreß, H.-J. and G. Lipsmeier (1995), Was gehört zum notwendigen Lebensstandard und wer kann ihn sich leisten? Ein neues Konzept zur Armutsmessung, *Aus Politik und Zeitgeschichte* (B 31-32): 35-49.
Andreß, H.-J., G. Lipsmeier, R. Samson and W. Strengmann-Kuhn (1995), *Einkommensanalysen mit Daten des Sozio-ökonomischen Panels: Beschreibung der Längsschnittdatei A_J mit Datenprüfungen und -ersetzungen und einer Sozialhilfe-Simulation*, Arbeitspapier des DFG-Projekts, Fakultät für Soziologie, Bielefeld: Universität Bielefeld.

Ashworth, K., R. Walker and P. Trinder (1997), *Benefit Dynamics in Britain: Routes on and off Income Support*, Working Paper of the Centre for Research in Social Policy No. 253S, Loughborough: Loughborough University.
Atkinson, A. B. (1989 [1984]), Take-up of Social Security Benefits, in A. B. Atkinson (ed.) *Poverty and Social Security*, Hemel Hempstead: Harvester Wheatsheaf: 190-207.
—— (1990), *A National Minimum? A History of Ambiguity in the Determination of Benefit Scales in Britain*, STICERD Welfare State Programme, Discussion Paper No. WSR/47, London: London School of Economics.
—— (1998), *Poverty in Europe*, Oxford: Blackwell.
—— (1999), *The Economic Consequences of Rolling Back the Welfare State*, Cambridge (Mass.): MIT Press.
Atkinson, A. B., K. Gardiner, V. Lechêne and H. Sutherland (1998), Comparing Poverty Rates across Countries: A Case Study of France and the United Kingdom, in S. P. Jenkins, A. Kapteyn and B. M. S. van Praag (eds.), *The Distribution of Welfare and Household Production: An International Perspective*, Cambridge: Cambridge University Press: 50-74.
Atkinson, A. B. and J. Micklewright (1983), On the Reliability of Income Data from the Family Expenditure Survey 1970-1977, *Journal of the Royal Statistical Society, Series A* 146 (1): 33-61.
Atkinson, A. B. and G. V. Mogensen (eds.) (1993), *Welfare and Work Incentives - a North European Perspective*, Oxford: Clarendon.
Atkinson, A. B., L. Rainwater and T. M. Smeeding (1995), *Income Distribution in OECD Countries: Evidence from the Luxembourg Income Study*, Paris: OECD.
Atkinson, A. B. and H. Sutherland (1998), Microsimulation and Policy Debate: A Case Study of the Minimum Pension Guarantee in Britain, in H. P. Galler and G. Wagner (eds.), *Empirische Forschung und wirtschaftspolitische Beratung*, Frankfurt (Main)/New York: Campus: 79-98.
Bäcker, G. and W. Hanesch (1998), Sozialhilfe und Erwerbstätigkeit: Zur Diskussion über den Erwerbstätigenfreibetrag, *Nachrichtendienst des Deutschen Vereins für öffentliche und private Fürsorge* 78 (9): 264-272.
Baldwin, P. (1990), *The Politics of Social Solidarity: Class Bases of the European Welfare State 1875-1975*, Cambridge: Cambridge University Press.
Bechtold, S., W. Bihler and D. Deininger (1993), Einmalige Leistungen der Hilfe zum Lebensunterhalt nach §21 BSHG im Jahr 1991, *Aus Wirtschaft und Statistik* (2): 113-125.
Beckerman, W. (1979), *Poverty and the Impact of Income Maintenance Programmes in Four Developed Countries - Case Studies of Australia, Belgium, Norway and Great Britain*, Geneva: International Labour Office.
Bedau, K.-D. and P. Krause (1998), Das Einkommen der privaten Haushalte nach unterschiedlichen Statistiken, *Wochenberichte des Deutschen Instituts für Wirtschaftsforschung* 64 (3): 209-233.
Behrendt, C. (2000a), Do Means-Tested Transfers Alleviate Poverty? Evidence on Germany, Sweden and the United Kingdom from the Luxembourg Income Study, *Journal of European Social Policy* 10 (1): 23-41.

—— (2000b), Lücken im sozialen Netz und Armutsrisiken in vergleichender Perspektive: Alleinerziehende und alleinstehende ältere Frauen in Deutschland, Großbritannien und Schweden, *Zeitschrift für Sozialreform* 46 (2): 137-173.

—— (2000c), Private Pensions - a Viable Alternative? Their Distributive Effects in a Comparative Perspective, *International Social Security Review* 53 (3): 3-26.

Bennett, F. (1998a), Social Policy Digest, *Journal of Social Policy* 27 (1): 99-121.

—— (1998b), Social Policy Digest, *Journal of Social Policy* 27 (3): 397-420.

Bergmark, Å. and P. Sandgren (1998), *Vilka faktorer bestämmer socialbidragskostnaderna? En analysis av kommunaler variationer*, Stockholm: Socialstyrelsen.

Berntsen, R. (1989), *Einkommensanalysen mit Daten des Sozio-ökonomischen Panels unter Verwendung von Generierten Einkommensdaten*, Arbeitspapier des Sfb 3: 'Mikroanalytische Grundlagen der Gesellschaftspolitik' No. 291, Frankfurt (Main): Johann Wolfgang Goethe-Universität.

—— (1992), *Dynamik in der Einkommensverteilung privater Haushalte: Eine empirische Längsschnittanalyse für die Bundesrepublik*, Frankfurt (Main)/New York: Campus.

Berthoud, R. (1983), *Study of the Reformed Supplementary Benefit Scheme*, London: Policy Studies Institute.

Bishop, J. A., J. P. Formby and L. A. Zeager (1996), The Impact of Food Stamps on US Poverty in the 1980s: A Marginal Dominance Analysis, *Economica* 63 (250, Supplement): S141-162.

Björklund, A. (1998), Income Distribution in Sweden: What Is the Achievement of the Welfare State? *Swedish Economic Policy Review* 5: 39-80.

Blackburn, M. L. (1994), International Comparisons of Poverty, *American Economic Review* 84: 371-374.

—— (1998), The Sensitivity of International Poverty Line Comparisons, *Review of Income and Wealth* 44 (4): 449-472.

Blackburn, M. L. and D. E. Bloom (1994), *Changes in the Structure of Family Income Inequality in the United States and Other Industrial Nations During the 1980s*, NBER Working Paper Series No. 4754, Cambridge (Mass.): National Bureau of Economic Research.

Blank, R. M. and P. Ruggles (1996), When Do Women Use Aid to Families with Dependent Children and Food Stamps?, *Journal of Human Resources* 31 (1): 57-89.

Block, F. (1987), Rethinking the Political Economy of the Welfare State, in F. Block, R. A. Cloward, B. Ehrenreich and F. F. Piven (eds.), *The Mean Season: The Attack on the Welfare State*, New York: Pantheon Books: 109-160.

Blundell, R. (2000), Work Incentives and 'in-Work' Benefit Reforms: A Review, *Oxford Review of Economic Policy* 16 (1): 27-44.

Böhnke, P. and J. Delhey (1999), *Poverty in a Multidimensional Perspective: Great Britain and Germany in Comparison*, Diskussionspapier der Arbeitsgruppe Sozialberichterstattung des Wissenschaftszentrums Berlin für Sozialforschung No. FS III 99-413, Berlin: WZB.

Bolderson, H. and S. Roberts (1995), New Restrictions on Benefits for Migrants: Xenophobia or Trivial Pursuits?, *Benefits* (January): 11-15.

Boss, A. (1999), *Sozialhilfe, Lohnabstand und Leistungsanreize*, Kieler Arbeitspapiere No. 912, Kiel: Institut für Weltwirtschaft an der Universität Kiel.

Bradshaw, J. R. (1995), Simulating Policies: An Example in Comparative Method, in B. Palier (ed.) *Comparing Social Welfare Systems in Europe, Vol. 1, Oxford Conference (France - United Kingdom)*, Paris: MIRE: 439-460.

—— (1997), Social Assistance in Comparative Perspective, in P. R. De Jong and T. R. Marmor (eds.), *Social Policy and the Labour Market*, Aldershot: Ashgate: 235-257.

Bradshaw, J. R. and U. Björnberg (1997), Lone Mothers, Policy and Employment in 20 Countries, in P. R. De Jong and T. R. Marmor (eds.), *Social Policy and the Labour Market*, Aldershot: Ashgate: 259-283.

Bradshaw, J. R. and L. I. Terum (1997), How Nordic Is the Nordic Model? Social Assistance in a Comparative Perspective, *Scandinavian Journal of Social Welfare* 6: 247-256.

Breuer, W. and D. Engels (1994), *Bericht und Gutachten zum Lohnabstandsgebot*, Schriftenreihe des Bundesministerium für Familie und Senioren No. 29, Bonn: German Ministry for Families and the Elderly.

—— (1998), *Grundinformationen und Daten zur Sozialhilfe*, Bonn: German Ministry for Health.

Brühl, A. (1992), *Mein Recht auf Sozialhilfe*, 9th edition, Munich: dtv.

—— (1998), *Mein Recht auf Sozialhilfe*, 15th edition, Munich: dtv.

Brungger, H. (1996), *The Use of Purchasing Power Parities in International Comparisons*, presented at the First Meeting of the Canberra Group, Expert Group on Household Income Statistics, Canberra (Australia), December 1996.

Buck, T. (1996), *The Social Fund: Law and Practice*, London: Sweet & Maxwell.

Buhmann, B., L. Rainwater, G. Schmaus and T. M. Smeeding (1988), Equivalence Scales, Well-Being, Inequality and Poverty: Sensitivity Estimates across Ten Countries Using the Luxembourg Income Study (LIS) Database, *Review of Income and Wealth* 34: 114-142.

Buhr, P. (1995), *Dynamik von Armut: Dauer und biographische Bedeutung von Sozialhilfe*, Opladen: Westdeutscher Verlag.

—— (1999), Vorbild Schweden? Armut und Sozialhilfe in unterschiedlichen Wohlfahrtsstaaten, *Leviathan* 27 (2): 218-237.

Bujard, O. and U. Lange (1978a), *Armut im Alter: Ursachen, Erscheinungsformen, politisch-administrative Reaktionen*, Weinheim/Basel: Beltz.

—— (1978b), *Theorie und Praxis der Sozialhilfe: Zur Situation der einkommensschwachen alten Menschen*, Schriftenreihe des Bundesministers für Jugend, Familie und Gesundheit No. 56, Stuttgart: Kohlhammer.

Bundesminister für Jugend, Familie und Gesundheit (ed.) (1985), *Regelsatz und Warenkorb in der Sozialhilfe: Eine Untersuchung zu Ausgaben- und Verbrauchsstrukturen bei Sozialhilfeempfängerhaushalten*, Schriftenreihe des Bundesministers für Jugend, Familie und Gesundheit, Bonn: Bundesminister für Jugend, Familie und Gesundheit.

Bundesministerium für Arbeit und Sozialordnung (1994), *Übersicht über das Sozialrecht*, Bonn: Bundesministerium für Arbeit und Sozialordnung.
—— (1997), *Übersicht über das Sozialrecht*, Bonn: Bundesministerium für Arbeit und Sozialordnung.
—— (1998), *Übersicht über das Sozialrecht (Stand 1. Januar 1998)*, Bonn: Bundesministerium für Arbeit und Sozialordnung.
Bundesministerium für Gesundheit (1996), *Sozialhilfereform*, Bonn: Bundesministerium für Gesundheit.
—— (1997), *Asylbewerberleistungsgesetz*, Bonn: Bundesministerium für Gesundheit.
Burchardt, T., J. Le Grand and D. Piachaud (1999), Social Exclusion in Britain 1991-1995, *Social Policy and Administration* 33 (3): 227-244.
Burkhauser, R. V., J. R. Frick and J. Schwarze (1997), A Comparison of Alternative Measures of Economic Well-Being for Germany and the United States, *Review of Income and Wealth* 43 (2): 153-171.
Burkhauser, R. V., T. M. Smeeding and J. Merz (1996), Relative Inequality and Poverty in Germany and the United-States Using Alternative Equivalence Scales, *Review of Income and Wealth* 42 (4): 381-400.
Burniaux, J.-M., T.-T. Dang, D. Fore, M. Förster, M. Mira d'Ercole and H. Oxley (1998), *Income Distribution and Poverty in Selected OECD Countries*, Economic Department Working Papers No. 189, Paris: OECD.
Byberg, I. (1998), *Arbetsmetoder och socialbidrag: En studie av olika faktorers betydelse för kommunernas socialbidragskostnader*, SoS-Rapport No. 1998:11, Stockholm: Socialstyrelsen.
Callan, T., B. Nolan and C. T. Whelan (1993), Resources, Deprivation and the Measurement of Poverty, *Journal of Social Policy* 22: 141-172.
Castles, F. G. and D. Mitchell (1993), Worlds of Welfare and Families of Nations, in F. Castles (ed.) *Families of Nations: Patterns of Public Policy in Western Democracies*, Aldershot: Dartmouth: 93-128.
Central Statistical Office (1999), *Documentation of the Family Expenditure Survey, 1994-1995*: The Data Archive, University of Essex.
Coleman, J. (1982), Income Testing and Social Cohesion, in I. Garfinkel (ed.) *Income-Tested Transfer Programs: The Case for and Against*, New York: Academic Press: 67-88.
Corden, A. (1995), *Changing Perspectives on Benefit Take-Up*, London: HMSO.
Corden, A. and P. Craig (1991), *Perceptions of Family Credit*, Report of the Social Policy Research Unit, London: HMSO.
Cornia, G. A. (1997), Child Poverty and Deprivation in the Industrialized Countries from the End of World War II to the End of the Cold War Era, in G. A. Cornia and S. Danziger (eds.), *Child Poverty and Deprivation in the Industrialized Countries, 1945-1995*, Oxford: Clarendon: 25-63.
Cornia, G. A. and S. H. Danziger (eds.) (1997), *Child Poverty and Deprivation in the Industrialized Countries, 1945-1995*, Oxford: Clarendon.
CPAG (1997a), *National Welfare Benefits Handbook 1997/98*, London: Child Poverty Action Group.

—— (1997b), *Rights Guide to Non-Means-Tested Benefits 1997/98*, London: Child Poverty Action Group.
—— (1998), *National Welfare Benefits Handbook 1998/99*, London: Child Poverty Action Group.
de Vos, K. and M. A. Zaidi (1997), Equivalence Scale Sensitivity of Poverty Statistics of Member States of the European Community, *Review of Income and Wealth* 43 (3): 319-333.
Deacon, B. and J. R. Bradshaw (1983), *Reserved for the Poor: The Means-Test in British Social Policy*, London: Martin Robertson.
Deleeck, H., K. Van den Bosch and L. De Lathouwer (1992), *Poverty and the Adequacy of Social Security in the EC - a Comparative Analysis*, Aldershot: Avebury.
Department of Social Security (1992), *Social Security Statistics 1992*, London: HMSO.
—— (1997), *Social Security Statistics 1997*, London: HMSO.
—— (1998), *Social Security Statistics 1998*, London: HMSO.
Deutscher Verein für öffentliche und private Fürsorge (1992), Empfehlungen des Deutschen Vereins für den Einsatz des Vermögens in der Sozialhilfe, *Nachrichtendienst des Deutschen Vereins für öffentliche und private Fürsorge* (5): 141-148.
Ditch, J. (1995), Comparing Discretionary Payments within Social Assistance Schemes, in B. Palier (ed.) *Comparing Social Welfare Systems in Europe, Vol. 1, Oxford Conference (France - United Kingdom)*, Paris: MIRE: 337-368.
Ditch, J., J. Bradshaw, J. Clasen, M. Huby and M. Moodie (1997), *Comparative Social Assistance: Localisation and Discretion*, Aldershot: Ashgate.
Dixon, J. (1999), Comparative Social Security: The Challenge of Evaluation, *Journal of Comparative Policy Analysis* 1: 61-95.
Douglas, M. and B. C. Isherwood (1979), *The World of Goods*, New York: Basic Books.
Duclos, J.-Y. (1992), *The Take-up of State Benefits: An Application to Supplementary Benefits in Britain Using the FES*, STICERD Welfare State Programme, Discussion Paper No. WSP/71, London: London School of Economics.
—— (1995), Modelling the Take-up of State Support, *Journal of Public Economics* 58 (3): 391-415.
Duncan, G. J., B. A. Gustafsson, R. Hauser, G. Schmaus, S. Jenkins, H. Messinger, R. A. Muffels, B. Nolan, J.-C. Ray and W. Voges (1995), Poverty and Social Assistance Dynamics in the United States, Canada, and Europe, in K. McFate, R. Lawson and W. J. Wilson (eds.), *Poverty, Inequality, and the Future of Social Policy*, New York: Russell Sage Foundation: 67-108.
Duncan, S. and R. Edwards (eds.) (1997), *Single Mothers in International Context: Mothers or Workers*, London: Taylor & Francis.
Eardley, T., J. Bradshaw, J. Ditch, I. Gough and P. Whiteford (1996a), *Social Assistance in OECD Countries, Volume I: Synthesis Report*, Department of Social Security Research Report No. 46, London: HMSO.

Bibliography 225

—— (1996b), *Social Assistance in OECD Countries, Volume II: Country Reports*, Department of Social Security Research Report No. 46, London: HMSO.
Eichhorn, H. and B. Fergen (1998), *Praxis der Sozialhilfe: Nachschlagewerk für Praxis und Lehre*, Mainz: Eichhorn & Fergen.
Elmer, Å. (1989), *Svensk socialpolitik*, Malmö: Liber.
Esping-Andersen, G. (1990), *The Three Worlds of Welfare Capitalism*, Cambridge: Polity.
—— (1999), *Social Foundations of Postindustrial Economies*, Oxford: Oxford University Press.
Euler, M. (1983), Erfassung und Darstellung der Einkommen privater Haushalte in der amtlichen Statistik, *Wirtschaft und Statistik* (1): 56-62.
—— (1992), Einkommens- und Verbrauchsstichprobe 1993, *Wirtschaft und Statistik* (7): 463-469.
European Commission (1999), *A Concerted Strategy for Modernising Social Protection*, Brussels: European Commission.
Evans, M. C. (1994), *Not Granted? An Assessment of the Change from Single Payments to the Social Fund*, STICERD Welfare State Programme, Discussion Paper No. WSP/101, London: London School of Economics.
Falkingham, F. (1985), *Take-up of Benefits: A Literature Review*, Benefits Research Unit Review Paper No. 1:1985, Nottingham: University of Nottingham.
Falkingham, J. and J. Hills (eds.) (1995), *The Dynamic of Welfare: The Welfare State and the Life Cycle*, London: Prentice Hall.
Fasselt, U. (1997), Sozialhilfe für Ausländer, in K. Barwig, K. Sieveking, G. Brinkmann, K. Lörcher and S. Röseler (eds.), *Sozialer Schutz von Ausländern in Deutschland*, Baden-Baden: Nomos: 315-329.
Findlay, J. and R. E. Wright (1996), Gender, Poverty and the Intra-Household Distribution of Resources, *Review of Income and Wealth* 42 (3): 335-351.
Flora, P. (ed.) (1986), *Growth to Limits: The Western European Welfare States since World War II (3 Volumes)*, Berlin: de Gruyter.
Flora, P. and A. J. Heidenheimer (eds.) (1981), *The Development of Welfare States in Europe and America*, New Brunswick: Transaction Books.
Ford, R. (1998), Lone Mothers' Decision of Whether or Not to Work: Childcare in the Balance, in R. Ford and J. Millar (eds.), *Private Lives and Public Responses*, London: Policy Studies Institute: 208-225.
Ford, R. and J. Millar (eds.) (1998), *Private Lives and Public Responses*, London: Policy Studies Institute.
Förster, M. F. (1994), The Effects of Net Transfers on Low Incomes among Non-Elderly Families, *OECD Economic Studies* (22): 181-221.
Foster, K. (1996), A Comparison of the Census Characteristics of Respondents and Non-Respondents to the 1991 Family Expenditure Survey, *Survey Methodology Bulletin* 38 (1): 9-17.
Freeman, G. P. (1986), Migration and the Political Economy of the Welfare State, *Annals of the American Academy of Political and Social Science* 485: 51-63.
Fridberg, T. (ed.) (1993), *On Social Assistance in the Nordic Capitals*, Kopenhagen: Socialforskningsinstituttet.

Fry, V. and G. Stark (1993), *The Take-up of Means-Tested Benefits, 1984-90*, London: Institute for Fiscal Studies.
George, V. and R. Lawson (1980), Introduction, in V. George and R. Lawson (eds.), *Poverty and Inequality in Common Market Countries*, London: Routledge & Kegan Paul.
Glatzer, W. and W. Hübinger (1990), Lebenslagen und Armut, in D. Döring, W. Hanesch and E. Huster (eds.), *Armut im Wohlstand*, Frankfurt (Main): Suhrkamp: 31-55.
Goodin, R. E., B. Headey, R. A. Muffels and H.-J. Dirven (1999), *The Real Worlds of Welfare Capitalism*, Cambridge: Cambridge University Press.
Gordon, D. and C. Pantazis (eds.) (1997), *Breadline Britain in the 1990s*, Aldershot: Ashgate.
Gordon, D. and P. Spicker (eds.) (1999), *The International Glossary on Poverty*, London: Zed Books.
Gornick, J. C., M. Meyers and K. Ross (1997), Supporting the Employment of Mothers: Policy Variation across Fourteen Welfare States, *Journal of European Social Policy* 7 (1): 45-70.
Gough, I., J. Bradshaw, J. Ditch, T. Eardley and P. Whiteford (1997), Social Assistance in OECD Countries, *Journal of European Social Policy* 7 (1): 17-43.
Goul Andersen, J., P. A. Pettersen, S. Svallfors and H. Uusitalo (1999), The Legitimacy of the Nordic Welfare States: Trends, Variations and Cleavages, in M. Kautto, M. Heikkilä, B. Hvinden, S. Marklund and N. Ploug (eds.), *Nordic Social Policy: Changing Welfare States*, London: Routledge: 235-261.
Goyder, J. (1985), Nonresponse on Surveys: A Canadian-United States Comparison, *Canadian Journal of Sociology/Cahiers canadiens de sociologie* 10 (3): 231-251.
—— (1987), *The Silent Minority: Nonrespondents in Sample Surveys*, Cambridge: Polity.
Groves, R. M. (1989), *Survey Errors and Survey Cost*, New York: John Wiley & Sons.
GSOEP (1996), *Desktop Companion to the German Socio-Economic Panel Study (GSOEP)*, Berlin: DIW.
Guibentif, P. and D. Bouget (1997), *Mindesteinkommen in der Europäischen Union: Ein sozialpolitischer Vergleich*, Lissabon: União des Mutualidades Portuguesas.
Gustafsson, B. A. (1986a), Bidragsmottagarna: Antal Och Inkomster, in Finansdepartementet [Swedish Ministry of Finance] (ed.) *Socialbidrag*, Stockholm: Swedish government.
—— (1986b), International Migration and Falling into the Income Safety Net: Social Assistance among Foreign Citizens in Sweden, *International Migration* 24: 461-483.
—— (1987), Som Ett Isberg? Om Underutnyttjande Av Socialbidrag, *Nordisk Socialt Arbede* 7 (3).
—— (1993), The Income Safety Net: Who Falls into It and Why?, in E. J. Hansen, S. Ringen, H. Uusitalo and R. Erikson (eds.), *Welfare Trends in the Scandinavian Countries*, Armonk/NY: Sharpe: 251-266.

—— (1998), Armut in Schweden: Veränderungen in Struktur und Dynamik im Zeitraum von 1975 bis 1993, *Zeitschrift für Sozialreform* 44 (4-5): 278-294.
Gustafsson, B. A., L.-C. Hydén and T. Salonen (1990), *Beslut Om Socialbidrag I Storstäder*, Skriftserie 4: 90 No.: Sekretariat för Sociala Studies.
Gustafsson, B. A. and M. Lindblom (1993), Poverty Lines and Poverty in Seven European Countries, Australia, Canada and the USA, *Journal of European Social Policy* 3 (1): 21-38.
Gustafsson, B. A. and H. Uusitalo (1990), The Welfare State and Poverty in Finland and Sweden from the Mid-1960s to the Mid-1980s, *Review of Income and Wealth* 36 (3): 249-266.
Haagenaars, A., K. de Vos and A. Zaidi (1994), *Poverty Statistics in the Late 1980s*, Luxembourg: Eurostat.
—— (1998), Patterns of Poverty in Europe, in S. P. Jenkins, A. Kapteyn and B. M. S. van Praag (eds.), *The Distribution of Welfare and Household Production: An International Perspective*, Cambridge (MA): Cambridge University Press: 25-49.
Habich, R., B. Headey and P. Krause (1991), Armut im Reichtum: Ist die Bundesrepublik Deutschland eine Zwei-Drittel-Gesellschaft?, in U. Rendtel and G. G. Wagner (eds.), *Zur Einkommensdynamik in Deutschland seit 1984*, Frankfurt (Main)/New York: Campus: 488-509.
Hall, A. S. (1974), *The Point of Entry: A Study of Client Reception in the Social Services*, London: Allen & Unwin.
Halleröd, B. (1991), *Den Svenska Fattigdomen: En Studie Av Fattigdom Och Socialbidragstagande*, Lund: Arkiv förlag.
—— (1995a), Making Ends Meet - Perceptions of Poverty in Sweden, *Scandinavian Journal of Social Welfare* 4: 174-189.
—— (1995b), The Truly Poor: Indirect and Direct Consensual Measurement of Poverty in Sweden, *Journal of European Social Policy* 5 (2): 111-129.
—— (1996a), Deprivation and Poverty: A Comparative Analysis of Sweden and Great Britain, *Acta Sociologica* 39 (2): 141-168.
—— (1996b), Generell Välfärd Eller Selektiv Fattigvård?, in J. Palme and I. Wennemo (eds.), *Generell Välfärd: Hot Och Möjligheter?*, Stockholm: Norsteds Tryckeri AB, 4: 35-64.
—— (1998), Poor Swedes, Poor Britons: A Comparative Analysis of Relative Deprivation, in H.-J. Andreß (ed.) *Empirical Poverty Research in a Comparative Perspective*, Aldershot: Ashgate: 283-312.
Halvorsen, K. (1993), Social Assistance Schemes in the Nordic Countries, in T. Fridberg (ed.) *On Social Assistance in the Nordic Capitals*, Kopenhagen: Socialforskningsinstituttet: 35-51.
Halvorsen, K. and S. Marklund (1993), The Growth of Social Assistance in the Nordic Countries During the 1980s, in T. Fridberg (ed.) *On Social Assistance in the Nordic Capitals*, Kopenhagen: Socialforskningsinstituttet: 67-87.
Hammar, T. (1999), Closing the Doors of the Swedish Welfare State, in G. Brochmann and T. Hammar (eds.), *Mechanisms of Immigration Control: A Comparative Analysis of European Regulation Policies*, Oxford: Berg: 169-201.

Hanefeld, U. (1987), *Das Sozio-ökonomische Panel: Grundlagen und Konzeption*, Frankfurt (Main)/New York: Campus.

Hanesch, W., W. Adamy, R. Martens, D. Rentzsch, U. Schneider, U. Schubert and M. Wißkirchen (1994), *Armut in Deutschland: Der Armutsbericht des DGB und des Paritätischen Wohlfahrtsverbands*, Reinbek: Rowohlt.

Hansbro, J. and K. Foster (1997), *Characteristics of Non-Response in the 1995-96 FES*, ONS Social Survey Report, London: Office for National Statistics.

Harding, A. (ed.) (1996), *Microsimulation and Public Policy*, Amsterdam: North-Holland.

Harris, G. (1998), *Income Distribution Data for the United Kingdom*, Robustness Assessment Report of the Canberra Group.

Harris, N. (2000a), The Shape and Characteristics of Social Security Today (Including Insurance, Pensions and Means-Tests), in N. Harris (ed.) *Social Security Law in Context*, Oxford: Oxford University Press: 155-206.

—— (2000b), Widening Agendas: The Social Security Reviews and Reforms of 1985-8, in N. Harris (ed.) *Social Security Law in Context*, Oxford: Oxford University Press: 119-154.

Hartmann, H. (1981), *Sozialhilfebedürftigkeit und 'Dunkelziffer der Armut': Bericht über das Forschungsprojekt zur Lage potentiell Sozialhilfeberechtigter*, Schriftenreihe des Bundesministers für Jugend, Familie und Gesundheit No. 98, Stuttgart: Kohlhammer.

—— (1985), Armut Trotz Sozialhilfe - Zur Nichtinanspruchnahme von Sozialhilfe in der Bundesrepublik, in S. Leibfried and F. Tennstedt (eds.), *Politik der Armut und die Spaltung des Sozialstaats*, Frankfurt (Main): Suhrkamp: 169-189.

Hauser, R. (1987), Comparing the Influence of Social Security Systems on the Relative Economic Positions of Selected Groups in Six Major Industrialized Countries: The Case of One-Parent Families, *European Economic Review* 31 (1-2): 192-201.

—— (1995a), Das empirische Bild der Armut in der Bundesrepublik Deutschland - ein Überblick, *Aus Politik und Zeitgeschichte* (B 31-32): 3-13.

—— (1995b), Die Caritas-Armutsuntersuchung aus der Sicht der Armutsforschung, in W. Hübinger and R. Hauser (eds.), *Die Caritas-Armutsuntersuchung: Eine Bilanz*, Freiburg im Breisgau: Lambertus: 12-25.

—— (1997), The Main Problems of International Comparative Poverty Research, in N. Ott and G. G. Wagner (eds.), *Income Inequality and Poverty in Eastern and Western Europe*, Heidelberg: Physica: 31-52.

Hauser, R., H. Cremer-Schäfer and U. Nouvertné (1981), *Armut, Niedrigeinkommen und Unterversorgung in der Bundesrepublik Deutschland*, Frankfurt (Main)/New York: Campus.

Hauser, R. and I. Fischer (1990), Economic Well-Being among One-Parent-Families, in T. M. Smeeding, M. O'Higgins and L. Rainwater (eds.), *Poverty, Inequality and Income Distribution in Comparative Perspective*, Hemel Hempstead: Harvester Wheatsheaf: 126-157.

Hauser, R. and W. Hübinger (1993a), *Arme unter uns - Teil 1: Ergebnisse und Konsequenzen der Caritas-Armutsuntersuchung*, Freiburg im Breisgau: Lambertus.
—— (1993b), *Arme unter uns - Teil 2: Dokumentation der Erhebungsmethoden und der Instrumente der Caritas-Armenuntersuchung*, Freiburg im Breisgau: Lambertus.
Hauser, R. and G. Wagner (1996), Die Einkommensverteilung in Ostdeutschland: Darstellung, Vergleich und Determinanten für die Jahre 1990 bis 1994, in R. Hauser (ed.) *Sozialpolitik im Vereinten Deutschland III*, Berlin: Duncker & Humblot, 208/III: 79-128.
Havemann, R. (1996), Reducing Poverty While Increasing Employment: A Primer on Alternative Strategies, and a Blueprint, *OECD Economic Studies* (26): 7-42.
Hedström, P. and S. Ringen (1990), Age and Income in Contemporary Society, in T. M. Smeeding, M. O'Higgins and L. Rainwater (eds.), *Poverty, Inequality and Income Distribution in Comparative Perspective*, Hemel Hempstead: Harvester Wheatsheaf: 77-104.
Heising, M. (1995 [1990]), *Armenpolitik in Nachkriegsdeutschland (1945-1964): Die Entwicklung der Fürsorgeunterstützungssätze im Kontext allgemeiner Sozial- und Fürsorgereform*, Dissertationen, Diplomarbeiten, Dokumentationen No. 29, Frankfurt (Main): Eigenverlag des Deutschen Vereins für öffentliche und private Vorsorge.
Huby, M. (1996), Reflections on the Social Fund, *Benefits* (January): 9-11.
Huby, M. and G. Dix (1992), *Evaluating the Social Fund*, London: HMSO.
Huby, M. and C. Whyley (1996), Take-up and the Social Fund, *Journal of Social Policy* 25 (1): 1-18.
Jahn, D. (1997), Das politische System Schwedens, in W. Ismayr (ed.) *Die Politischen Systeme Westeuropas*, Opladen: Leske & Budrich: 91-124.
Jansson, K. (1994), Use of Administrative Registers for Income Statistics in Sweden, *Statistical Journal of the United Nations* 11: 211-221.
—— (1998), *Income Distribution Data for Sweden: Robustness Assessment Report*, Manuscript No. Stockholm: Statistiska Centralbyrån.
Jäntti, M. (1996), Poverty in the United States and Europe: A Review, *Review of Income and Wealth* 42 (2): 233-240.
Jäntti, M. and S. H. Danziger (2000), Income Poverty in Advanced Countries, in A. B. Atkinson and F. Bourguignon (eds.), *Handbook on Income Distribution*, Amsterdam: Elsevier: 309-378.
Johnson, P. and J. McCrae (1998), Robustness of FES Income Data, 1985-92, in J. Banks and P. Johnson (eds.), *How Reliable Is the Family Expenditure Survey? Trends in Incomes and Expenditures over Time*, London: Institute for Fiscal Studies: 17-66.
Julkunen, I. (1993a), The Silent Discontent - Attitudes Towards Welfare Service among Long-Term Recipients of Social Assistance, in T. Fridberg (ed.) *On Social Assistance in the Nordic Capitals*, Kopenhagen: Socialforskningsinstituttet: 183-200.

—— (1993b), Social Welfare Agencies in the Nordic Capitals, in T. Fridberg (ed.) *On Social Assistance in the Nordic Capitals*, Kopenhagen: Socialforskningsinstituttet: 52-66.

Kangas, O. E. (2000), *Distributive Justice and Social Policy: Some Aspects on Rawls and Income Distribution*, Luxembourg Income Study Working Paper Series No. 221, Luxembourg.

Kangas, O. E. and V.-M. Ritakallio (1998a), Different Methods - Different Results? Approaches to Multidimensional Poverty, in H.-J. Andreß (ed.) *Empirical Poverty Research in a Comparative Perspective*, Aldershot: Ashgate: 167-204.

—— (1998b), *Social Policy or Structure? Income Transfers, Socio-Demographic Factors and Poverty in the Nordic Countries and in France*, Luxembourg Income Study Working Paper Series No. 190, Luxemburg: LIS.

Kassella, T. and U. Hochmuth (1989), *Ein synthetisches Mikrodatenfile des Haushaltssektors für steuerpolitische Simulationen*, Arbeitspapier des Sfb 3: 'Mikroanalytische Grundlagen der Gesellschaftspolitik' No. 299, Frankfurt (Main): Johann Wolfgang Goethe-Universität.

Kayser, H. and J. R. Frick (2000), *Take It or Leave It: (Non-)Take-up Behavior of Social Assistance in Germany*, DIW Discussion Papers, Berlin: DIW.

Kemp, P. (1995), Housing Benefit: Some Peculiarities of the British System, *Benefits* (September/October): 1-5.

Kenworthy, L. (1998), *Do Social Welfare Policies Reduce Poverty? A Cross-National Assessment*, Luxembourg Income Study Working Paper Series No. 188, Luxemburg: LIS.

—— (1999), Do Social Welfare Policies Reduce Poverty? A Cross-National Assessment, *Social Forces* 77 (3): 1119-1139.

Kerr, S. A. (1982), Deciding About Supplementary Pensions: A Provisional Model, *Journal of Social Policy* 2 (4): 505-517.

Kersbergen, K. van (1995), *Social Capitalism: A Study of Christian Democracy and the Welfare State*, London: Routledge.

Klanberg, F. (1979), Einkommensarmut 1969 und 1973 bei Anlegung verschiedener Standards, *Sozialer Fortschritt* 28 (6): 127-131.

Klinger, R. (1998), Pauschalierung der Hilfe zum Lebensunterhalt nach dem BSHG: Reformvorschlag der Landkreise als örtliche Sozialhilfeträger, *Nachrichtendienst des Deutschen Vereins für öffentliche und private Fürsorge* 78 (1): 5-9.

Korpi, W. (1975), Poverty, Social Assistance and Social Policy in Postwar Sweden, *Acta Sociologica* 18 (2-3): 120-141.

Krämer, W. (1997), *Statistische Probleme bei der Armutsmessung, Gutachten im Auftrag des Bundesministeriums für Gesundheit*, Baden-Baden: Nomos.

—— (2000), *Armut in der Bundesrepublik: Zur Theorie und Praxis eines überforderten Begriffs*, Frankfurt (Main)/New York: Campus.

Krause, P. (1997a), *Calculating Annual Social Assistance Benefit Payments for the GSOEP since 1995*, Berlin: DIW.

—— (1997b), *Zur Messung von Einkommensarmut am Beispiel des vereinigten Deutschlands: Methodische Ansätze und empirische Analysen auf Grundlage der Daten des Sozio-ökonomischen Panels (SOEP)*, PhD Thesis, Bochum: Ruhr-Universität Bochum.

Krause, P., B. Butrica, W. Strengmann-Kuhn and J. Schwarze (1996), *Dokumentation (Teil 2): Schätzung der Sozialhilfe-Beträge für die Jahre 1992-1994*.

Laan, P. van der (1998), *Reconciliation of Income Statistics with Aggregated Data*, presented at the Second Meeting of the Canberra Group, Expert Group on Household Income Statistics, Voorburg (Netherlands), 9-11 March 1998.

Le Grand, J. and D. Winter (1987), The Middle Classes and the Defence of the British Welfare State, in R. E. Goodin and J. Le Grand (eds.), *Not Only the Poor: The Middle Classes and the Welfare State*, London: Allen & Unwin: 147-168.

Leibfried, S. (1976), Armutspotential und Sozialhilfe in der Bundesrepublik: Zum Prozeß des Filterns der Ansprüche auf Sozialhilfe, *Kritische Justiz* 4: 377-393.

—— (1992), Towards an European Welfare State? On Integrating Poverty Regimes into the European Community, in Z. Ferge and J. E. Kolberg (eds.), *Social Policy in a Changing Europe*, New York/Frankfurt (Main): Campus/Westview: 245-279.

Leisering, L. (1995), Armutspolitik und Lebenslauf: Zur politisch-administrativen Relevanz der lebenslauftheoretischen Armutsforschung, in W. Hanesch (ed.) *Sozialpolitische Strategien Gegen Armut*, Opladen: Westdeutscher Verlag: 65-111.

Leisering, L. and S. Leibfried (1999), *Time, Life & Poverty: Social Assistance Dynamics in the German Welfare State*, Cambridge: Cambridge University Press.

Leisering, L. and W. Voges (1993), *Secondary Poverty in the Welfare State. Do Social Security Institutions Create Their Own Clients? An Application of Longitudinal Analysis*, Working Paper of the Zentrum für Sozialpolitik, Bremen No. 10/93, Bremen: Zentrum für Sozialpolitik.

Leisering, L. and R. Walker (eds.) (1998), *The Dynamics of Modern Society: Poverty, Policy and Welfare*, Bristol: Policy Press.

Lipsky, M. (1979), *Street-Level Bureaucracy: Dilemmas of the Individual in Public Services*, New York: Russel Sage.

—— (1980), Poverty and Administration: Perspectives on Research, in V. T. Covello (ed.) *Poverty and Public Policy: An Evaluation of Social Science Research*, Cambridge (MA): Schenkman: 164-188.

—— (1991), The Paradox of Managing Discretionary Workers in Social Welfare Policy, in M. Adler, C. Bell, J. Clasen and A. Sinfield (eds.), *The Sociology of Social Security*, Edinburgh: Edinburgh University Press: 212-228.

Lipsmeier, G. (1993), *Zu Repräsentation des unteren Einkommensbereichs im Sozioökonomischen Panel (SOEP)*, Arbeitspapier des DFG-Projekts der Fakultät für Soziologie, No. 10, Bielefeld: Universität Bielefeld.

Lødemel, I. (1989), *The Quest for Institutional Welfare and the Problem of the Residuum: The Case of Income Maintenance and Personal Social Care Policies in Norway and Britain 1946 to 1966*, PhD Thesis, London: London School of Economics.

—— (1992), *European Poverty Regimes*, presented at the International Research Conference on Poverty and Distribution.

—— (1997), *The Welfare Paradox: Income Maintenance and Personal Social Services in Norway and Britain, 1946-1966*, Oslo: Scandinavian University Press.

Lødemel, I. and B. Schulte (1992), Social Assistance: A Part of Social Security or the Poor Law in New Disguise?, in European Institute of Social Security (ed.) *Reforms in Eastern and Central Europe: Beveridge 50 Years After*, Leuven: Acco: 515-538.

Mack, J. and S. Lansley (1985), *Poor Britain*, London: Allen & Unwin.

Mannion, R., S. Hutton and R. Sainsbury (1994), *Direct Payments from Income Support*, Department of Social Security Research Report No. 33, London: HMSO.

Marsh, A. and S. McKay (1993), *Families, Work and Benefits*, London: Policy Studies Institute.

Marshall, T. H. (1965), *Class, Citizenship and Social Development*, New York: Doubleday.

Mau, S. (1997a), Ideologischer Konsens und Dissens im Wohlfahrtsstaat: Zur Binnenvariation von Einstellungen zu sozialer Ungleichheit in Schweden, Großbritannien und der Bundesrepublik Deutschland, *Soziale Welt* 47: 17-38.

—— (1997b), *Ungleichheits- und Gerechtigkeitsorientierungen in modernen Wohlfahrtsstaaten: Ein Vergleich der Länder Schweden, Großbritannien und der Bundesrepublik Deutschland*, Discussion Paper No. FS III 97-401, Berlin: WZB.

Mayer, S. (1995), A Comparison of Poverty and Living Conditions in the United States, Canada, Sweden, and Germany, in K. McFate, R. Lawson and W. J. Wilson (eds.), *Poverty, Inequality, and the Future of Social Policy*, New York: Russell Sage Foundation: 109-152.

McFate, K., T. Smeeding and L. Rainwater (1995), Markets and States: Poverty Trends and Transfer System Effectiveness in the 1980s, in K. McFate, R. Lawson and W. J. Wilson (eds.), *Poverty, Inequality, and the Future of Social Policy*, New York: Russell Sage Foundation: 29-66.

Millar, J. (1989), *Poverty and the Lone-Parent: The Challenge to Social Policy*, Aldershot: Avebury.

Minas, R. and S.-Å. Stenberg (2000), *På tröskeln till bidrag: Mottagningen av nya socialbidragsansökningar på sju socialkontor i Sverige*, CUS-skrift No. 2000:1, Stockholm: Socialstyrelsen.

Minderhoud, P. (1999), Asylum Seekers and Access to Social Security: Recent Developments in the Netherlands, United Kingdom, Germany and Belgium, in A. Bloch and C. Levy (eds.), *Refugees, Citizenship and Social Policy in Europe*, London: Macmillan: 132-148.

Bibliography 233

Ministerie van Sociale Zaken en Werkgelegenheit (1995), *Unemployment Benefits and Social Assistance in Seven European Countries*, Werkdokumenten No. 10, The Hague: Ministerie van Sociale Zaken en Werkgelegenheit.
Mitchell, D. (1991), *Income Transfers in Ten Welfare States*, Aldershot: Avebury.
Moffitt, R. A. (1983), An Economic Model of Welfare Stigma, *American Economic Review* 73 (5): 1023-1035.
—— (1992), Incentive Effects of the U.S. Welfare System: A Review, *Journal of Economic Literature* 30 (1): 1-61.
Muffels, R. (1993), Deprivation Standards and Style of Living Indicators, in J. Berghman and B. Cantillon (eds.), *European Face of Social Security: Essays in Honour of Herman Deleeck*, Aldershot: Avebury: 43-59.
Muffels, R., J. Berghman and H.-J. Dirven (1992), A Multi-Method Approach to Monitor the Evolution of Poverty, *Journal of European Social Policy* 2: 193-213.
Müller, C. (1998), *Der Rückgriff auf Angehörige von Sozialhilfeempfängern: Ein Leitfaden*, Baden-Baden: Nomos.
Neumann, U. (1999), Verdeckte Armut in der Bundesrepublik Deutschland: Begriff und empirische Ergebnisse für die Jahre 1983 bis 1995, *Aus Politik und Zeitgeschichte* (B 18): 27-32.
Neumann, U. and M. Hertz (1998), *Verdeckte Armut in Deutschland*, Bonn: Friedrich-Ebert-Stiftung.
Nolan, B. and C. T. Whelan (1996a), The Relationship between Income and Deprivation, *Revue économique* (3): 709-717.
—— (1996b), *Resources, Deprivation and Poverty*, Oxford: Clarendon.
Oberbracht, D. (1993), *Die Parlamentarisierung des sozialhilferechtlichen Regelsatzes*, Nomos Universitätsschriften No. 103, Baden-Baden: Nomos.
Obinger, H. and U. Wagschal (1997), Drei Welten des Wohlfahrtsstaates? Das Stratifizierungskonzept in der clusteranalytischen Überprüfung, in S. Lessenich and I. Ostner (eds.), *Welten des Wohlfahrtskapitalismus: Der Sozialstaat in vergleichender Perspektive*, Frankfurt (Main)/New York: Campus: 109-136.
OECD (1996), *Enhancing the Effectiveness of Active Labour Market Policies: Evidence from Programme Evaluations in OECD Countries*, Economic Department Working Papers No. 56, Paris: OECD.
—— (1997), *The Tax/Benefit Position of Employees*, Paris: OECD.
—— (1998a), *The Battle against Exclusion: Social Assistance in Australia, Finland, Sweden and the United Kingdom*, Paris: OECD.
—— (1998b), *The Battle against Exclusion: Social Assistance in Belgium, the Czech Republic, the Netherlands and Norway*, Paris: OECD.
—— (1999a), *The Battle against Exclusion: Social Assistance in Canada and Switzerland*, Paris: OECD.
—— (1999b), *Social Expenditure Database 1980/1996*, Paris: OECD.
Office for National Statistics (1998a), *Family Expenditure Survey, 1996-1997 [Computer File]*, Colchester (Essex): The Data Archive [distributor].
—— (1998b), *Family Expenditure Survey User Documentation, 1996-97*, London: Office for National Statistics.

Olsson, S. (1986), Sweden, in P. Flora (ed.) *Growth to Limits: The Western European Welfare States since World War II, Vol. 1*, Berlin: de Gruyter: 1-116.

Oorschot, W. van (1991), Non-Take-up of Social Security Benefits in Europe, *Journal of European Social Policy* 1 (1): 15-30.

—— (1995), *Realizing Rights: A Multi-Level Approach to Non-Take-up of Social Security Benefits*, Aldershot: Avebury.

—— (1998), Failing Selectivity: On Extent and Causes of Non-Take-up of Social Security Benefits, in H.-J. Andreß (ed.) *Empirical Poverty Research in a Comparative Perspective*, Aldershot: Ashgate: 101-132.

Oorschot, W. van and L. Halman (1998), *Blame or Fate, Individual or Social? An International Comparison of Popular Explanations of Poverty*, presented at the 14th World Congress of Sociology, Montréal/Canada, 26 July - 1 August 1998.

Oorschot, W. van and P. Kolkhuis Tancke (1989), Het Niet-gebruik van Sociale Zekerheid: Feiten, Theorieën, Onderzoeksmethoden; Cosz Series No. 16, The Hague.

Orthbandt, E. (1980), *Der Deutsche Verein in der Geschichte der Deutschen Fürsorge: zum Hundertjährigen Bestehen des Deutschen Vereins*, Schriften des Deutschen Vereins für Öffentliche und Private Fürsorge No. 260, Frankfurt (Main): Eigenverlag des Deutschen Vereins für öffentliche und private Vorsorge.

—— (1986), *Tarife, Richtsätze, Regelsätze: Dokumentarischer Bericht über eine hundertjährige Problemdiskussion*, Dissertationen, Diplomarbeiten, Dokumentationen No. 8, Stuttgart: Kohlhammer.

Oxley, H., J.-M. Burniaux, T.-T. Dang and M. Mira d'Ercole (1999), Income Distribution and Poverty in 13 OECD Countries, *OECD Economic Studies* 1997 (II): 55-94.

Pahl, J. (1989), *Money and Marriage*, London: Macmillan.

Pedersen, A. W. (1999), *The Taming of Inequality in Retirement: A Comparative Study of Pension Policy Outcomes*, Fafo Report No. 317, Oslo: FAFO.

Pierson, P. (1994), *Dismantling the Welfare State? Reagan, Thatcher, and the Politics of Retrenchment*, Cambridge: Cambridge University Press.

Piven, F. F. and R. A. Cloward (1971), *Regulating the Poor: The Functions of Public Welfare*, New York: Pantheon Books.

Prinz, A. (1983), Die Finanzierung der Sozialhilfe im Finanzverbund zwischen Bund, Ländern und Gemeinden, *Finanzarchiv* 41: 431-451.

Radner, D. B. (1997), Noncash Income, Equivalence Scales, and the Measurement of Economic Well-Being, *Review of Income and Wealth* 43 (1): 71-88.

Rahilly, S. (2000), Social Security, Money Management, and Debt, in N. Harris (ed.) *Social Security Law in Context*, Oxford: Oxford University Press: 431-459.

Rainwater, L. (1982), Stigma in Income-Tested Programs, in I. Garfinkel (ed.) *Income-Tested Transfer Programs: The Case for and Against*, New York: Academic Press: 19-46.

—— (1999), Poverty among Children and Elders in Europe and North America, in S. Ringen and P. R. de Jong (eds.), *Fighting Poverty: Caring for Children, Parents, the Elderly and Health*, Aldershot: Ashgate: 33-52.
Rainwater, L. and T. M. Smeeding (1998), Demography and Income Packaging: What Explains the Income Distribution?, in H. P. Galler and G. G. Wagner (eds.), *Empirische Forschung und wirtschaftspolitische Beratung*, Frankfurt (Main)/New York: Campus: 99-118.
Rake, K. (1999), Accumulated Disadvantage? Welfare State Provision and the Incomes of Older Women and Men in Britain, France and Germany, in J. Clasen (ed.) *Comparative Social Policy: Concepts, Theories and Methods*, Oxford: Blackwell: 220-246.
Rendtel, U. (1990), Teilnahmebereitschaft in Panelstudien: Zwischen Beeinflussung, Vertrauen und sozialer Selektion, *Kölner Zeitschrift für Soziologie und Sozialpsychologie* 42 (23): 280-299.
Rendtel, U., G. Wagner and J. Frick (1995), Eine Strategie zur Kontrolle von Längsschnittgewichtungen in Panel-Erhebungen: Das Beispiel des Sozio-ökonomischen Panels (SOEP), *Allgemeines Statistisches Archiv* 79: 252-277.
Richardson, A. and J. Naidoo (1978), *The Take-up of Supplementary Benefits: A Report on a Survey of Claimants,*: Chelsea College, University of London.
Riksförsäkringsverket (1998a), *Bostadsbidrag*, Stockholm: Riksförsäkringsverket.
—— (1998b), *Bostadstillägg Till Pensionärer*, Stockholm: Riksförsäkringsverket.
Ringeling, A. (1981), The Passivity of the Administration, *Policy and Politics* 9 (3): 295-309.
Ringen, S. (1987), *The Possibility of Politics: A Study in the Political Economy of the Welfare State*, Oxford: Clarendon.
—— (1988), Direct and Indirect Measures of Poverty, *Journal of Social Policy* 17 (3): 351-365.
Riphahn, R. T. (1998), Immigrant Participation in the German Welfare Program, *FinanzArchiv* 55 (2): 163-185.
—— (2000), *Rational Poverty or Poor Rationality? The Take-up of Social Assistance Benefits*, Discussion Paper No. 124, Bonn: Institute for the Study of Labor.
Roller, E. (1995a), Political Agendas and Beliefs About the Scope of Government, in O. Borre and E. Scarbrough (eds.), *The Scope of Government (Beliefs in Government, Vol. 3)*, Oxford: Oxford University Press: 55-86.
—— (1995b), The Welfare State: The Equality Dimension, in O. Borre and E. Scarbrough (eds.), *The Scope of Government*, Oxford: Oxford University Press: 165-197.
Room, G. (1990), *'New Poverty' in the European Community*, London: Macmillan.
Rosenhek, Z. (1999), The Exclusionary Logic of the Welfare State: Palestinian Citizens in the Israeli Welfare State, *International Sociology* 14 (2): 195-215.
Ross, C. E. and J. R. Reynolds (1996), The Effects of Power, Knowledge, and Trust on Income Disclosure in Surveys, *Social Science Quarterly* 77 (4): 899-911.
Rowlingson, K. and C. Whyley (1998), 'The Right Amount to the Right People?' Reducing Fraud, Error and Non-Take-up of Benefit, *Benefits* (January): 7-10.

Sachße, C. and F. Tennstedt (1988), *Geschichte der Armenfürsorge in Deutschland, Band 2: Fürsorge und Wohlfahrtspflege 1971 bis 1929*, Stuttgart: Kohlhammer.

—— (1998), *Geschichte der Armenfürsorge in Deutschland, Band 1: Vom Spätmittelalter bis zum 1. Weltkrieg (2. Aufl.)*, Stuttgart: Kohlhammer.

Sainsbury, D. (ed.) (1999), *Gender and Welfare State Regimes*, Oxford: Oxford University Press.

Sainsbury, R. (2000), Social Security Decision Making and Appeals, in N. Harris (ed.) *Social Security Law in Context*, Oxford: Oxford University Press: 207-230.

Salas, R. and I. Rabadan (1998), Lifetime and Intertemporal Inequality: Income Smoothing, and Redistribution: A Social Welfare Approach, *Review of Income and Wealth* 44 (1): 63-79.

Salonen, T. (1993), *Margins of Welfare*, Torna: Hällestad Press.

—— (1997), *Övervältringar från socialförsäkringar till socialbidrag*, Meddelanden från Socialhögskolan No. 23.03.11997: 8, Lund: University of Lund.

—— (1998), *Övervältringsstudie 1997: Effekter av besparingar inom socialförsäkringsområdet for kommunernas socialbidrag*, Arbetsreport, Lund: University of Lund.

Sawyer, M. (1976), *Income Distribution in the OECD Countries*, OECD Economic Outlook - Occasional Studies No. Paris: OECD.

Scheiwe, K. (1994), Labor Market, Welfare State and Family Institutions: The Links to Mothers' Poverty Risks. A Comparison between Belgium, Germany and the United Kingdom, *Journal of European Social Policy* 4 (3): 201-224.

Schellhorn, W. (1989), Neues Bedarfsbemessungssystem für die Regelsätze der Sozialhilfe: Ableitung der Regelsätze für sonstige Haushaltsangehörige, *Nachrichtendienst des Deutschen Vereins für öffentliche und private Fürsorge* (5): 157-161.

Schnell, R. (1991), Wer ist das Volk? Zur Faktischen Grundgesamtheit bei 'Allgemeinen Bevölkerungsumfragen': Undercoverage, Schwererreichbare und Nichtbefragbare, *Kölner Zeitschrift für Soziologie und Sozialpsychologie* 43 (1): 106-137.

—— (1993), Homogenität sozialer Kategorien als Voraussetzung für 'Repräsentativität' und Gewichtungsverfahren, *Zeitschrift für Soziologie* 22 (1): 16-32.

—— (1997), *Nonresponse in Bevölkerungsumfragen: Ausmaß, Entwicklung und Ursachen*, Opladen: Leske & Budrich.

Schoch, D. (1995), *Sozialhilfe: Ein Leitfaden für die Praxis*, Köln: Heymanns.

—— (1998), Das Sozialgesetzbuch - ein Buch mit sieben Siegeln? Ein Beitrag zum Verwaltungsverfahren in der Sozialhilfe, *Zentralblatt für Sozialversicherung, Sozialhilfe und Versorgung* 52 (5): 129-144.

Schulte, B. and P. Trenk-Hinterberger (1986), *Sozialhilfe: Eine Einführung*, 2nd edition, Heidelberg: C. F. Müller.

Schulz, J. (1989), *Armut und Sozialhilfe*, Stuttgart: Kohlhammer.

Schwarz, B. (1986), Socialbidrag i bidragssystemet, in Finansdepartementet [Swedish Ministry of Finance] (ed.) *Socialbidrag*, Stockholm: Swedish government.

Schwarze, U. (1994), *Einkommensarmut und Privatverschuldung in Schweden: Sozialhilfe und 'haushaltsökonomische Beratung' dargestellt am Beispiel der Stadt Malmö*, Dissertationen, Diplomarbeiten, Dokumentationen No. 25, Frankfurt (Main): Eigenverlag des Deutschen Vereins für öffentliche und private Vorsorge.

Sell, S. (1998), Weiterentwicklung der Sozialhilfe an der Schnittstelle zwischen Leistungsbezug und Erwerbstätigkeit? Zur Neuregelung der Freibeträge für Erwerbstätige Sozialhilfeempfänger, *Sozialer Fortschritt* 47 (2): 27-30.

Shaver, S. (1998), Universality and Selectivity in Income Support: An Assessment of the Issues, *Journal of Social Policy* 27 (2): 231-254.

Shaw, A., R. Walker, K. Ashworth, S. P. Jenkins and S. Middleton (1996), *Moving Off Income Support: Barriers and Bridges*, Department of Social Security Research Report No. 53, London: HMSO.

Siegenthaler, J. (1996), Poverty among Single Elderly Women under Different Systems of Old-Age Security: A Comparative Review, *Social Security Bulletin* 59 (9): 31-44.

Simmel, G. (1908), Der Arme, in *Soziologie - Gesammelte Werke*, Berlin: Duncker & Humblot, 2: 345-374.

Skocpol, T. (1991), Targeting with Universalism: Politically Viable Politics to Combat Poverty in the United States, in C. Jencks and P. E. Peterson (eds.), *The Urban Underclass*, Washington D.C.: Brookings Institution: 411-436.

Smeeding, T. M. (1997), *Financial Poverty in Developed Countries: The Evidence from LIS: Final Report to the UNDP*, Luxembourg Income Study Working Paper Series No. 155, Luxemburg: LIS.

Smeeding, T. M., M. O'Higgins and L. Rainwater (eds.) (1990), *Poverty, Inequality and Income Distribution in Comparative Perspective*, Hemel Hempstead: Harvester Wheatsheaf.

Smeeding, T. M. and K. Ross (1999), *Social Protection for the Poor in the Developed World: The Evidence from LIS*, Luxembourg Income Study Working Paper Series No. 204, Luxemburg: LIS.

Smeeding, T. M., K. Ross, P. England, K. Christopher and S. McLanahan (1999), *Poverty and Parenthood across Modern Nations: Findings from the Luxembourg Income Study*, Luxembourg Income Study Working Paper Series No. 194, Luxemburg: LIS.

Smeeding, T. M., P. Saunders, J. Coder, S. Jenkins, A. J. M. Hagenaars, R. Hauser and M. Wolfson (1993), Poverty, Inequality, and Family Living Standards Impacts across Seven Nations: The Effect of Noncash Subsidies for Health, Education and Housing, *Review of Income and Wealth* 39 (3): 229-256.

Smeeding, T. M. and G. Schmaus (1990), The LIS Database: Technical and Methodological Aspects, in T. M. Smeeding, M. O'Higgins and L. Rainwater (eds.), *Poverty, Inequality and Income Distribution in Comparative Perspective*, Hemel Hempstead: Harvester Wheatsheaf: 1-19.

Social Security Advisory Committee (1992), *The Social Fund: A New Structure*, London: HMSO.

Socialstyrelsen (1997a), *Försörjningsstöd och övrigt economisk stöd - om ändringar i socialtjänstlagen och socialtjänstförordningen 1998*, Meddelandeblad No. 275/97, Stockholm: Socialstyrelsen.

—— (1997b), *Social and Caring Services in Sweden 1996*, Stockholm: Socialstyrelsen.

—— (1998), *Från collegium medicorum till socialstyrelsen*, Stockholm: Socialstyrelsen.

Stapf, H. (1997), Old Age Poverty in Selected Countries of the European Union - Are Women Disproportionally Affected?, in N. Ott and G. G. Wagner (eds.), *Income Inequality and Poverty in Eastern and Western Europe*, Heidelberg: Physica: 125-146.

Statistisches Bundesamt (1997), *Sozialhilfe, Fachserie 13, Reihe 2*, Stuttgart: Metzler-Poeschel.

—— (1998), *Statistik der Sozialhilfe: Ausgaben und Einnahmen (Arbeitsunterlage)*, Wiesbaden: Statistisches Bundesamt.

Steffen, J. (1995), *Die wesentlichen Änderungen in den Bereichen Arbeitslosen-, Renten-, Krankenversicherung und Sozialhilfe (HLU) in den vergangenen Jahren*, Bremen: Arbeiterkammer Bremen.

Stumpfögger, N. and U. Wiethoff (1989), *Armutsverwaltung: Kritik und Perspektive der Sozialhilfe*, Berlin: Sigma.

Stuttard, N. (1996), *Reconciliation of UK Household Income Statistics with the National Accounts*, presented at the Meeting of the Expert Group on Household Income Statistics, Canberra (Australia), 2-4 December 1996.

Sunesson, S., S. Blomberg, P. G. Edebalk, L. Harryson, J. Magnusson, A. Meeuwisse, J. Petterson and T. Salonen (1998), The Flight from Universalism, *European Journal of Social Work* 1 (1): 19-29.

Svallfors, S. (1991), The Politics of Welfare Policy in Sweden: Structural Determinants and Attitudinal Cleavages, *British Journal of Sociology* 42 (4): 609-634.

—— (1995), The End of Class Politics? Structural Cleavages and Attitudes to Swedish Welfare Policies, *Acta Sociologica* 38 (1): 53-74.

—— (1997), Worlds of Welfare and Attitudes to Redistribution: A Comparison of Eight Western Nations, *European Sociological Review* 13 (3): 283-304.

Svensson, B.-M. (1993), *Socialbidrag: Normer Och Kostnader - En Jämförande Undersökning*, Stockholm: Svenska kommunförbundet.

Task Force on Statistics on Social Exclusion and Poverty (1998), *Recommendations of the Task Force on Statistics on Social Exclusion and Poverty (DOC E2/TFSEP/20/98)*, Luxembourg: Eurostat.

Taylor-Gooby, P. (1974), *Means-Tests and Social Policy (MPhil Thesis)*, York: University of York.

—— (1985), *Public Opinion, Ideology and State Welfare*, London: Routledge & Kegan Paul.

Thomas, D. (1990), Intra-Household Resource Allocation: An Inferential Approach, *Journal of Human Resources* 25 (4): 635-664.

Titmuss, R. (1974), *Social Policy*, London: Allen & Unwin.

Townsend, P. (1979), *Poverty in the United Kingdom: A Survey of Household Ressources and Standards of Living*, Berkeley: University of California Press.
—— (1987), Deprivation, *Journal of Social Policy* 15 (2): 125-146.
Tschoepe, A. (1987), Neues Bedarfsbemessungssystem für Regelsätze in der Sozialhilfe nach § 22 BSHG, *Nachrichtendienst des Deutschen Vereins für öffentliche und private Fürsorge* 67 (12): 433-442.
Veit-Wilson, J. (1992), Muddle or Menacity? The Beveridge Committee and the Poverty Line, *Journal of Social Policy* 21 (3): 269-301.
—— (1998), *Setting Adequacy Standards: How Governments Define Minimum Incomes*, Bristol: Policy Press.
Voges, W. and G. Rohwer (1991a), Receiving Social Assistance in Germany: Risk and Duration, *Journal of European Social Policy* 2: 175-191.
—— (1991b), Zur Dynamik des Sozialhilfebezugs, in U. Rendtel and G. G. Wagner (eds.), *Lebenslagen im Wandel - zur Einkommensdynamik in Deutschland seit 1984*, Frankfurt (Main)/New York: Campus: 510-531.
Voges, W. and A. Weber (1996), Sozialhilfebezug von Ausländern und Zuwanderern, in P. Buhr and W. Voges (eds.), *Kommunale Sozialberichterstattung. Erfassung regionaler Disparitäten*, Opladen: Leske & Budrich.
Wagner, G. G., J. Schupp and J. Rendtel (1994), Das Sozio-ökonomische Panel (SOEP) - Methoden der Datenproduktion und -aufbereitung im Längsschnitt, in R. Hauser, N. Ott and G. G. Wagner (eds.), *Mikroanalytische Grundlagen der Gesellschaftspolitik, Bd. 2: Erhebungsverfahren, Analysemethoden und Mikrosimulation*, Berlin: Akademie Verlag: 70-112.
Walker, C. (1993), *Managing Poverty: The Limits of Social Assistance*, London: Routledge.
Walker, R., G. Dix and M. Huby (1992), *Working the Social Fund*, London: HMSO.
Westerhäll, L. (1997), Social Assistance and Migrant Workers: Regulation No. 1612/68 from a Swedish Perspective, in E. Eichenhofer (ed.) *Social Security of Migrants in the European Union of Tomorrow*, Osnabrück: Universitätsverlag Rasch: 73-89.
Whelan, B. J. (1993), Non-Monetary Indicators of Poverty, in J. Berghman and B. Cantillon (eds.), *European Face of Social Security: Essays in Honour of Herman Deleeck*, Aldershot: Avebury: 24-42.
Whiteford, P. and S. Kennedy (1995), *Incomes and Living Standards of Older People: A Comparative Analysis*, Department of Social Security Research Report No. 34, London: HMSO.
Wienand, M. (1997a), Regelsatzfestsetzung nach dem Statistikmodell auf dem Gerichtlichen Prüfstand: Anmerkungen zu den Regelsatzurteilen des Bundesverwaltungsgerichts, *Nachrichtendienst des Deutschen Vereins für öffentliche und private Fürsorge* 77 (6): 196-199.
—— (1997b), Sozialhilfe, in M. Wienand, V. Neumann and I. Brockmann (eds.), *Fürsorge*, Opladen: Leske & Budrich, 6.8.

Index

adequacy 11, 49-51, 59, 87, 90, 103-4, 108, 111-3, 127-8, 130, 133, 138-44, 147, 155-7, 189, 204-6
asylum seekers 38, 62, 93-6
Australia 6, 16-18, 21-7, 83-5, 211-2
Austria 8-10, 83
Beckerman ratio 18-21, 29-31, 35, 210
Belgium 18, 22, 25-7, 83, 212
benefits
   administration 166, 182, 186-7
   cash 26, 54-5, 213
   categorical 36, 119
   in kind 4, 94-6
   indexation 103, 113-6, 126
   level 10-11, 17, 94, 101-10, 113-5, 127-33, 136-40, 147-52, 155, 164, 179, 191, 204-8
   one-off benefits 103, 107-9, 121-4, 127, 131, 140, 143, 156, 160, 164, 185, 201
   premiums 119-20, 152
   simulation of 128, 140-50, 155
   special premiums 99, 103, 117, 120-1, 142
   standard benefit rates 76, 95, 103-21, 125-7, 130, 142, 185
   take-up 11, 20, 39, 49, 51, 87, 101, 125, 141, 144, 147-8, 155-66, 173-80, 184-201, 204-7
   targeting 46, 97, 193
Beveridge, William I. 105
Bismarck, Otto von 6
Canada 6, 16, 21-5, 83-4, 211-2
capital 48, 67-8, 77-9, 98, 123, 130, 137, 153, 199

charity 158, 197, 200
child benefit 104, 179
children 1, 15-16, 22-5, 35-7, 57, 71-5, 91, 94, 98, 104, 107, 117-21, 129-40, 147-52, 155, 159, 162, 179-82, 195, 198, 212
decommodification 7
Denmark 7, 16, 22, 25, 83, 110, 211-2
dependency 163
deprivation, multidimensional 13, 58
disability 10, 92, 99, 103, 120, 127, 131, 163, 185
discretion 4, 7-8, 95, 108-11, 117-25, 143, 160, 163-6, 180, 183-90, 193-95, 199-201, 204, 207-8
divorce 24, 154
earnings 4, 24, 37, 50, 66-9, 98-102, 108, 113-6, 128-30, 136, 148, 153, 162, 173, 176-7, 209
economic growth 30
education 26, 36, 64, 77-8, 90-1, 105
effectiveness 1-5, 18-22, 25-33, 39, 44-51, 54, 59, 86, 89, 96-101, 105, 108, 112, 138-41, 147, 162, 187, 191-3, 203-7, 212
efficiency 19-21, 27, 97, 122, 160
elderly 10, 21-2, 26, 47, 59, 77, 98, 103, 108-10, 114, 119-21, 131-2, 135-8, 142, 147-9, 152-5, 161, 177, 182, 195, 197-8
elderly women 148, 153-5
eligibility 7, 10-11, 49-51, 87-9, 92-101, 106-8, 118-9, 124, 127, 141, 144, 148, 155-9, 162-4, 178, 183, 192-3, 198-200, 204-9

employment 24, 65-7, 77-9, 91-2, 96, 99, 118, 140-2, 153, 180, 204, 209
self-employment 60, 63, 67-8, 77, 92, 100, 195, 199
unemployment 3, 36-7, 47, 50, 64, 67-8, 79, 108, 130, 142, 150, 166, 170-3, 182
work incentives 7, 101, 104, 143
entitlement 3, 7-8, 51, 67, 72, 89-91, 97-100, 106-8, 117-9, 124-48, 152-66, 171-3, 178, 180-1, 184-5, 189-200, 208
equivalence scale 15, 24, 35-8, 41, 54-5, 70, 73-7, 80-5, 103, 111, 118, 134-40, 146-7, 152, 210, 213, 214-6
institutional 75-6, 137-8, 146
family 1-2, 6, 9, 15-16, 21, 24-5, 33-8, 42, 45, 50, 57, 60, 65, 69-75, 91-8, 103-4, 107-8, 117-22, 128-52, 155, 159, 162-4, 179-81, 185, 190, 194-5, 198, 201, 204, 207, 211-3
Family Expenditure Survey (United Kingdom) 60, 64-8, 79, 194-5, 211, 220, 223-5, 228-9, 233
Finland 7, 16, 22, 25-8, 53, 110, 211-212
France 16-18, 21-2, 25-7, 83-5, 211
German Socio-Economic Panel (GSOEP) 60-1, 64-9, 80, 197, 211-3
Germany 6-13, 16-17, 21-2, 25-7, 31, 35-47, 51, 54-5, 58-62, 67-71, 74-85, 89-96, 99, 103-20, 124-7, 130-55, 161, 165-207, 211-8
health care 77, 127
health insurance 78
homeless 63, 119, 196-7
household
 definition of 16, 23, 43, 46, 70, 71-2, 143, 205, 210

household size (see also equivalence scale) 15, 22-4, 34-8, 41, 45, 73, 80, 132, 136, 212-5
 private 2, 5, 11, 18, 37, 50-1, 57, 60-2, 71-3, 76, 86, 106, 125
household definition 16, 23, 43, 46, 70-2, 143, 205, 210
housing allowance 10, 36, 66-9, 103, 109, 122, 125-6, 143, 156, 195, 199
housing cost 10, 36, 69, 76, 90, 103, 113-7, 125-7, 131-7, 141-3, 180, 194, 217, 218
immigrants 38, 93
income
 disposable income 4, 22-4, 33-5, 40, 45, 54-5, 59, 73, 76-7, 130, 136, 143, 156, 212-4
 disregard 97, 129-30, 142, 181, 190, 199-201, 206-9
 income disregard 63, 92, 97-9, 130
 inequality 21
 market income 22-3, 26, 32, 47-9, 77, 98
 non-cash 77
 redistribution of 1, 6, 20, 23, 32, 47, 176, 203
 sources of 49, 66-7, 77, 132, 140, 210
 transfers 1, 4, 17-49, 66-9, 77, 116, 209, 212-5
income support (United Kingdom) 10, 36-8, 66-8, 90-2, 95, 98-9, 105, 109, 113-6, 120-5, 131, 143, 170, 174, 177-80, 184-5, 195, 200
income survey 209
 data quality 67
 non-response 63-6, 100, 196
 non-sampling errors 63-5, 141, 148, 209
 sample size 100, 196, 211

sampling and non-sampling errors
  63-6, 141, 148, 209
sampling errors 63, 66
sampling process 63
undercoverage 63
institutions 6, 62-3, 68, 94, 100, 105,
  122, 196
Ireland 8, 83, 175
Italy 16, 22, 85, 211, 212
Japan 6, 8, 83-5
labour market 4, 18, 57, 79, 94,
  99-100, 171, 209
Luxembourg 6, 13, 16, 21-2, 33, 36,
  60, 71, 78, 83-5, 100, 103, 127,
  141-2, 210-2
Luxembourg Income Study (LIS) 6,
  11-15, 21-8, 33-8, 41-2, 45, 54-5,
  60-2, 65, 68-84, 100, 103, 127-8,
  133-6, 149-51, 194, 198, 210-5
means-test 4, 33, 91, 125, 158-9,
  163-4, 185-6, 190, 205
means-tested benefits 3, 11, 33-49,
  54-5, 66, 75, 152, 195, 213-5
men 63
micro-simulation 196
middle class 29, 61, 64, 102
migrants 93, 96, 177, 207
minimum income benefit 2, 31, 127,
  130, 134, 144, 150, 177-8
minimum income guarantee 2, 32
model family approach 128, 140-2,
  146-9, 152, 155
Netherlands, the 16, 21-2, 27, 83-5,
  211-2
New Zealand 6
Nordic countries 7, 175
Norway 7, 16-18, 21-2, 27, 110, 208,
  211-2, 220, 232-3
pensions 18, 22-4, 29, 35, 66-9, 114,
  130, 142, 153, 177-9, 200
poor law 3, 201
poverty
  absolute poverty 81-5

alleviation of 1-4, 11, 21-2, 26-33,
  39, 47-50, 90, 97-101, 104, 113,
  118, 125-7, 157, 162, 191-3,
  204-6, 209
consumption 56
definition of 14, 144
in old age 121
intensity 14-16, 31-46, 70-4, 144-
  5, 149-50, 153-5, 205, 214-5
intensity of 17, 39, 44
measurement 4, 51-6, 59, 65, 78,
  86, 147, 204, 209
persistence of 1-3, 17, 27, 31, 47,
  86, 101, 155, 205, 209
poverty gap 20, 39, 44-7
poverty line 4, 11-16, 19-23, 29,
  32-6, 39-47, 54-60, 71, 76, 80-5,
  96-7, 101-2, 134-9, 144-5,
  149-51, 155, 191, 204-6, 210-4
poverty rate 9-10, 14-18, 21-8,
  31-2, 39-42, 46-7, 58, 63-4,
  70-4, 77- 85, 100, 133, 138,
  143-55, 205, 210-2, 215
poverty trap 98
profile of 14-18, 31, 71, 81
relative poverty 4, 13, 26, 34,
  54-5, 80-5, 128, 134, 206
poverty regime 6-8
pregnancy 120, 127, 131
public policies 30, 157
public policy 2, 8, 30, 49, 60, 67-9,
  93-4, 104-13, 116-8, 121, 125-6,
  169, 176-9, 182, 194
refugees 93-5, 111, 130
replacement rate 128
retrenchment 29, 102-3, 108, 112,
  117, 166
right of appeal 96, 187-90
right, social 2, 6-7, 100
single parent 10, 21, 66, 75-7, 98-9,
  118-21, 129-31, 135-42, 147-50,
  195, 198
social assistance 3-11, 30-1, 38,
  47-51, 55, 75, 86-103, 107-12,

117-20, 127-9, 136-40, 143, 146, 152, 155-7, 160-9, 173-9, 183-5, 189-93, 198-209
access to 89, 182-3, 204, 207-8
administration 166, 182, 186-7
administrative discretion 4, 7-8, 95, 108-11, 117-25, 143, 160, 163-66, 180, 183-90, 193-5, 199-201, 204, 207-8
attitudes towards 61, 162-5, 175-7, 190
claiming process 157-65, 180, 184, 190
direct payments 184
dynamics 174
expenditure 3, 112, 166-9, 173-5
family liability 181, 201, 207
indexation 103, 113-6, 126
level 10-11, 17, 94, 101-10, 113-5, 127-33, 136-40, 147-55, 164, 179, 191, 204-8
one-off benefits 103, 107-9, 121-4, 127, 131, 140, 143, 156, 160, 164, 185, 201
premiums 119-20, 152
programme structure 11, 47-51, 157-8, 163-6, 178, 190, 193, 200, 204
recipients 54, 102-3, 126, 130-2, 135, 140-2, 164, 171, 175-7, 185-7
regime 6-8, 208
renewal of claims 164, 190
simulation of entitlements 128, 140-50, 155
special premiums 99, 103, 117, 120-1, 142
standard benefit rates 76, 95, 103-21, 125-7, 130, 142, 185
take-up 11, 20, 39, 49-51, 87, 101, 125, 141, 144, 147-8, 155-66, 173-80, 184-201, 204-7
social exclusion 86

social expenditure 3-5, 18, 25-7, 32, 166-8, 203, 210
social fund (United Kingdom) 95, 109, 120-4, 131, 184-5, 188, 201
social insurance 3, 7-10, 31, 35, 46-50, 77, 93, 114, 126, 130, 173, 177, 182, 186, 201
social policy 1-2, 4-7, 31-2, 140, 188, 203, 210
socialbidrag (Sweden) 10, 36, 72, 114, 126, 175
Sozialhilfe (Germany) 10, 36, 98, 121, 186
  Hilfe in besonderen Lebenslagen 36, 112, 119, 167-72
  Hilfe zum Lebensunterhalt 36, 119, 169-72, 181
Spain 83-5
stratification 176
students 16, 37, 43, 59, 62, 68, 71-3, 90-2, 96, 100, 199
Sweden 5-13, 16-17, 21-3, 27-8, 31-46, 51, 54-5, 58-62, 67-76, 80-81, 84-5, 89-100, 103-19, 124-7, 130-3, 137-43, 146-56, 165-83, 187-95, 198-208, 211-8
taxation 1, 18, 21-5, 28, 32-4, 77, 104, 109-12, 116, 127, 177, 212
United Kingdom 6-16, 21-2, 25-8, 31-2, 35-46, 54-5, 58, 67-8, 74-7, 81-4, 89-92, 95-6, 109, 113-20, 125-7, 131, 146, 166-9, 174-81, 184, 187, 190, 194-200, 203-5, 208, 211-8
United States 6, 16, 21-9, 78, 83-5, 111, 174, 211-2
wages and salaries 24, 50, 68-9, 98, 101-2, 113-6, 128-30, 209
welfare state 1-35, 46-50, 55, 59, 82, 86, 93, 101-3, 110, 136, 166, 173-8, 181, 190, 201-6, 209-10
welfare state regime 3, 6-9, 21-3
women 119-20, 147-8, 153-5, 198
young people 59, 72, 90, 142, 199